ESCORT

40 PROFILES WITH PHOTOGRAPHS OF MEN WHO SELL SEX

BY DAVID LEDDICK
AND HERIBERTO SANCHEZ
PHOTOGRAPHS BY DAVID VANCE

WHITE LAKE PRESS

TO RAY REILLY
WHO FIRST INSISTED WE DO THIS BOOK

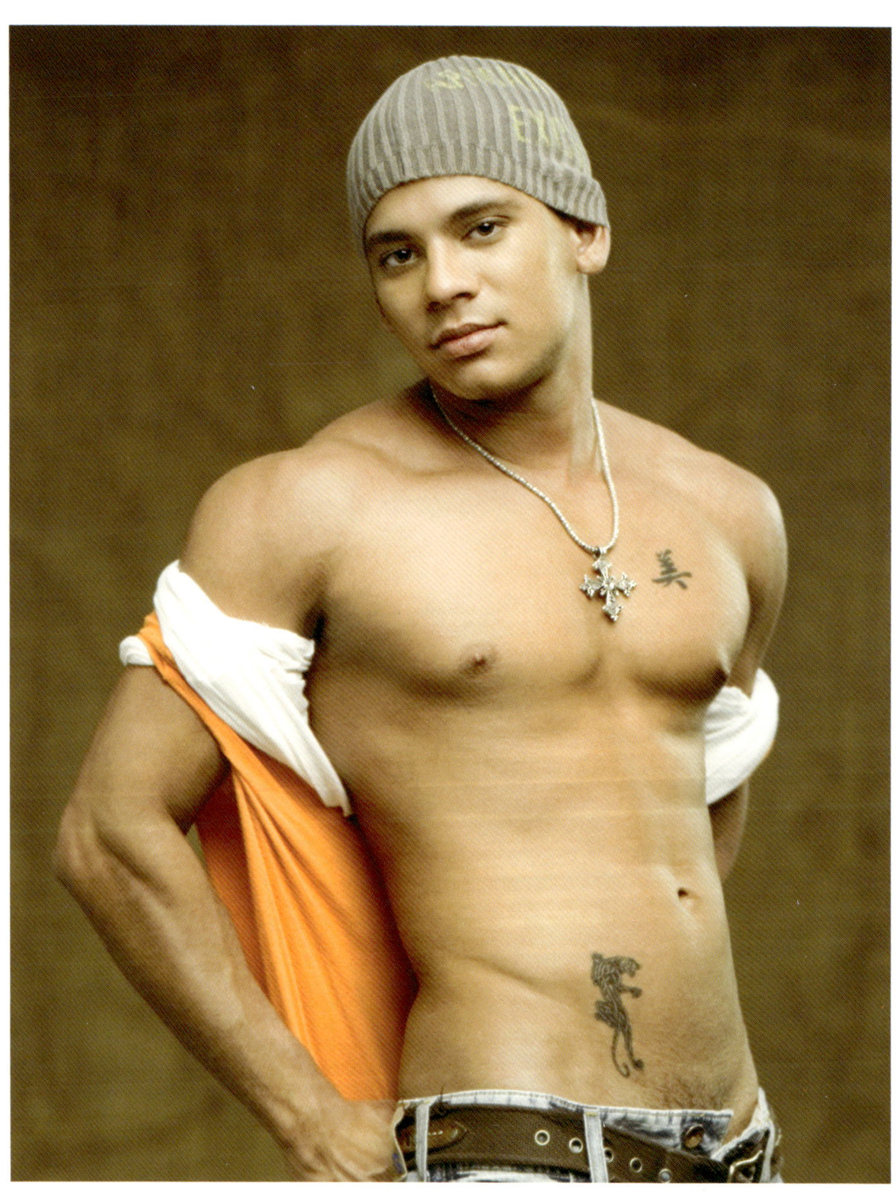

INTRODUCTION
DAVID LEDDICK

When I proposed the name "Escort" for this book some of my acquaintances demurred and thought it should be called something more vernacular like "Hustlers." But I think its name is suggestive of a change in attitude in the 21st Century about men who sleep with other men for money. And in this my publishers agree with me and have encouraged me to make this exploration of the changing attitudes towards the sex activities that surround us.

Exchanging sex for money is a very ancient practice, but has generally been considered a taboo subject for polite conversation or even polite recognition. In what has always been the puritanical atmosphere of the United States, many people pass through their lives knowing very little about the selling and buying of sex and are delighted to ignore it. Others would like to know more about it but have suffered through lives of repression and inexperience. Never fulfilled. Never knowledgeable. Satisfied perhaps that they have not sinned. But somehow one doubts it.

The Internet has changed everything. Now it is possible for everyone to confront their desires directly. Many times assignations are made between strangers, only for romance, excitement, experimentation. Sometimes there have been offers of money. And from these casual encounters have come services like *men4rent* and many others where fantasies can be fulfilled. Now we see that below the surface of conformity there is a turmoil of sexual needs and interests that literature and art have explored for centuries, but that our own country has been reluctant to accept and discuss and admit to until the advent of the Internet.

So here is an initial step below the surface of hypocrisy. Here are the advertisements that these men place. Interviews where the reader can find out who they are, where they come from, what they think about their lives. And portraits by that very talented photographer of men, David Vance.

Here they are as they really are: the mysterious men behind the advertising of escorts.

OPPOSITE: ELI DURAN

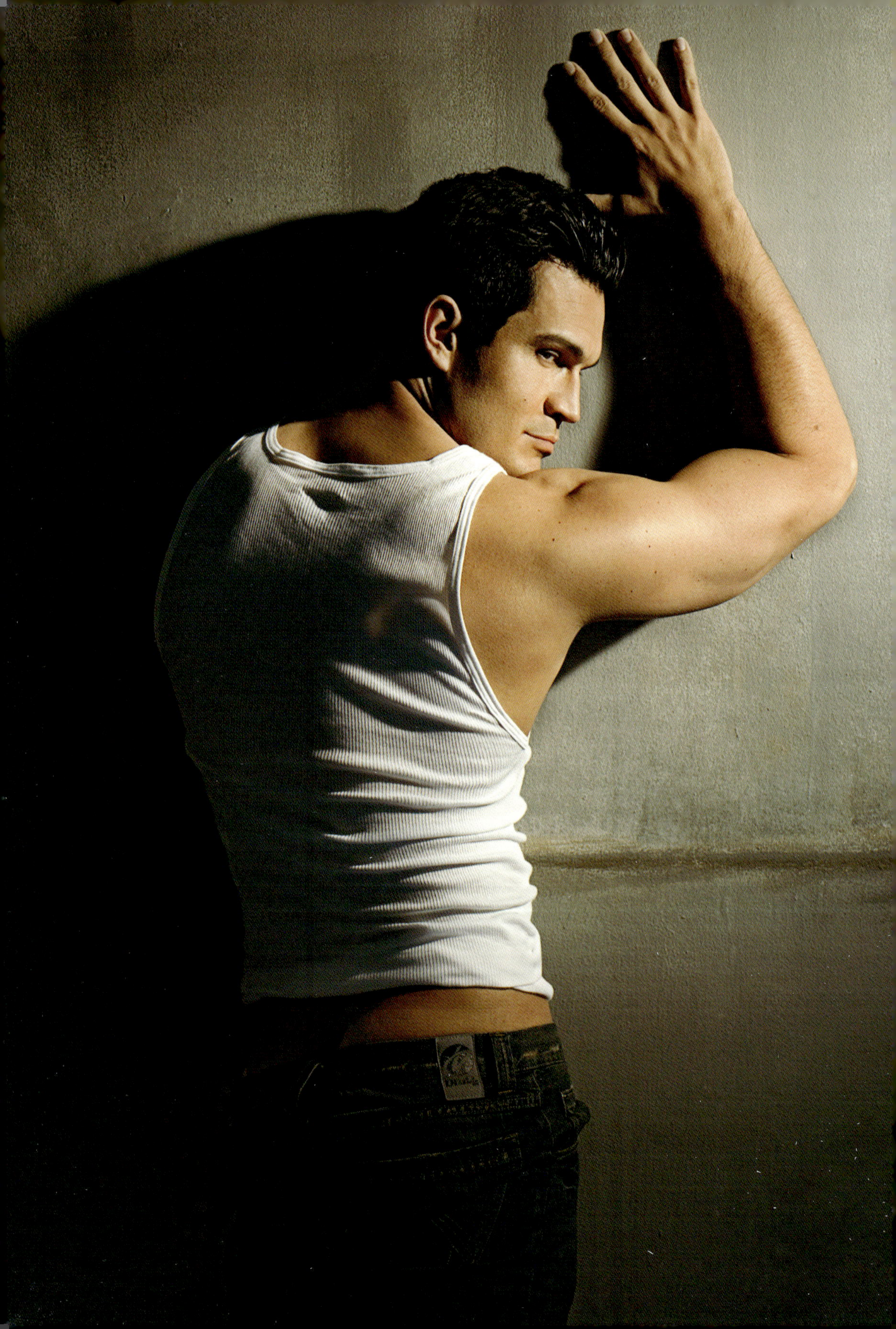

REFLECTING ON ESCORTS

HERIBERTO SANCHEZ

I've never escorted nor hired one. But I have always had a fascination, a curiosity about the men that do it. What are they like? What brings them to do it? Economic need? Higher than normal libidos? Or sexual addiction? Needing to work as an escort to bring food to the table versus liking it; is one better than the other?

This book will give some insights into the lives and minds of male escorts. It is by no means a clinical study. The subjects were picked randomly from magazine publications and escorts' advertising on Internet sites. The methodology was simple. We found the ads and contacted the escorts via telephone or email. We invited them to a casual lunch. After interviewing, David Vance photographed them. The escorts in turn would get pictures from the photo shoot and were all paid a courtesy fee.

Who hasn't wondered what their price might be after watching "Indecent Proposal," when dapper Robert Redford offers one million dollars to sleep with Demi Moore, who's character is married to working class Woody Harrelson? What would you do for a million? Does considering a million versus one hundred make you a different person? Or are you whoring at any price?

In the search for escorts to interview, an escort, Colby Cruise, who turned us down, asked, "Why would anyone want to glamorize prostitution?" And I told him we did not consider it glamorizing but humanizing. And we hoped to reveal a mystery fascinating to many people. A lot of people want to know about the lives behind the man in the escort ad. It is an interesting subject matter that has scarcely been explored. Attitudes are changing from what people thought about "hustlers" to current views about male "escorts." Many escorts run their work like a business. We've found many people from different walks of life and nationalities in this line of work. Some have difficulties with this work and feel caught up with no way out, while others are at ease and report enjoying what they do. That is the subject we are exploring and reporting on. We're not in the business of making moral judgments.

Sidney Biddle Barrows, aka The Mayflower Madam, a New York socialite from an old New England family who was caught running a house of prostitution of educated and sophisticated girls for New York elite clients said, "If you can give it away, why can't you sell it?"

The explosion of male escorting is an internet phenomenon. Who knew there were so many clients with so much money? This book is about the supply and there is certainly a demand. Since prostitution is illegal in this country, many escorts advertise their hourly rate for time only. Many include a disclaimer such as: "All rates are for time only, I do not sell sex for money. What happens during this time together is private and confidential between myself and the client."

As opposed to other career fields where the salary disparity has historically favored men, there is a big disparity in income in favor of women in escorting. In the business of escorting, women do make a lot more than men, as in fashion modeling.

Reflecting on the photo shoots, there were many amusing moments. Such as Bull Stanton's permanent hard-on during the shoot. Bull had a raging hard-on and teased his boyfriend, asking him to fluff him by poking him with his sizable member. Even poking it in his ears.

Chris, our supposedly straight escort, was allergic to cats and had trouble keeping himself from sneezing when David Vance's cats were roaming around and trying to jump on the sofa where he was posing. I was on the sidelines shooing them off.

The dynamic strip dance and charm of Jamie Lee; the shyness and sex appeal of Cody Johnson; Chris' polite sensitive boy next door allure; Seth's everlasting card throwing, which had to be taken and retaken until the cards flew just right. All of these shoots were memorable.

During an on-location shoot, Marcos David was on a tree branch but just when the photographer was ready to shoot, I called out, "Stop!" He looked great nude but was wearing his muddy sneakers, which did not look good. So I approached his spread-eagled legs with his impressive erect member inches away from my face. I very business-mindedly attempted to ignore it as it pointed straight at me, gingerly unfastening his laces, shoes and removing his socks. A few annoying gnats started hovering over his penis and my face. Without thinking I blew in the general direction to shoo them away. Later I found out the photographer had taken a picture of the back of my head with the model's legs spread at the sides of my ears. When showed the picture, some escorts thought I was there to be a fluffer. I replied as Tallulah Bankhead had when caught in bed with a married man, "It's all a lie!"

There were surprises. I often wondered what it would be like if I set up an appointment and had someone I knew previously show up. It finally happened with Eduardo. While we were waiting for him, my cell phone rang. As I answered I saw Eduardo right in front of me calling me. We knew each other from the gym. We recognized each other and there was no embarrassment on Eduardo's part.

Some friends thought mine was a dream job, but as in any production job, it certainly had its drawbacks. There was dealing with flaky people, no-shows, excuses like dogs dying, spider bites that send people to the Emergency Room where they lose their phones. I think I've heard them all.

At other times there was drama right before a shoot. We found out about breakups just before a shoot, when the partner is a no-show. Another time the escort was so strung up that it was difficult to apply make up. A handsome guy, it was sad to see him twitching while make-up was being applied on him.

Then there were courageous escorts like our special featured escort, Mike Jones, who exposed the hypocrisy of religious right wing preacher, Ted Haggard, the President of the New Life Church as well as a leader of thousands of evangelists and advisor to President George Bush. The Rev. Ted Haggard in his private life sought "massage" services from Mike Jones, a gay masseur, from whom the Rev. got more for his money including sex and drugs. This was a man who said he did not understand "Gay Pride" and that having a gay pride parade was like having a "murderers day parade."

Then there was the afternoon with German Master Dieter, his size and musculature very commanding. As he modeled for the camera his facial expressions switched from a very disarming, gentle smile to a masterful glare. He admitted it was the first time someone had applied make-up on him and photographer David Vance admitted it was his first time photographing a Leather Master. I said to David, "Every sentence you address to him must be finished by 'Sir'." Then David Vance started spraying him with a silver colored paint. He was quite a mess to clean up. It was like washing a car. This man was so big! There I was in the backyard with a bucket of warm soapy water and a large sponge, scrubbing his back and those hard to reach places. He didn't mind that the hose water was cold. He said he was in the military so he was not bothered. Such a charming guy, he carried the heavy bronze statue we had used in the shoot with one arm as if it were a light shopping bag. The photographer's assistant and myself had struggled together to get it out of the car and into the studio.

During the interviews, some of the escorts were nervous about speaking or exposing themselves verbally. Kevin Thomas and Alexander, too, were both very nervous in the interview. Later in the shoot, Kevin was completely at ease undressing before the camera. Cody was shy during the photo shoot. I, on my end, being the one making them comfortable and helping build their trust in the project, was I the escorts' escort? Seducing them to perform for the project?

MIKE JONES

MASSAGE BY MIKE

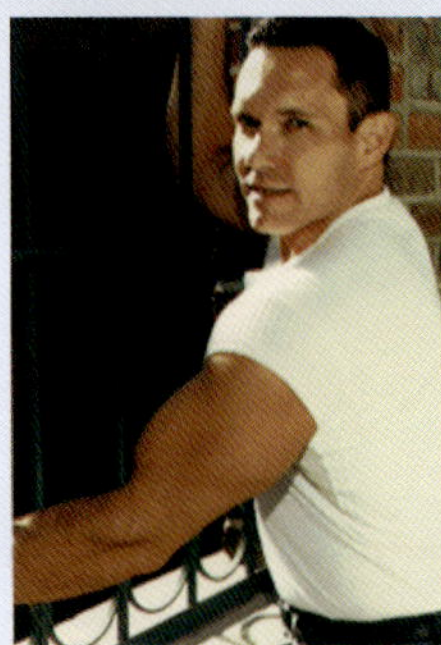

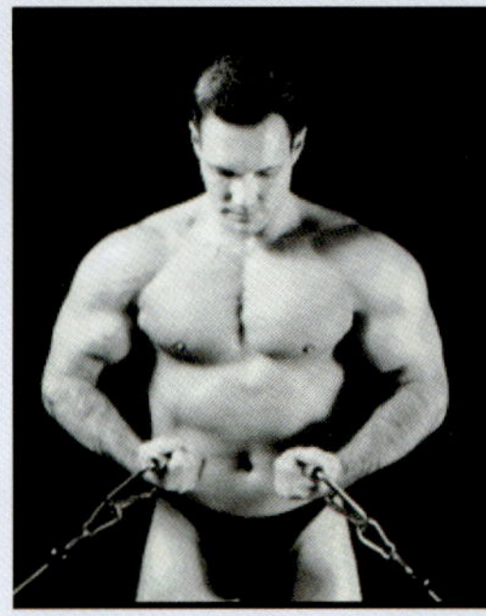

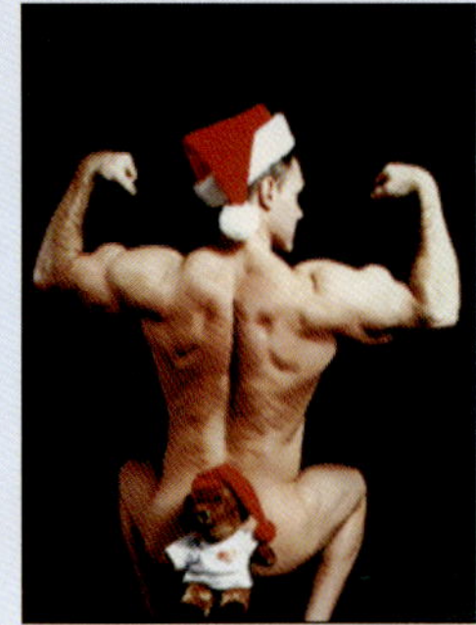

DON'T BE DISAPPOINTED AGAIN!!!!

Voted best massage and personal trainer for the years *2000, 2001 and 2002* by readers of the community newspaper Out Front Colorado. Former state bodybuilding and powerlifting champion.

I offer a deep tissue and swedish style massage with the pleasure of the **man in mind.** If you like a strong **muscle man** to bring pleasure to you then please call me. I am a **muscle stud** with a friendly personality and a caring heart. When the Broadway shows play in town the cast and crew call upon me for massage.

I am 5"8 and weigh 190 lbs.
My arms are 18 inches.
My chest is 47 inches.
My waist is 32 inches.
My thighs are 24 inches.
I have brown hair and blue eyes.

My rates are as follows:

In calls at my place in Capitol Hill of Denver: $70.00 per hour $90.00 1 1/2 hrs.

Out calls start at $100.00.

PLEASE CALL # 303-861-8779
E-MAIL Massageandmuscle@aol.com

Hours and days vary depending on availability.

A national scandal precipitated Mike Jones to the attention of the American public. He's the escort who blew the whistle on the Reverend Ted Haggard in Denver. And may very well have caused a seismic shift in voter attitudes just before the Democrats took over in the 2006 national election. It was interesting that when he was picked up at the airport he emerged under the sign TED/United Airlines. Ironically, he flew Ted for his interview and photographs.

Here's how he tells the story: "I had been seeing a client for some three years in Denver, whom I only knew as Art from Kansas City. I just assumed he was someone who came to town regularly on business. Over the years that I had been seeing him, he had become a regular client and we explored quite a few different things sexually.

"One evening I was watching television. For some reason I happened to be watching the History Channel and there was a discussion of the Anti-Christ. And there was Art from Kansas City. Except it wasn't Art, it was some local minister. His name was flashed on the screen but I was so surprised I missed it.

"The next morning I went to the gym at 5:00 A.M., which I regularly do, and that's when I knew I was supposed to do something. Because there on the screen of one of the televisions was Daystar (the religious channel). Out of the blue, there it was. And there was Art, and there was his name. The Reverend Ted Haggard. I knew who he was because there had been talk about him leading a movement to approve a constitutional amendment defining marriage as only between one man and one woman. I realized that I had to do something about it.

"I went to a local television station and they talked to me a long time. They sat on the story a long time. Three months passed and they didn't do anything, so I went to a local radio station. I was on the radio the next day with my story. When the television station heard about the radio interview, they went to Colorado Springs to confront Ted Haggard. The news broke at 10:00pm on November 1st 2006. Obviously, they were very scared of doing something about it if I was lying. I gave them all the details I could, but obviously I had only very recently found out my client's real identity myself."

For all the interviews and attention he has received, Mike Jones remains a pleasant, amusing, easy-going man who looks far younger than his 49 years. His regular gym attendance has paid off and he has a strong, good-looking body to go with his open, upbeat appearance.

He is from what has to be an early Denver family, now numbering four generations. They were early settlers who came to Colorado in the late 1800s. One of his great-grandmothers was born in Central City, one of the earliest gold-mining towns. Family history recounts that she was a Madam who ran a house of ill repute. The family went to Fort Morgan, Colorado where his grandmother went to high school. One of her classmates was the famous bandleader Glenn Miller.

Mike's father was a police officer and his mother organized statewide bowling tournaments. He has two brothers, one older and one younger. His brother eventually became a professional bowler. Mike went to high school in Edgewater, a town near Denver.

He remembers, "I started working out when I was thirteen. I was being bullied in school and I thought, 'I'll show them.' I used the equipment that they had at the school. In high school I entered bodybuilding and power lifting contests and won state titles.

"After leaving high school I had some small jobs and continued working out. I had a fake I.D. and went to some bars and men came on to me and I realized that some people were willing to pay. Before then I had hung out in stores that sold X-rated videos to make sexual contacts.

"I knew I was gay when I was five but I didn't know what that meant. I knew I was interested in boys my own age. I had my first sexual experiences when I was six with two brothers who had a clubhouse next door. I could reach orgasm although there wasn't any ejaculation. I used to hump a pole on the playground, too. It was back when torment begins when you hear negative things about being gay.

"After I began escorting I also opened a gym, which I ran for five years and I also studied massage. I had a relationship for five-years with a divorced man. He had five children. I used to escort when he was busy with the kids. That was during the period when I was 30 to 38 years old. Then he left me for someone younger. I have had opportunities to date since then but I have to admit that I find it hard to be intimate with someone when I am also escorting.

"Of course some clients fall for me. They bring me presents like watches and things but I never get personally involved with a client. I would say that about 80% of my clients are married, but even so, they sometimes fall into that wanting me to be a boyfriend. The boyfriend syndrome thing. I would also say that about 20% are clergy. Priests, pastors, ministers, a lot of clients are from out of town. They are regular visitors who are in Denver on holiday or on business.

"I've also had politicians, movie stars and pro-athletes among my clients. When they come to my apartment I never use my bedroom. I have a massage table where they can have a massage or not, as they choose." When asked if there is specific age group, Mike says that it isn't the case. "My clients range from their twenties all the way to their eighties." He has had some unusual clients, though. "One client said, 'I'm a large man.' Then 350 pounds showed up. I just can't get excited. When that happens I just lay there on the floor and they get the "Express" instead of the "Deluxe" package."

The massage fee is only $100 and Mike explains that he does have straight clients who only want a massage. If there is sex involved the fee goes up to $200.

Though he advertises he also finds that clients can be found when he goes to the piano bar at Brown's Palace hotel. He says, "I could have had tons of sugar daddies, but I have never wanted that. I'm too independent. I'm a Taurus, the Bull."

Discussing some of the unusual aspects of his work, Mike Jones says, "You hear about men liking to watch two women fool around. I had a man who came to see me because his wife wanted to see me having sex with her husband. Then they wanted to see me having sex with the wife. It was kind of a turn on. I have always been an exhibitionist. I don't mind being watched while I'm having sex.

"I can be very verbal and aggressive, too. I was in many leather contests. I was in the Mr. Rocky Mountain Leather competition and went to the finals. I came in second place for the title of Mr. Drummer in San Francisco. I came in second in a contest on Fire Island. I've won thousands of dollars in those competitions. I can be really dominant. I'm very good at smacking ass. A friend of mine in New York said, 'You can be the nicest, sweetest guy I know. But you can be the nastiest son of a bitch, too.' But I can turn it on and off, too."

Returning to the subject of Reverend Haggard he adds, "He always showed up in blue jeans and a long-sleeved polo shirt. He loved my collection of cock rings. I had lots of stuff like that from my leather days. I'm over all that now.

"He had a fantasy of having sex with college age guys, 18 to 22. He asked me if I could organize an orgy but we never got around to that. He rented x-rated videos and wanted some 'extreme' videos. They didn't have any at the store. They had his phone number to let him know when his videos were in. He was taking more risks than just with me. He wasn't a bad client but I didn't want to die with regrets. I didn't want to go through life regretting that I didn't expose that fraud.

"And of course I have had a lot of criticism as well as congratulations. I was besieged with e-mails after the news broke and many escorts said they felt I had violated the escort code by talking about a client. But I don't mingle with other escorts and massage therapists in Denver so it's not a real problem."

For the future Mike Jones plans to stay in great shape. He has a workout program of a half-hour of cardio and one hour of weights every day and points out, "I'm also a very good tennis player."

As far as his private life is concerned, he says, "I would like to have a personal relationship. I'd like to share the rest of my life with someone."

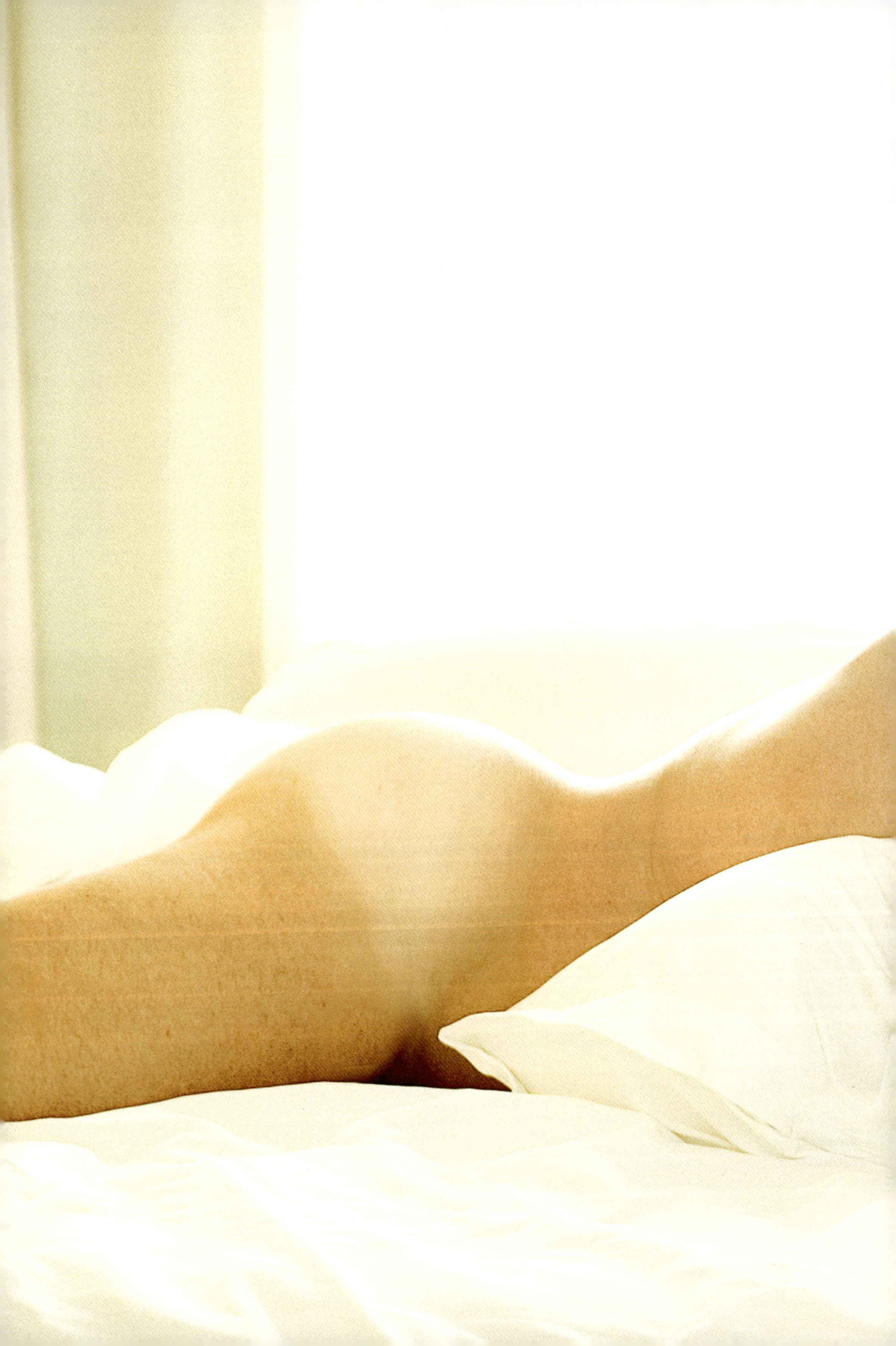

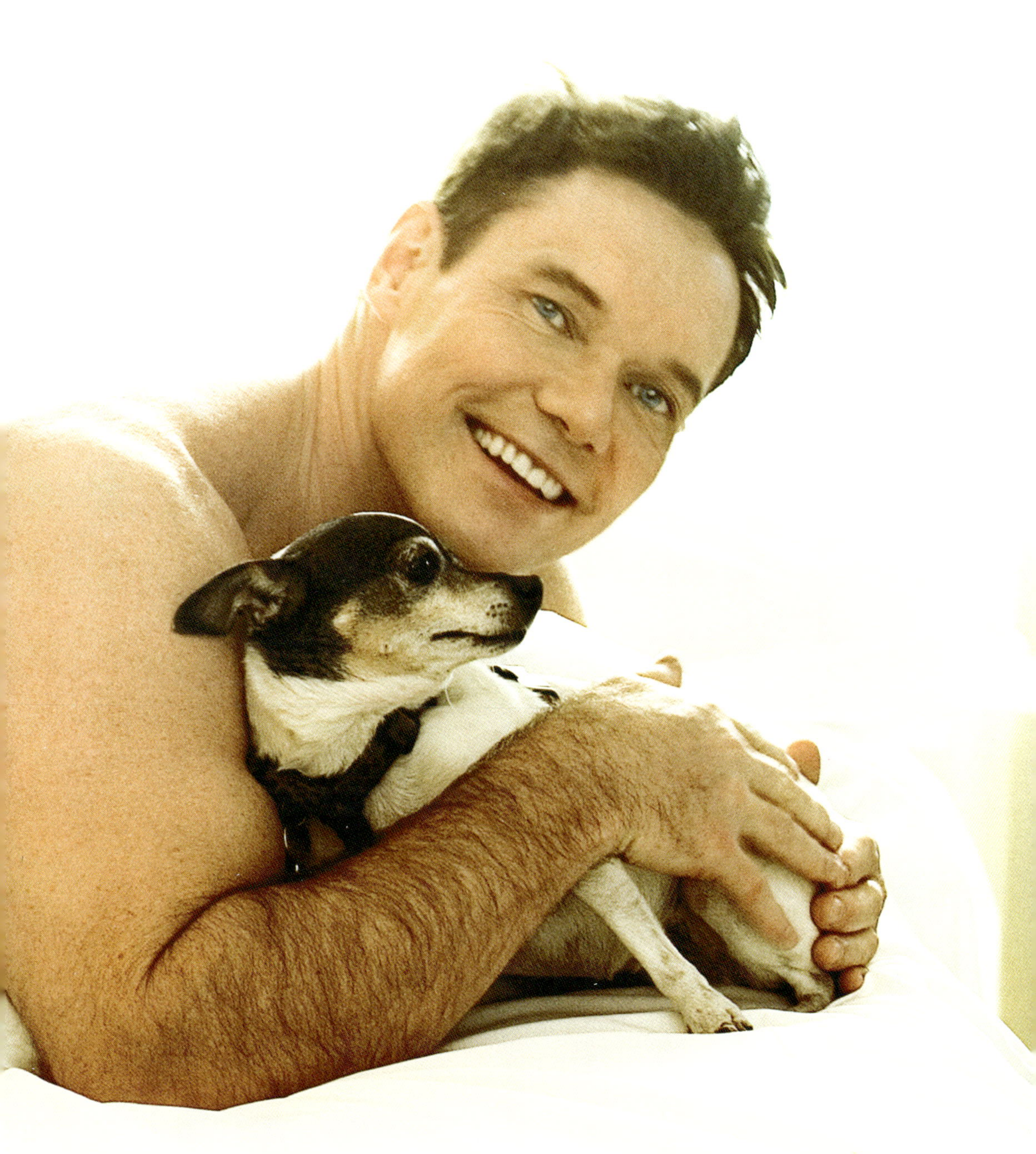

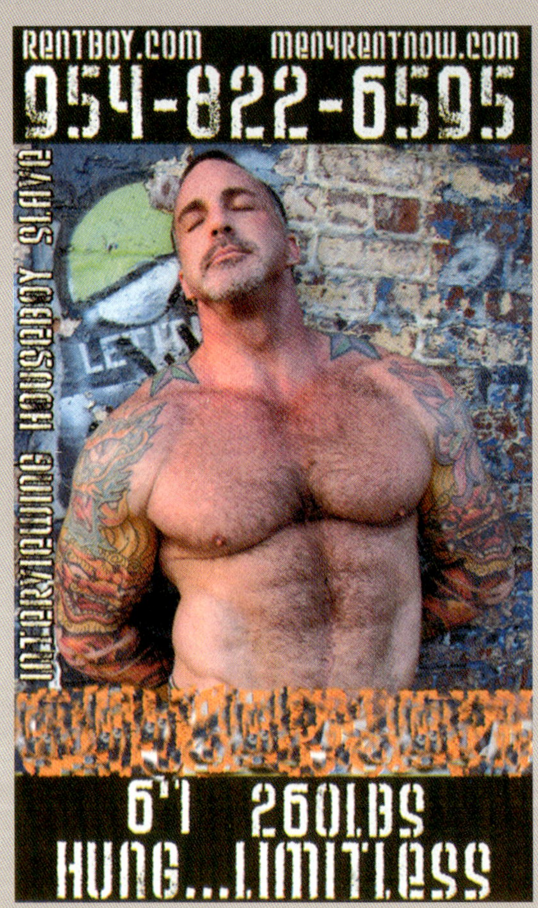
RENTBOY.COM
MEN4RENTNOW.COM
954-822-6595
INTERNATIONAL HOUSEBOY SLAVE
6'1 260LBS
HUNG...LIMITLESS

BULL STANTON

Big and boisterous, kind and complicated, this is Bull Stanton. One of the major and most interesting of male escorts of the last ten years, Bull Stanton, surprisingly, was married to his second wife until May of 2005. His divorce is not yet final. For most of their married life together in Tampa, Fla. she had nothing but approval for his providing escort services. He says, "She had no objection to the income."

Born originally in Rhode Island, Bull Stanton moved as a ten-year-old to Fort Lauderdale, Fla. He began playing sports and started body building soon after and was an All American high school footballer. He attended the University of Miami for two years but injuries to his knees brought his football career to an end.

He married a cheerleader from that school and the newlyweds moved to Los Angeles where he became one of the first personal trainers, that being a brand new career choice in those years. He had continued his bodybuilding during this time and was Mr. Southern States in 1984 and Mr. Los Angeles in 1986. On the West Coast he trained with the same man who trained bodybuilding champion Bob Paris. This man had been the life partner of Bob Paris also.

He says "I was always faithful to my wife." but at the age of 28 he found himself involved with a female bodybuilder and re-married. With his new wife he moved to Tampa, Fla. to pursue his personal training work, and his bodybuilding. In 1992, he became Mr. America.

When personal training slumped he placed a training ad in a local gay magazine. Among the responses were inquiries as to what he might be willing to do sexually. He found that his wife encouraged him to pursue work as an escort.

Local Tampa men were his clients and also many men came to Tampa to see him. He says, "Some clients want to meet with you three times a week on a regular basis, some fewer, but like many fields of work regular clients are essential."

He also traveled to cities like San Francisco and New York and lived permanently in San Francisco for 18 months at one time.

In the escort business there are on-line reviews by clients and all those about Bull Stanton compliment him on his cordiality, conversational skills, and very energetic sexuality.

His busiest schedule? "Sometimes in New York I have calls six or seven times a day for a week. That's a lot. I have to rest up afterwards. "Strange or difficult clients? He says this is very rare. Only once did he think he might have to fight his way out of a situation. "If I have a bad client I wonder what I did wrong."

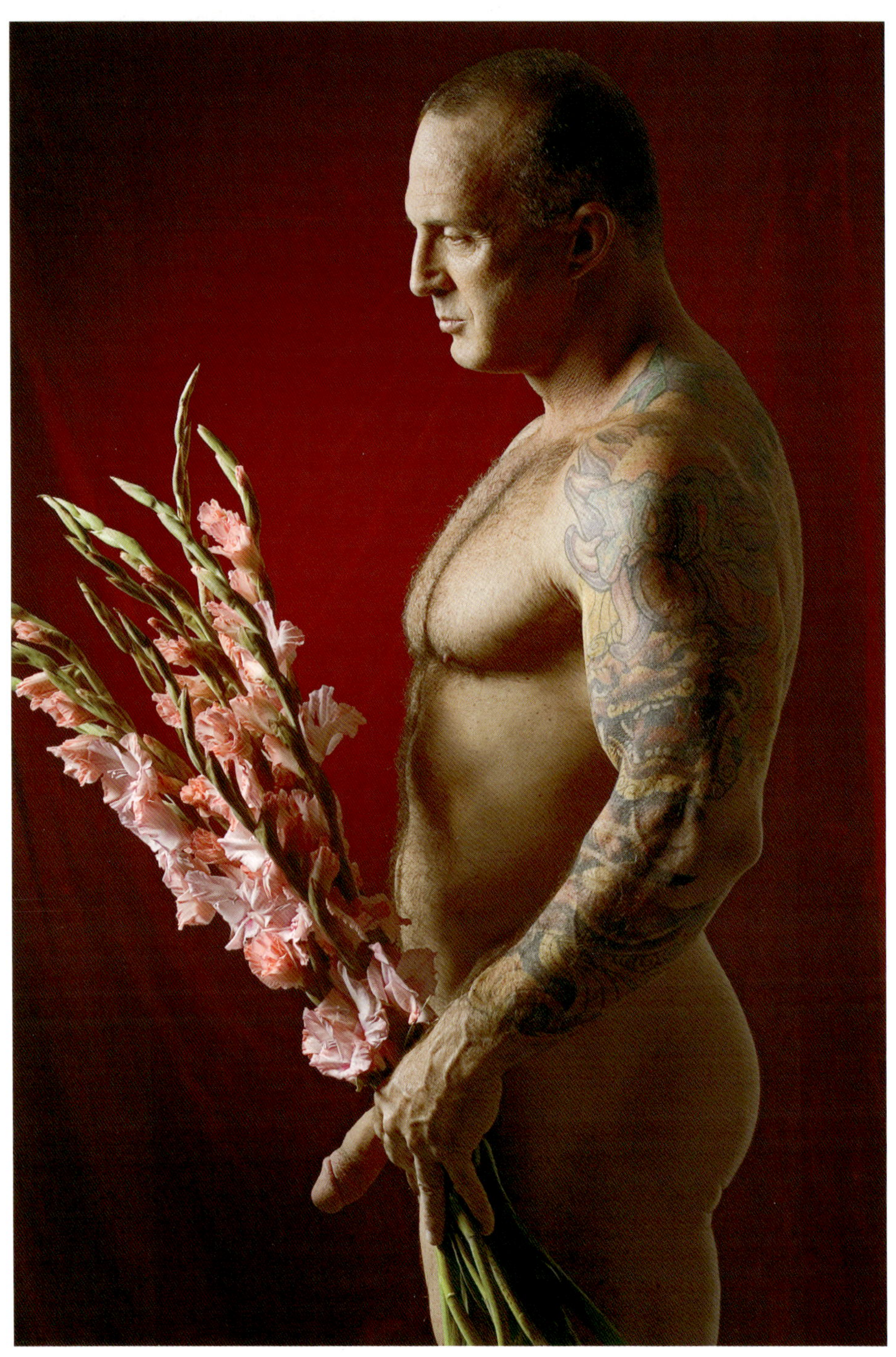

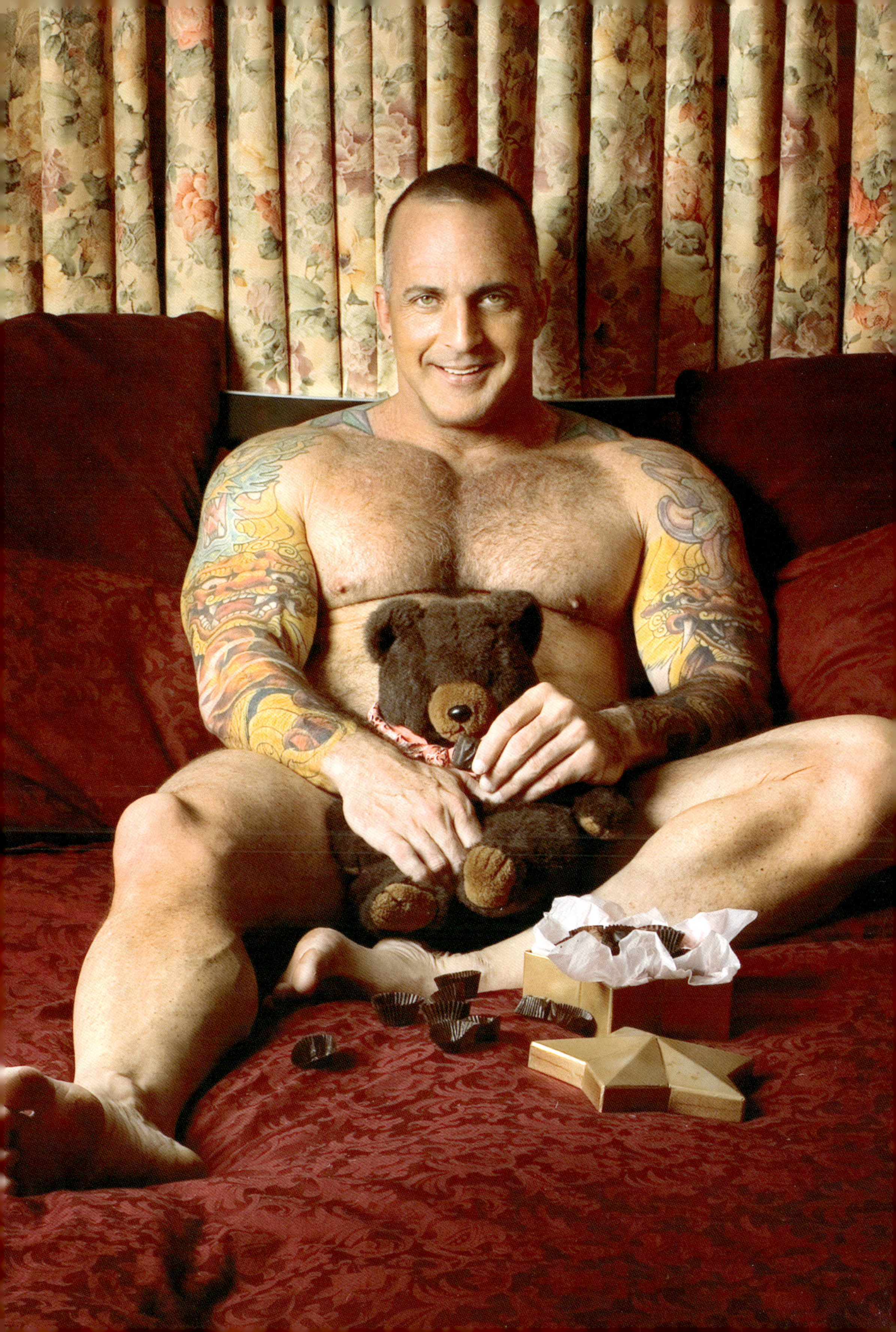

SCOTT AND JOSH

In their life together Scott and Josh run their escort service very much as a business. It began with their finding a computer in a dumpster. They repaired it and began their business. They laugh about how bad their first photographs were, which they took of each other with a cellphone. They still do but now the photos are more expert. They hijacked Josh's mother's Internet line so they could receive email, and their business began.

They keep track of how many appointments each of them have a week and how much was earned. Their rates are fixed. One price for one man per appointment. A higher price if it requires going to Miami Beach or other nearby cities. A higher price for booking the two of them together, which is frequently done.

In their on-line and magazine advertising they place separate advertisements but note that it is possible to book them together. Although the advertising doesn't mention it, they are now in the Fort Lauderdale world and are known to be hirable as a team. They say about forty percent of their assignments are together and at the moment they average about sixteen assignments a week.

Josh says, "Our customers are not by any means older, wealthier men. We have many young good-looking men whom we later find out are well known. Even athletes. Sometimes we stumble upon them in magazines. Just last week we saw a professional tennis player's photo and recognized him. When the German Olympic swim team was in Fort Lauderdale we had clients. They use assumed names when they book us.

Working as a team or separately can bring them some amusing moments. Josh tells of an older client who called him in and as they engaged in the sex act looking over the yacht basin, drenched in moonlight, the client told him. "Oh, be careful, please. I haven't had sex in months." And Josh had to smother a laugh, knowing the same man was Scott's client the night before.

Scott has been called for assignments where a female escort is also involved. But it may resolve itself as voyeurism or something like that. As for the aspect of danger, Josh says, "We always know where each other is when we work separately. And 40% of the time we work together." They only take overnight assignments as a team.

"Some clients are quite young and the expense is a major financial outlay for them but they want to do it. We've had clients as young as eighteen. We never make any kind of financial adjustment. Our rates are our rates. This is a business." he adds. Josh mentions that they sometimes will also have assignments where the client is a young and good-looking man who feels that his attractiveness will not make it necessary to pay for

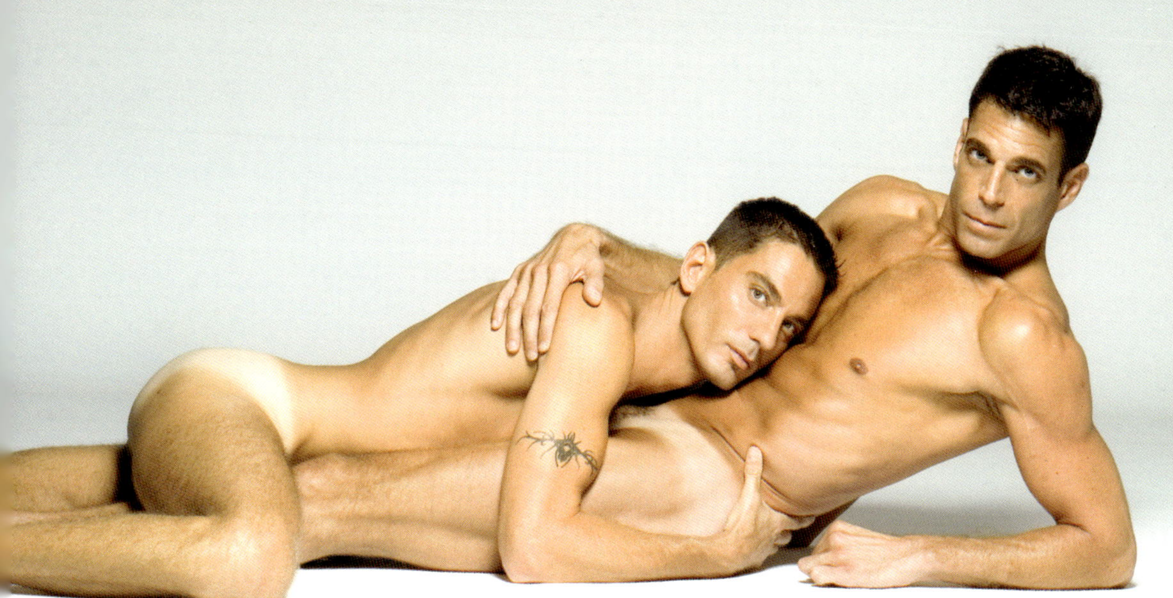

escort services. They always refuse this.

Scott talks about clients, "Some clients want what we call 'The Boyfriend Experience'. We don't allow them to think that that is a possibility. We may not tell them that we have a partner, but we don't lead them on." When asked if some wealthier clients may hire escorts as a form of "shopping" for a new lover, Scott says, "That is definitely a pattern we see. There may be escorts out there that are looking for that also. Some kind of permanent arrangement. But that is not the case for either of us. We have each other." Both men also confirm what other escorts have said. It is not so much the physical attractiveness of a client that can excite them but how interested the client is in having sex. The more aroused the client the more exciting it is for them they both agree, alone or together.

As for how their escort servicing affects their relationship, Scott will tell you, "They are completely separate things. I am a very sexual person and I enjoy my time spent with a client but it has nothing to do with Josh. Making love to someone with whom you are truly in love is completely different for me."

Josh adds, "Of course there is jealousy to contend with. You just can't ignore that completely. But after all is done, we know that we can count on each other to come home." They say, "We've tried to keep small town values. We don't mingle much with the gay world of Fort Lauderdale."

For anyone interested in working in the business they say, "Stay away from drugs. Keep it all business. Never think you're going to meet that person. No matter who they are and what they look like, however they are… remember, it's only an hour."

They have not been able to save much money and they have no plan or desire to segue-way into some other kind of business. Josh says, "I've been in the restaurant business and I have no desire to do that again. Something may occur to us but for the moment we're just doing what we're doing. The important thing for us is that we don't want to lose each other."

SCOTT

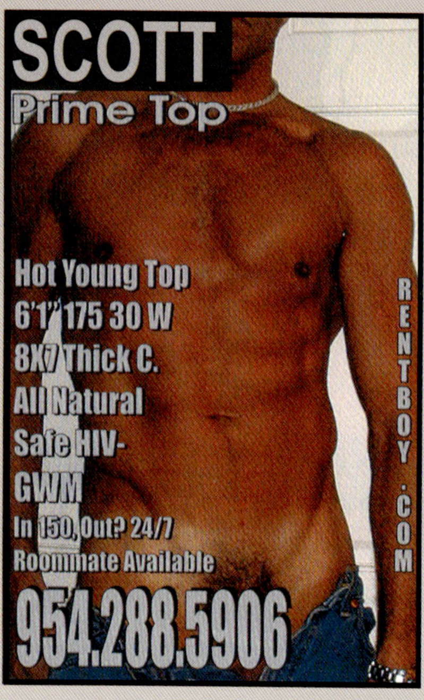

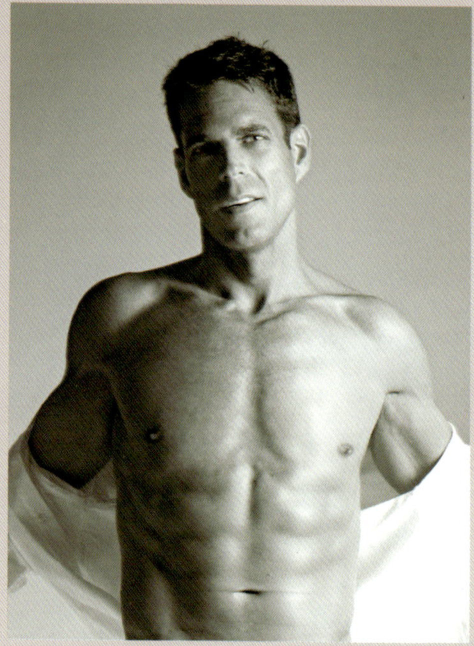

Scott as he calls himself, has a steely gaze. He is a quiet man and although he has a well-muscled body he is not a gym bunny. He runs and swims to maintain his physique. He lives in Fort Lauderdale, which is an excellent city to live in if you want to run and swim and also maintain an allover tan. Scott lives there with his partner Josh. They both work as escorts.

Scott has an unusual story, even for a male escort. In his mid-thirties, he is originally from the Northeast. Previously married, he has only been doing escort work for less than two years. Brought up in rural surroundings, he married his high school girlfriend at the time they were both finishing college. She was from a very strict Catholic background with a domineering father. He had planned a career in law enforcement but upon graduation worked in the automobile business. Scott says, "I didn't really want to be married. I knew I was homosexual. I did it largely to rescue her from her family. I wasn't in love with her. But I loved her and I still do."

As a young couple they lived and worked in a small town near one of the larger

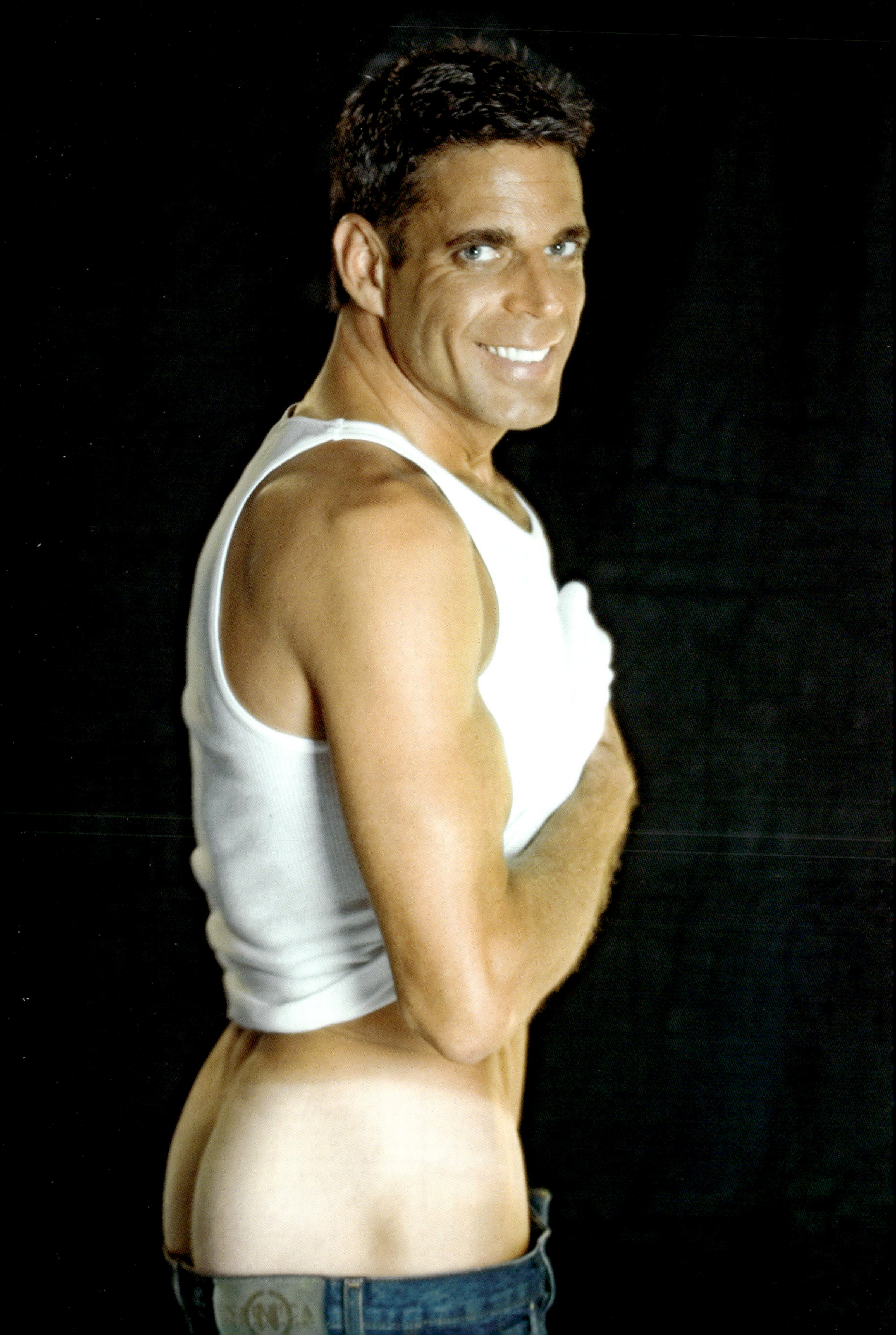

cities in that part of the country. After several years of marriage Scott felt compelled to explore the homosexual side of his nature. He had heard of a gay bar in a nearby town and went there. It was his first time in a gay bar and that night he met an older man who was to become his lover for the next ten years.

This man was handsome, married with children and lived in another small town not far from Scott. They met regularly. Of him, Scott says, "He was smart and insightful and he was able to play upon my insecurities and manipulate me. No one ever told me I was handsome or attractive or sexy and neither did he. I felt unattractive and I didn't like my situation and I felt I had to tell my wife." Which he did.

She did not want to break up their marriage. Appearances were everything in her provincial network of friends and family. She agreed that Scott could continue to meet his lover and she and the lover became very close friends as well, speaking almost every day. The lover even colluded with both the wife's family and Scott's family when they believed Scott was ill and needed medical attention. For the last few years of his relationship with his lover Scott lived with him and worked as a truck driver traveling all over the country. He still kept in close touch with his wife. He says, "I felt particularly unattractive then. I had a beard, wore wool shirts, I felt ugly."

Scott finally escaped his situation when he took a break and returned to his hometown and spent time with a woman friend who was a single mother. This woman forthrightly told him that he was not ill and the he was being urged to try to change his essential character so as to remain in a situation that was not good for him. Scott tells of his return from this visit, "I was met at the airport by my lover. True, we had been living together for several years but it was not good. When I got there he was in high spirits and had an evening of dinner and theater all planned. As luck would have it, that was the day that it had been made possible for same-sex marriages to take place in our area. In the car he said, 'What do you think of that?' I said, 'I don't like the idea. I don't like the idea for you and me.' And our relationship was over."

His relationship with his family has been for all practical purposes severed. From strictly religious farming community backgrounds, they disapproved of Scott's homosexuality completely. His father said, "It's a waste of a man." Of the rest of the family, he says, "I had an uncle, my mother's youngest brother, who was very supportive. He was a truck driver and traveled the whole country, so he had a wider view of what the world's about. When I was driving a truck myself we used to meet all over the place. Louisiana, Oklahoma, you name it. He was a great guy. He died recently in his early sixties of lung cancer and I miss him a lot. Of the whole family he was the only one I felt really loved me and cared what happened to me."

Not wanting to continue his marriage or his relationship with his lover, Scott went into the deep countryside and stayed for several months. One evening he visited a gay bar that was quite a distance from his home. And there he met Josh. This was the first time visiting this bar for both of them. Their life together began that night.

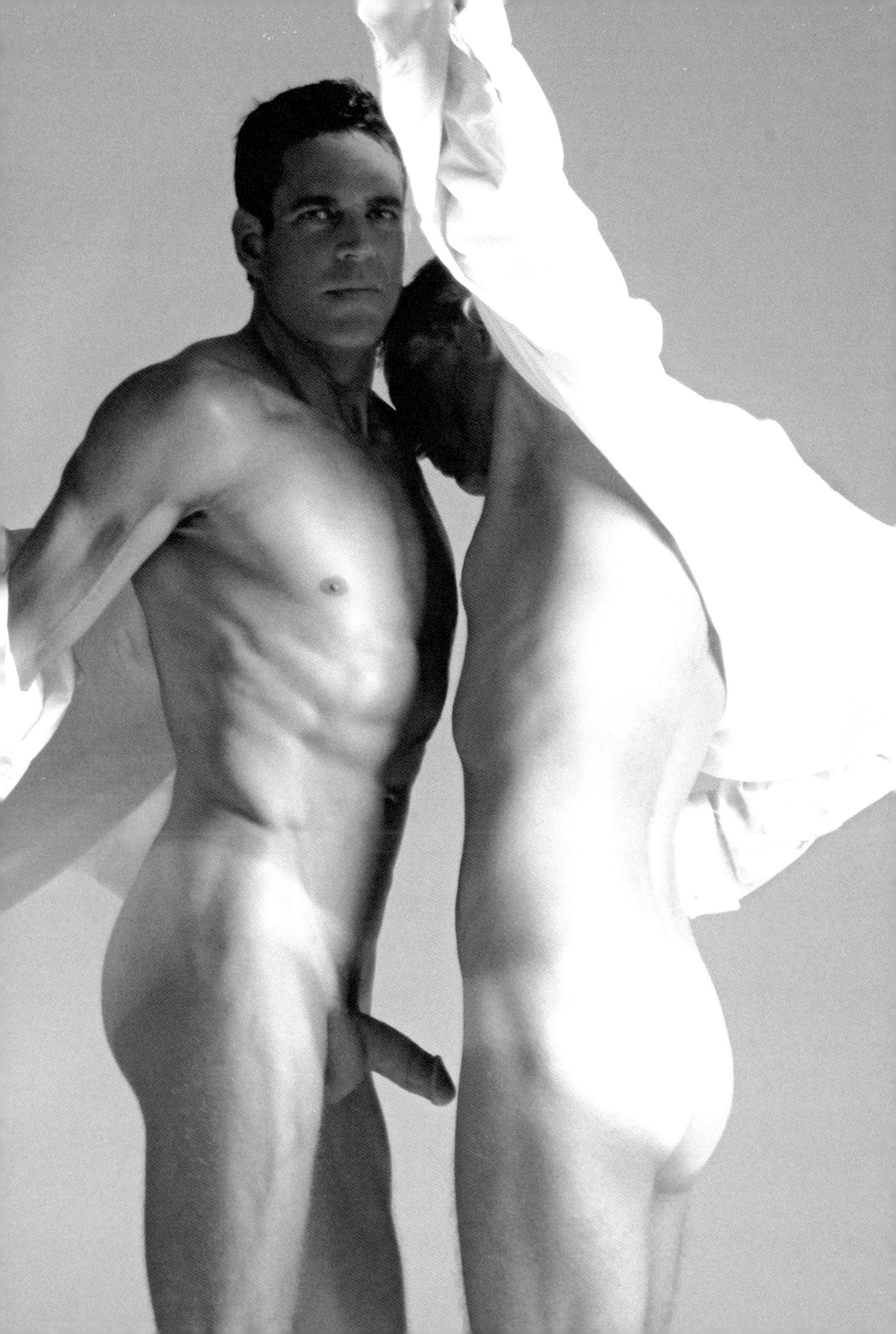

JOSH

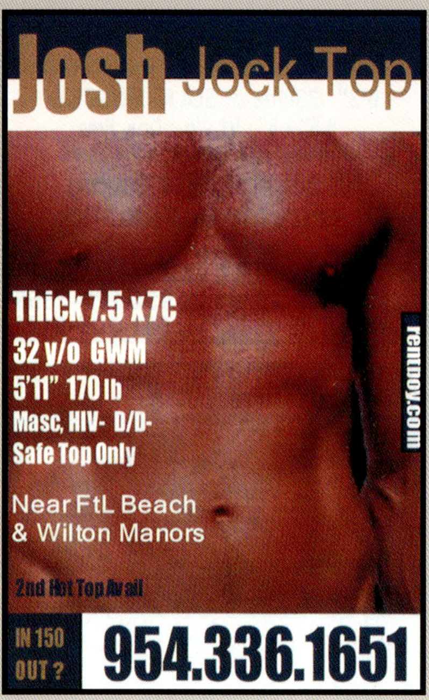

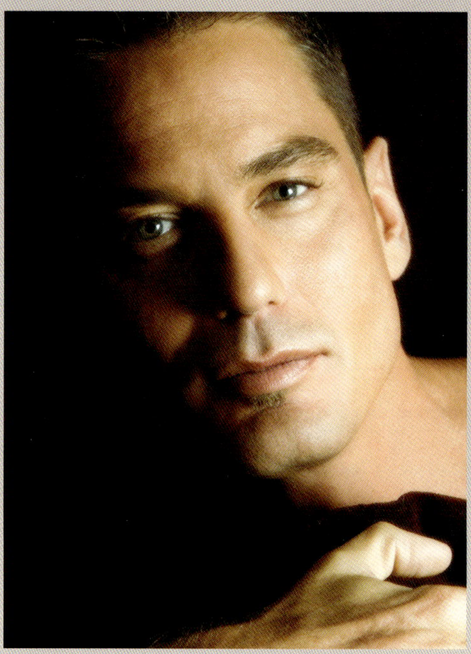

Josh has striking green-gray eyes, not unlike his lover Scott, and a brilliant smile to boot. In his tanned face the effect is immediate.

Josh's history is quite different from his lover Scott's. Coming from roughly the same region, he was aware of his homosexuality as a teenager and acted upon it. "I slept with lots of other boys when I was thirteen, fourteen and older. There was one, then there were two, and then there were lots of us. Sometimes in groups."

His parents were not unsophisticated and among their friends were gay couple. His mother and father wintered in Fort Lauderdale and the gay friends were neighbors. Their son's homosexuality did not alter their relationship with him once they were told.

Soon after graduating from a nearby college where he studied political science; Josh began a long relationship and with his lover he owned a restaurant; he abandoned his plan to study law. There were many ups and downs during their ten-year relationship and it finally foundered. It was at this time that Josh went to the gay bar, also quite distant from his home, where he encountered Scott. They went to a pool party, invited by a local wealthy gay man, and from there went to Scott's home in the rural village where he was living. They spent three months together but there was hostility to the gay couple. The villagers made it clear they weren't ready for two male lovers to be living together in their community.

Josh and Scott decided to make a visit to Fort Lauderdale, familiar to Josh because of his parents' friends. In Florida they found a much freer and welcoming atmosphere. Although they had only come on vacation they did not return North. They rented an apartment and got jobs.

When asked how they transited into becoming male escorts, Josh replies, "I don't know. People seemed to just think we were. At a party an older woman asked me if we were escorts and I guess put the idea into my head. We were both working as waiters for a really terrible boss and one day we had a row with him and quit."

He goes on, "We went to a cyber-café and put up some cell phone photos of ourselves and some details as escorts on the internet and left. I told Scott, 'I can't allow you to do it without me.' I though Scott would get the first call as he was the initiator of the idea. We weren't ten minutes away from the café driving home before I was the one who got a phone call. And so it started."

He laughs and adds, "That first escort request was a nightmare. It was for ten o'clock at night. I was very nervous all day long. Then it started pouring rain. I drove around the corner and ran out of gas and had to park in a neighboring churchyard. Then I walked through the rain to get some gas. After all this, I had to drive to Boca Raton, not very near. Finally I got there and it was fine. A gated community. A very cultivated and interesting German gentleman whom I enjoyed meeting. He was very understanding and very polite. It all worked out very well. He's still a client to this day."

He says he has many young clients. One particularly is a very regular client whom Josh calls, "A bottom in training." He adds, "I always try to remember with my clients that someday I'll probably be calling escorts myself, and try to act accordingly." Josh goes on, "I have worked in the service sector and we bring that attitude to our work. If I brought you a potpie and you were pleased, then I would have done my job. If we have a difficult client we blame ourselves for not having screened the client better." He adds that if the client is taking drugs it is rarely a successful call.

Josh's relationship with his parents is quite different from Scott's. "All my mother is interested in is when we're going to get married. She wants to give us a big party and have us be married by a lesbian minister in her church," he says. His parents do not know of his current work and he does not plan to tell them. He says, "Scott and I were in Fort Lauderdale with nothing. Terrible jobs. A terrible apartment. Salvation Army furniture. No future really. And now we live very well. We have a nice home. Part of our business is conducted at our apartment. I don't know where we are going next but we've gotten somewhere."

KEVIN THOMAS

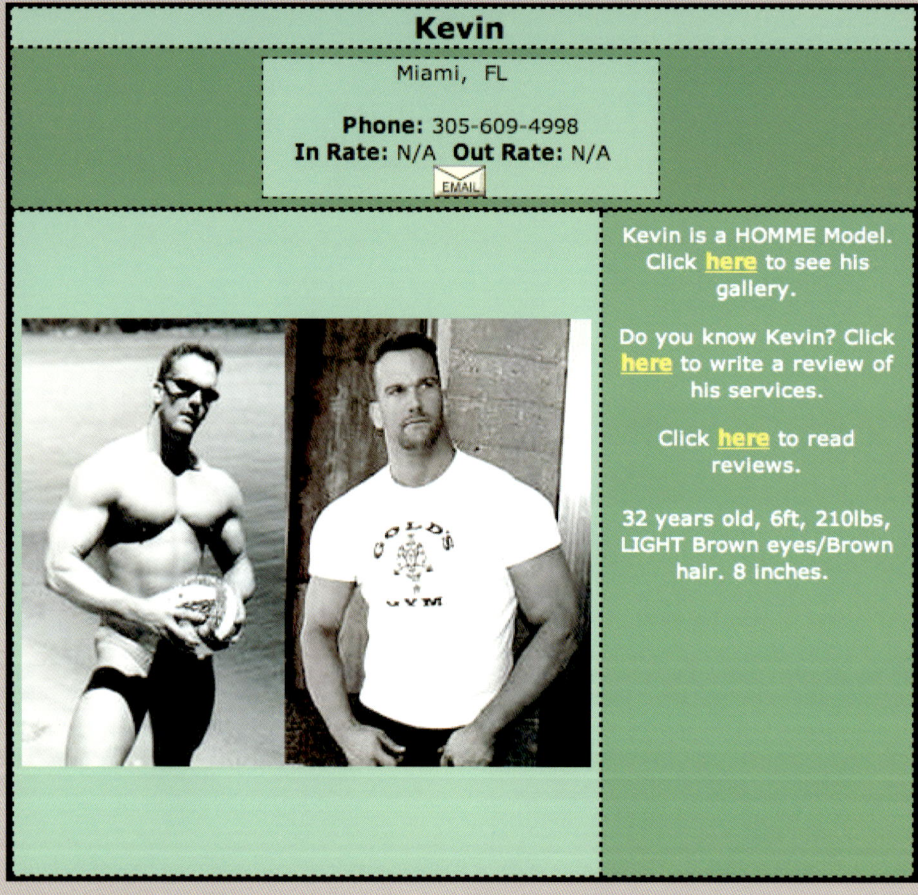

Kevin Thomas is big and brawny but there's something astute about him. He has a jovial smile, piercing pale blue eyes and an easy-to-talk to manner, but occasional comments reveal that he is very much aware of who he is and where he is.

Coming from New Jersey and a sizable family, of whom he is the youngest, he feels comfortable in his career as an escort. He is not in close contact with his family. Only one sister has some idea of how he earns his living. He feels in many ways he was heading for some kind of career like escorting from an early stage of his life. Kevin says,

"Female and male escorting are very different. Everyone sometimes gets into a hard place and needs cash. But with men there is the lover of the male body. As I am very sexual, a lot of excitement comes into play also. My work can be a pleasure.

"When I was a teenager and I realized that there were such things as male strippers I thought that would be a very cool thing to do. Other kids wanted to be firemen or policemen. I was always fascinated with making money out of arousal. When I was a teenager I imagined athletes from my school making love to girls when I masturbated, but after a while those girls weren't there anymore," he adds.

Kevin went to school in his home state and has a degree to teach. A degree he has never used. In his teen years he became very interested in a religious organization, a national church with televised services with which he was involved for his last high school years and through college. This church had strict ideas about sex and members were told even masturbation was wrong. Kevin had no sexual experience at all until he was twenty. "I was never comfortable in the gay world when I was in college," he adds.

He says, "Finally my feelings just got too strong. I had to do something so I went to a bathroom in the college library that had a reputation and there I met a man with a gigantic penis. I'm not somebody who cares particularly about that kind of thing, but I had to bring him back to my dorm room. We fooled around and afterwards I felt so guilty I didn't have sex again for a year."

The religious framework of his life collapsed when the church he belonged to was revealed to have a grave misappropriation of funds and the charismatic minister was found guilty of incest with his daughters. The church ceased to be and Kevin was left without the support of the organization of which he says, "I guess you could call it a cult."

As a college student working at a local chain restaurant for very little money, he had heard of a bar in New York called "Rounds" where it was possible for an escort to meet clients. He went there and says of the experience, "I was so green. I knew nothing. At the restaurant I would sometimes take home as little as fifty dollars when I worked lunch. I thought if I could do better than that then I've got something going." Some clients took advantage of him. Others filled him in on what other escorts were earning.

In his early twenties he went back and forth between a series of low paid and uninteresting jobs and working as an escort. Now he is a full-time escort working out of Miami. He says he has two or three calls a day but there are slow periods and then very active times. When he first came to Miami he worked in an insurance company. But he says, "I don't have the greatest work ethic." He likes the free time escorting allows him.

He has also done some porn films for Falcon Studios. He reports of his first film, "It was the first time I had ever bottomed. It wasn't a fun experience."

Kevin Thomas has a companion whom he is reluctant to call a lover. This man was originally a client. At one time a doctor, his companion is now unable to practice because of a too liberal use of recreational drugs. Kevin's companion has some family

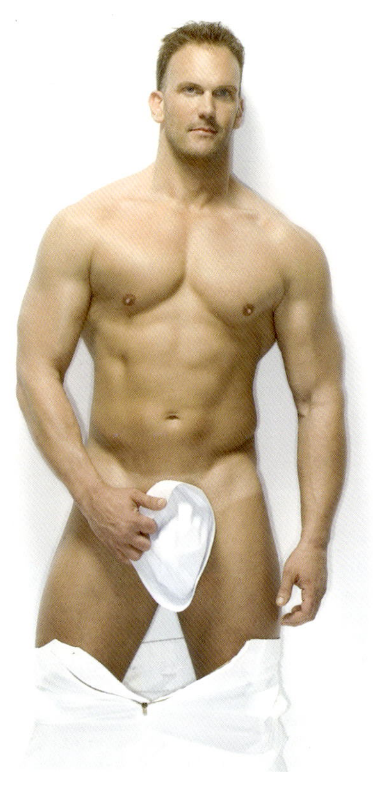

money and a strong interest in sexual experimentation. Kevin says of him, "He has been a great help to me in the understanding of myself. He figured me out. He is astute and can clearly see my personality characteristics, both good and bad. He knows my insecurities. Because of that he has been able to manipulate me frequently. We are together but we are companions, not lovers."

When asked if he has ever been in love his answer is, "Only once and I didn't like the feeling. He was a Cuban bartender with lots of muscles and we dated for a short time. I could feel myself caring about him too much and I did not like the loss of control over my own feelings. So I broke it off. I don't know to what degree he cared about me."

As with some other escorts, Kevin considers himself a very sexual person and believes this is what makes it possible for him to do the kind of work he does. He says, "I'm a bit of a chameleon and can role play easily, from romantic mushy-mushy to very carnal. Once I had to play a kidnapped superhero. Clients offer some very explicit scenarios. I do not mind being chained or having a mask on." He also agrees with other escorts' statements that the client's interest in having sex is more provocative than their physical appearance.

He says of those awkward moments between meeting a client and actually going to bed together, "It's just a matter of getting the chicken into the pot. The chicken wants to go into the pot but sometimes is shy or awkward. My job is to make that easy." It is clear that a successful escort has to have social abilities and creating a calm and confident atmosphere has to be one of them. Kevin says pointedly, "Sex can make people open their wallets much more than other things."

He only remembers one difficult client, who took him to a very remote seaside home and then became paranoid on cocaine, locking himself in his bedroom. Kevin had to wait until dawn for the client to regain his equilibrium and return him to New York City.

He says that sometimes his companion and he hire male escorts themselves when the urge takes them. He admits that he is not as business oriented as some of his competitors. Of his future he says, "I'm just taking it one day at a time."

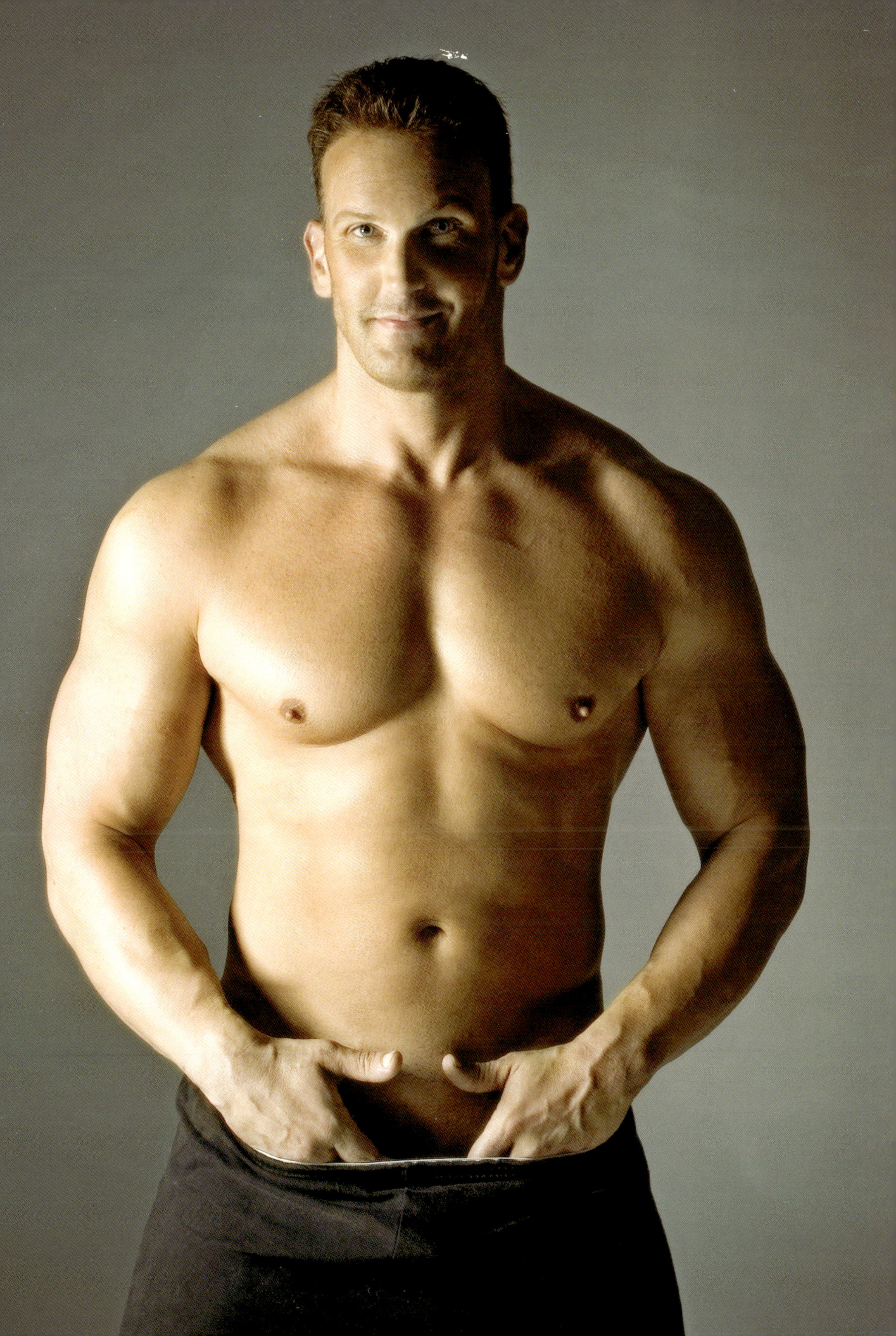

JAIME LEE

Jaime Lee gives a whole new meaning to the word entrepreneur. This handsome, muscular native of Panama has ventured into the escort business largely motivated by a desire to help his family. Through his work his mother and his three siblings have been rescued from poverty and have launched solid, secure lives, both financially and emotionally.

Jaime Lee arrived in Miami at the age of 17 without working papers. In his first year in this country he took any work he could find: construction, selling papers, anything. His luck changed when he was working as a food server in a chain restaurant and a young student from Michigan came down the line. They spoke, exchanged numbers and began a long-distance telephone relationship.

After three months the student called and invited Jaime to share a house in a Detroit suburb. In Michigan Jaime flourished, albeit working three jobs to earn money to

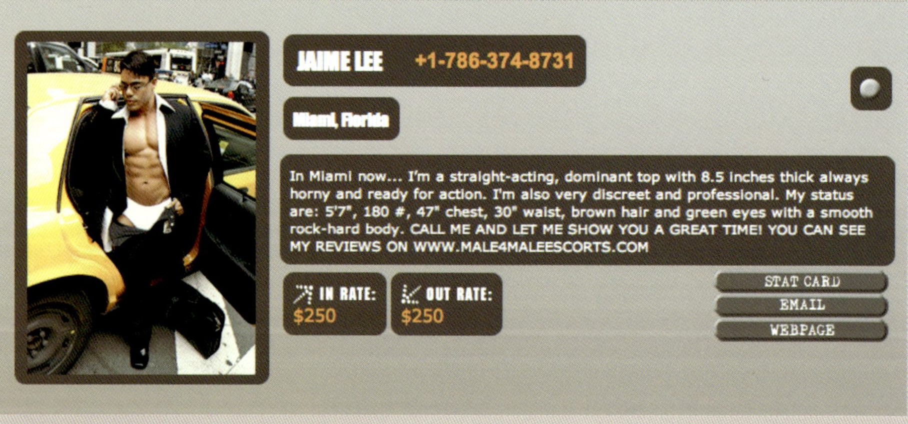

send to his family in Panama. He was sleeping five hours a night and sending most of the money he earned home.

He says of that period, "I really went to Michigan to learn English. I knew that if I stayed in Miami I'd never learn. And it was there that I also began to go to the gym regularly. Working at Wendy's and not exercising I blew up to 215 pounds. I went on a diet of salads at Wendy's and lost weight."

His relationship with the student soured after a year and a half. He explains, "He was preparing to be a preacher and was a very serious Bible student. My mother brought us up in the practice of Buddhism. My friend just couldn't stop giving long religious harangues and so finally I moved out." His work impressed his employers at the clothing store and he advanced there, both in responsibilities and salary. In the suburb where he lived he had frequently seen a neighbor mowing his lawn. An older man who worked shirtless and had an impressive body. Jaime admired him and finally stopped one day and introduced himself. He thought to himself, "I'm going to make him want me."

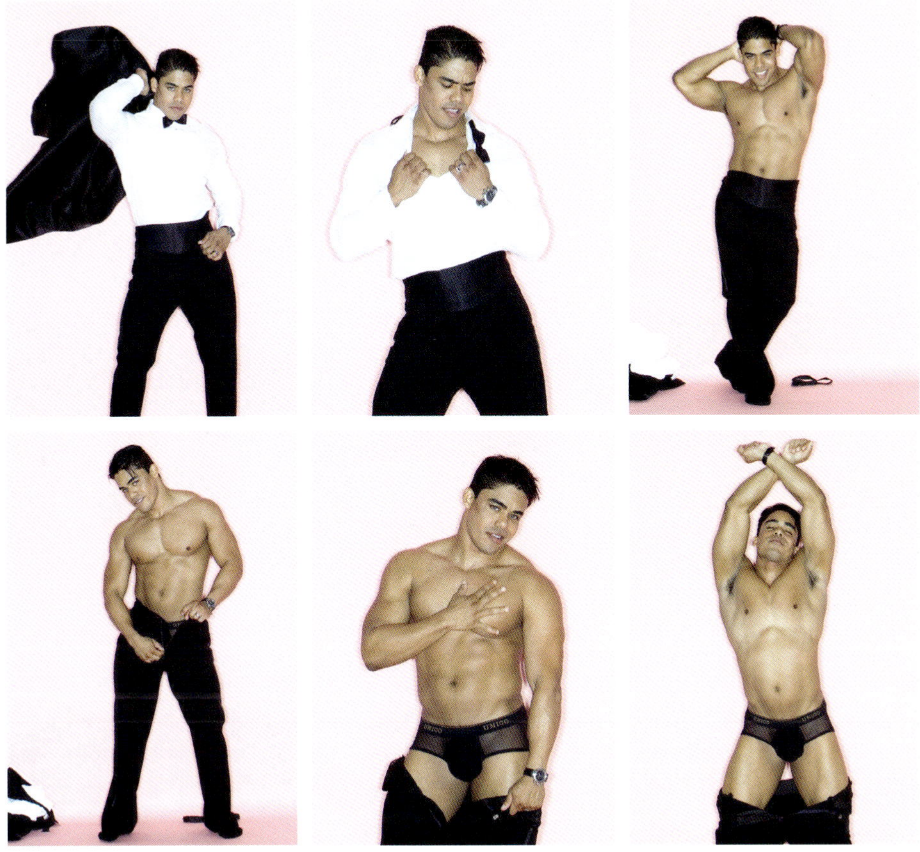

The man obviously liked Jaime yet seemed unwilling to start a relationship. Jaime understood one day when his new acquaintance showed him a photo of his former lover who had died of AIDS. Jaime guessed that this man, too, was seropositive and chose this way to tell him. Knowing this, Jaime persuaded him that he didn't care and they became lovers.

When Jaime was asked by the chain store of clothiers he worked for if he would like to manage a store in Miami, he jumped at it. His language skills were a key factor. He speaks Spanish and Portuguese as well as English. The move was not a problem for his lover, who was a financial advisor working from home. By this time Jaime had helped one brother come to the United States and settle in Houston, where he is employed and happily married. His sister also was able to emigrate, become educated, and move up to a good car and a good job. She recently married and lives in Miami. Jaime says, "I have to do the right thing by them. I told myself many times, if I make a little mistake they will have to pay for it. The hardest thing was not seeing them for three years. I had a Social Security card, filed taxes but was not allowed to leave the U.S. When I brought my sister here she wasn't a baby anymore and I missed that."

His relationship with the financial advisor worsened when Jaime wanted to start handling his own money. He felt he had to build credit history on his own and become legal. Until then he had turned over his paycheck to his lover and received an allowance. Now 25, he wanted more financial freedom. His lover wouldn't give it to him and he departed. He adds, "Everything is 'ours' when things are fine. When you break up things suddenly become 'mine'." He left the relationship with very little.

Shortly after, he spent an evening at a bar with friends. He participated in a wet T-shirt contest and as the winner was asked to dance at the bar. He danced on his days off from midnight to 3:00 A.M. His tips came to about $300 a night.

The difference in income was so great that Jaime became a full-time dancer, working five nights a week in different clubs. He heard about the Gaiety, a club in New York. He applied there many times and says, "Only the most beautiful men worked there. I pestered them for a long time and finally they took me. You could work seven or ten straight days, six shows a day, but only once every three months. They constantly wanted new faces. Two Greek women ran the Gaiety. They paid performers $50 a show, which came to about $500 a week."

Dancers were allowed to work as escorts on their afternoon break. No sexual contact was permitted in the theater. Doing this, in one ten day period Jaime earned $15,000. However, the police began raiding the Gaiety and just at that time a Gaiety client said, "You need a website." And Jaime set up *eastcoastboy.com*. He subsequently did a solo masturbation video for "Muscle Hunk," a video distribution company that advertised on the back of fitness magazines. He does not see this as porn but as a business strategy. The video was linked to his website and that changed his life. "I got 180 calls the first day. That is the day I became Jaime Lee and my life changed," he says. He is now available on *rentboy.com*, where he has been for five years.

Jaime Lee has inquiries on his website that range from questions about his workout routine, his hair cut, his weight and his bathing suit to invitations to be flown to Japan. He has many regular clients and travels a great deal to visit them and frequently to travel with them. He has recently been on a long trip to Japan with a client, and has visited other countries as well. He has a number of single gay clients who fly him to their home cities to keep them company. He points out, "I was out of town 85% of the time last year. The upside is visits to many interesting places."

When in Miami he may have three to ten engagements a week. Jaime books his own regular visits to other cities and when in these places may have four to five engagements a day. "Most are mutual masturbation sessions," he says. "They want a top but they don't really want to be topped. They want someone to take charge. For the most part they want to cuddle and kiss and masturbate."

He explains that over 80 percent of his clients are between their early forties to their late sixties. He has three to ten clients per week. About fifty percent of them are married. As for getting aroused for clients he says, "As long as they play with my nipples I can always get aroused."

His strangest request was from a man who called him and wanted him to come to the Raleigh Hotel pool and flirt with the man's wife. He was to suggest going to her room and when they did then have a three-way with her husband and her. Jaime refused. "It would be too easy for that to be a police set up," he says. "And what if I got the wrong woman? No way."

At this time Jaime Lee has a very nice house in a beautiful part of Miami, an expensive car and a very satisfactory lifestyle. He has been able to buy a home for his mother in Panama and is happy that his father has returned to her after a number of other women and children.

In the future Jaime Lee sees investing in real estate as his move into another line of business. His advice to those interested in escorting, "It's like any other job. You have good days and bad days. I practice safe sex and get tested every six to eight months for every sexually transmitted disease. My doctor is aware of my work."

"You have to be mentally strong. Most of my clients are powerful men who are in control of their lives. They want the escort to take over. You have to be stable to do that. It can take its toll on you and become mechanical. You can't get money crazy or lose your sense of sexual excitement."

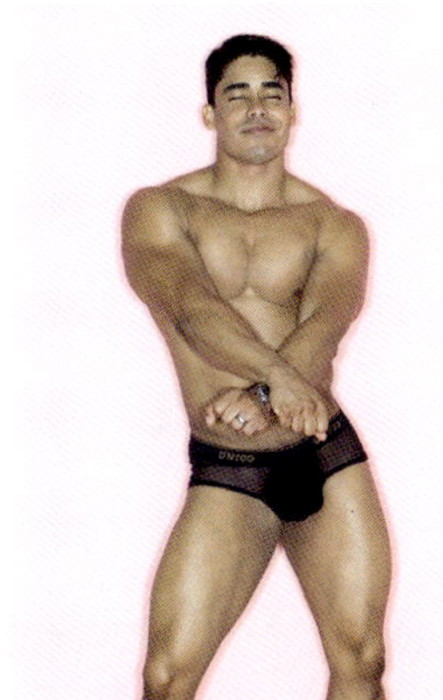

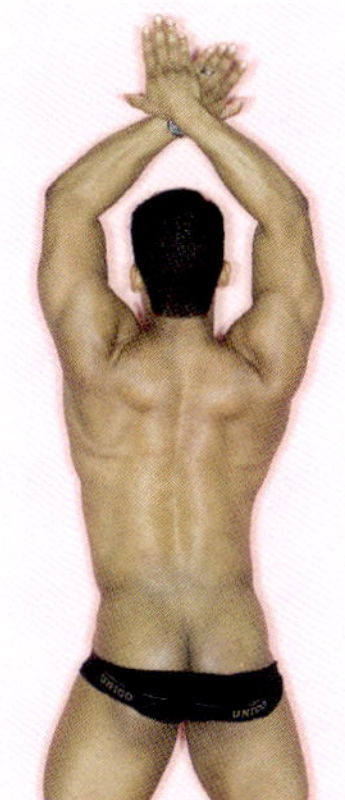

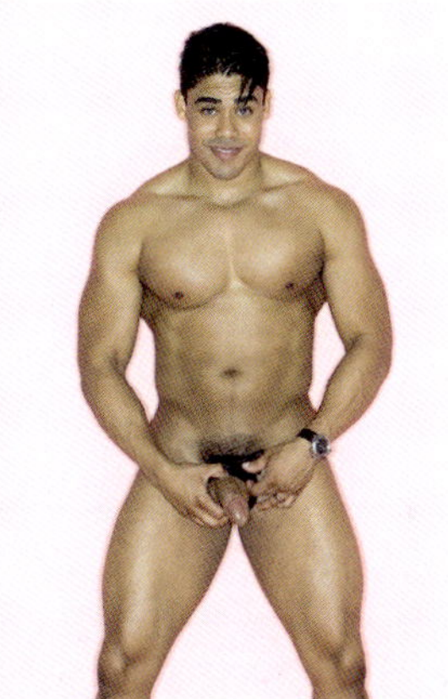

TYLER MICHAELS

Tall, blond, athletic looking Tyler Michaels is the prototypical American jock. The kind of guy so many high school boys had a secret crush on. No wonder he gets so many calls from well to-do middle-aged men who have never had sexual contact with another man before. Finally they've worked up the nerve... and earned enough money... to fulfill their dreams. Even if they are married and have a family.

Tyler Michaels is what he seems. Brought up on a farm, which his family didn't work. A high school athlete who played collegiate baseball at the large Middle-Western school he attended. He's not pretending to be anything he's not.

He fell in love while in college and went with his lover to another large university town in the Middle West. Tyler worked there while the other man was pursuing an advanced degree. Once that was completed they moved to Minneapolis to launch their careers.

Tyler worked as a publicist for a publishing firm there and found the work petty and unfulfilling. When his relationship broke up, about which he remains bitter, he moved to Chicago and continued working in promotion and publicity for several different publishers. At the same time he began making contact with other men online.

"That's how I began working as an escort. Men wanted to meet me and suggested that they were willing to pay for it. And also men would come up to me in bars, even on the street, and suggest we meet for money. And I did it from time to time. Very casually and not often. I didn't like my job and it seemed an okay thing to do. Then I got fired." Tyler says.

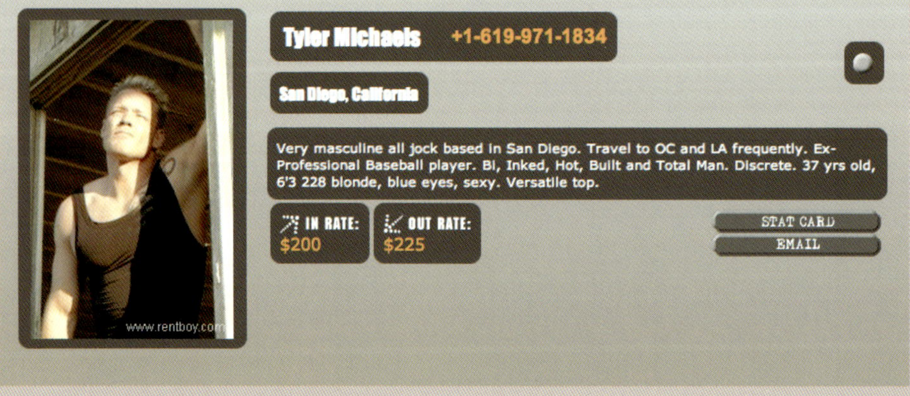

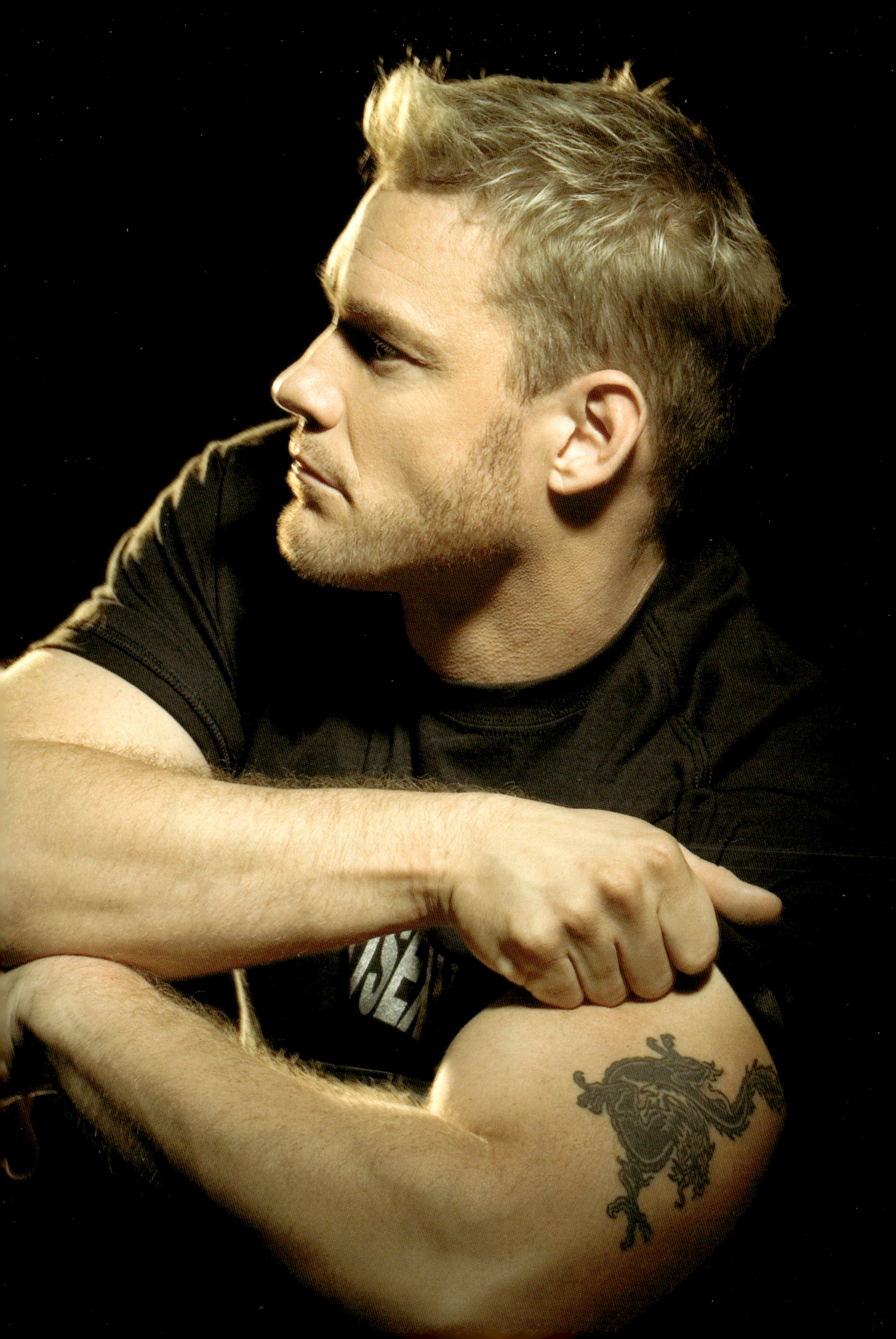

When he was fired he got a substantial sum of severance pay and decided to move to California. In San Diego he says he has a few friends who know what he does for a living but his new career as a full-time escort takes up almost all of his time. He travels a good deal, visiting highly placed CEOs and Presidents of major companies who do not want to hire escorts in their own cities to avoid gossip and notoriety. He has one of the higher rates for escort services.

Tyler Michaels does not have a lover and does not wish to have one. He believes that what he does for a living would be an enormous hurdle for another person to accept. When asked if he at times meets men who are not clients and spends romantic evenings with them he answers, "Yes, I do occasionally. But while we're making love I think 'There goes another $500 I could have earned'."

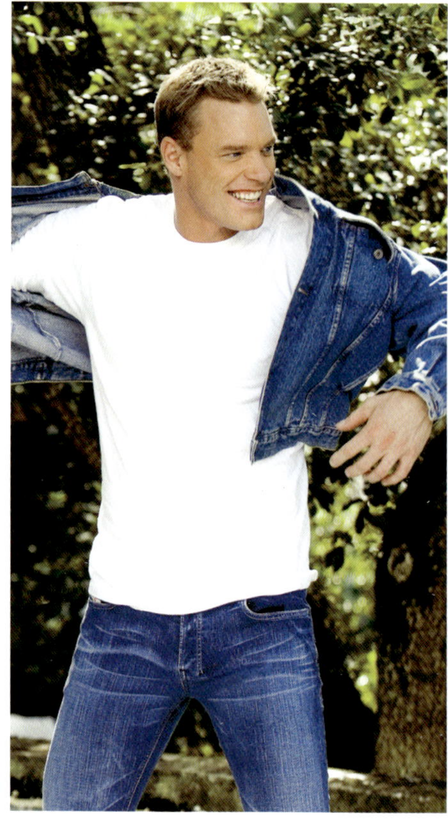

Talking about his work Tyler says, "My clients are falling into two major groups lately. I have these older, successful men who have never had sex with another man before. I have a lot of them. And then I have men who want to have a three-way with a woman. But the woman is there to give orders. She's supposed to say things like, 'Now you have to suck his...' things like that. I tell clients I don't know any women who will do that. And I don't."

He tells of a recent assignment which began with a trainer from Palm Springs who called and asked him to stand in for him with an important client. There was a very precise scenario that began with meeting the client at the airport and was followed with very specific things to say and do. When Tyler met the client he recognized the voice immediately. The client had posed as his own trainer so as to prepare a very exact series of events. He didn't want to be embarrassed by asking/suggesting anything in person. As a major president of a large company he was used to giving orders.

Tyler adds, "It's all about power and control. These men have to control everything they do. They don't want to have improvisations in their lives, even with a male escort."

Asked if he was saving money and what his overall plan is, Tyler finishes his interview by saying, "I'm saving money but not as much as I would like to. As for a plan, I don't really have one. Yet."

GERONIMO

Geronimo is a dark eyed Latin charmer with all the personal glamour of a 1930s movie star. He seems not too firmly attached to his identity as a male escort. And he is actually quite convincing when he explains that he is truly concerned with making other people happy. His parents are from Colombia and the Dominican Republic but he was born in New York. He has the happy disposition of someone from the islands combined with the adaptability to reality of a big city dweller.

As a child he lived in Puerto Rico, attended school there and in the Dominican Republic, his mother's home country. He finished high school in New York. At eighteen he was already married and the father of a child. His married life lasted for eight years. During most of this time he also had male lovers. He tells of his first relationship: "I was shopping in New York for a few things for the new baby. It was Gay Pride weekend. Walking down the street I saw this man in a window. He beckoned for me to come in. And I did. He was Puerto Rican and we became lovers. I was very much in love with him for six years."

His wife never knew of this lover. Geronimo worked for a computer company at this time and often worked a late shift. In this way it was possible for him to see his male lover without arousing suspicion. He kept a separate apartment that his wife knew nothing about and he began to see other men there also. Finally he felt he had to tell his wife about his secret life. She decided to stick their marriage out anyway. But eventually she decided to separate and took him to court for child custody. It all became too much for Geronimo.

He says, "My mom is a very religious Catholic. She doesn't know I'm an escort. But one Christmas I just sat the whole family down… sister, brother, spouses… and told

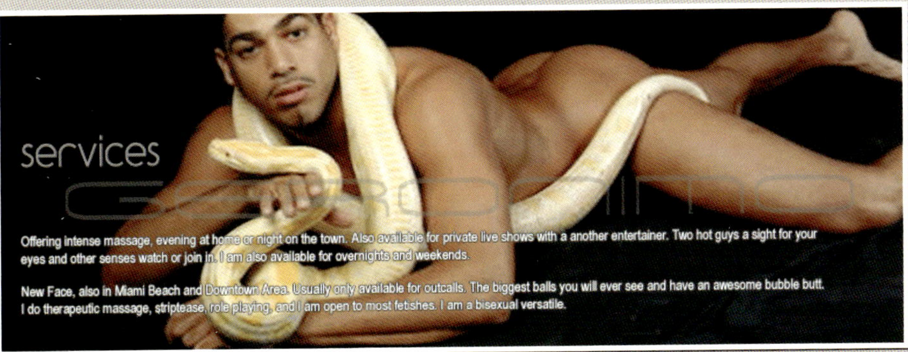

them I was gay." He had been living in Miami for three years at this point and after explaining everything to them he began a new life. His wife returned to Philadelphia with their child and he began a relationship with an attractive Italian man he met at the beach. He says of this man, "Friends are better than lovers. The relationship lasts longer. We are more like brothers."

"So when my friend suggested that we make ourselves available as a threesome with a porn star he knew, I wasn't at all sure that I was going to like it. My friend has a business he calls Beauty Dungeon where men can have hair removed from their bodies and their appearance improved, as well as exploring sex. We offered clients a large variety of sex experiences including voyeurism, single interaction, multiple involvements, lots of variations. Treatments were $40. Service was $300. The phone did not stop ringing. We were very successful."

Geronimo has done covers for an S&M magazine but did this work in New York at a time he was still married. His face wasn't shown and he reports, "They wanted me to continue doing them because sales shot up when I was on the cover but that is not at all my scene. And I moved at about that time."

At the present time he works for Wally Hurrell, who has the Horizontal Way company. He works both as a receptionist and locates new talent. Geronimo also works for a number of the cluster of online companies owned by Hurrell. He appears on *handsomemodel.com* and also *bigcocksociety.com*. He has worked in the past for *rentboy.com* and says of that organization that they are "wonderful people."

Geronimo likes his work. He says, "I believe an escort offers companionship. You give the client a nice time. Our job is to make the other person happy. I like to make people feel good. I always tell them on the phone that I offer them a massage. When we talk afterwards clients say 'You made my fantasy come true'. For instance, a client may call me up, we'll go to Cirque de Soleil have dinner. I'm very flexible. We don't have to have sex. I think my massages relax clients. I offer a nude erotic massage. If they are shy I massage them with their clothing on and relax them into undressing."

He states that he has never had a frightening client but occasionally deals with a strange one. "Like the man who wanted me to smoke a cigar, fuck him and watch the football game. All at the same time. After demanding, 'First, handcuff me'." Geronimo's service usually includes a massage and he always travels with oil, powder for men who don't want to go home with scented oil on their skin, condoms, lube, all the necessary materials for his work. He is concerned about disease and refuses any clients who want bareback.

A friend charges $1200 a night. "I've charged $700 and gotten repeats. Plus getting a dinner, a show and staying at a nice hotel. Why be greedy?" In the future he would like to be a chef. He purportedly excels at Colombian cuisine. "I love to cook and my goal is to have my own restaurant. When I hit 40 I want to be set up," Geronimo says. He concludes, "I'm a friendly person and I like to meet people. I think it will all fit together."

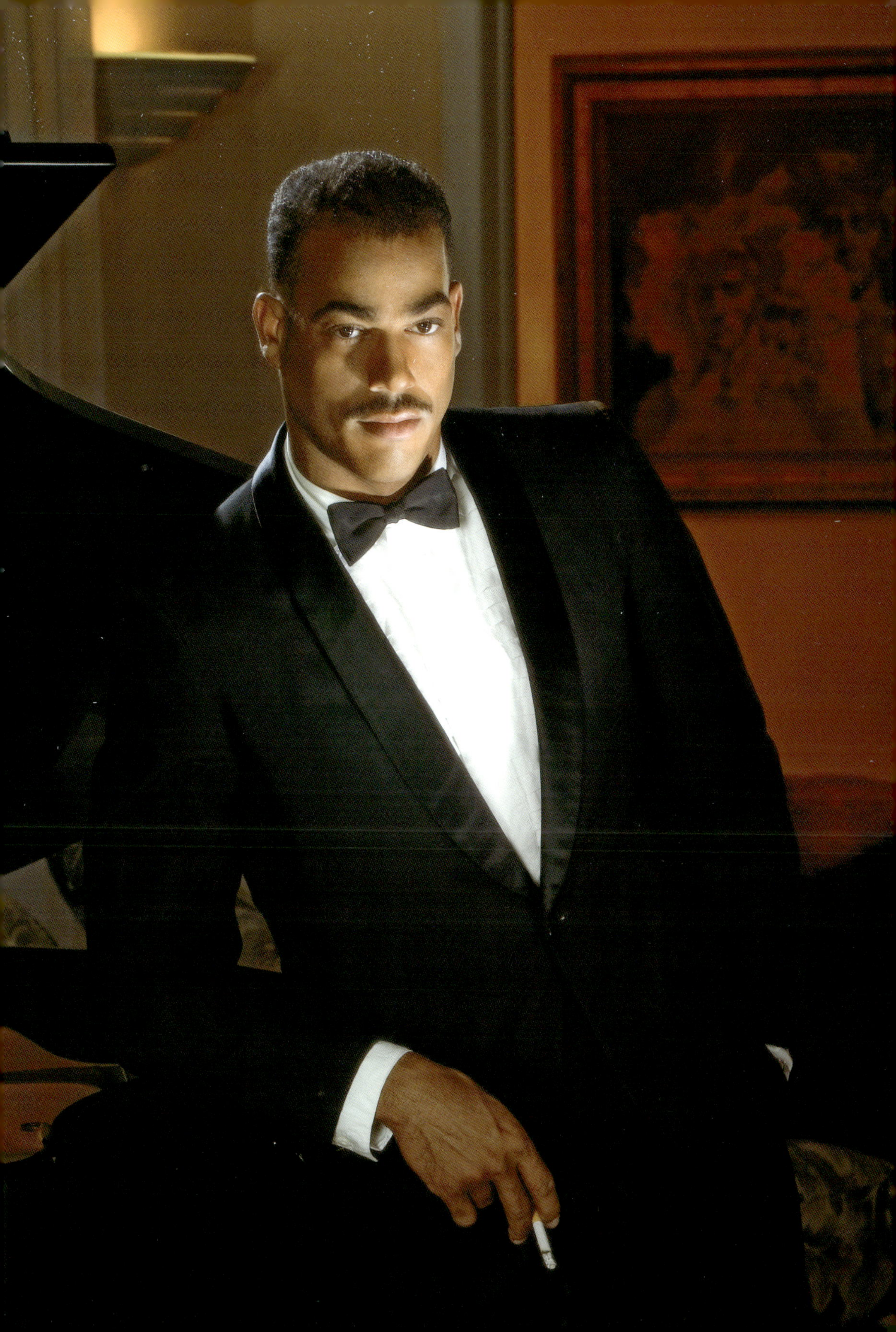

MARLONE STAR

Marlone Thomas. Also know as Marlone Star. So handsome. Sigh. Marlone's career as an escort has developed from his very successful career as a show dancer. He works both in Chicago and Orlando at present.

He is used to an itinerant life as he was an Army brat, traveling about with his family as they were posted from one base to another. He joined the Army himself at sixteen, which was permissible with family consent, and trained for five years to work as an Army nurse. His original commitment for three years was extended for two more. He explains that his family worked in nursing in the Army and it was something he felt comfortable doing. While in the Army he was married to a lesbian, for the most part because of the benefits that were available to married couples. He was stationed in Hawaii at this time.

He began dancing in Honolulu while he was in the Army at private parties. A gifted dancer, he had been seen in a nightclub and asked to work. This pay was $150 for half an hour and although it was forbidden to military personnel Marlone decided to do it, forbidden or not. He was with his wife at this time but they were leading increasingly separate lives. He led this double career and double life in Hawaii for two years without being caught, a court martial looming over his head all the time.

When he was transferred to Fort Lewis in Washington State he began dancing in Seattle at a club called Mr. Paddywack. At a club one night he met a stripper, performed on an amateur night and began to work, again illegally. He did this for two more years until he finished his military service.

His background is in fact a further cry from his present lifestyle than one might suspect. He was brought up in the Pentecostal church where women do not wear pants, jewelry or makeup and morals are strictly observed. His own father died when he was still a baby and his mother remarried when he was three. His stepfather was stationed in Germany and that is where he finished high school. He says there was no cursing, drinking or smoking pot in those days.

He realized he was gay when he was 17 but had no masturbation fantasies about men. His wet dreams were about women and he had girlfriends. He has five sisters who are all medical technicians in the Army and his mother is a General Practitioner. His father is a Supply Sergeant.

His first sexual experience with another man was aboard an airplane when he was transferred to Hawaii. He wasn't 18 yet. There were only 50 passengers in a plane that could carry 250. He was seated by himself near a window when another man came over and sat down beside him. After some conversation the man said, "Is it a myth that black men have large cocks? If it's that big I'll suck it."

Marlone says, "I don't know why but I said to him, 'I'm going to pull it out on the count of one- two- three-!" Then they went to a bathroom together and Marlone says that it was so exciting he told himself, "This can't be bad. I know it doesn't fit the rules. You're supposed to have sex if you're married. But this is important to me."

In the reception battalion when he arrived he met other gay men and this was the first time he entered another man and was entered. Once he was in Hawaii he learned his way around the gay world more seriously. He asked a cab driver to take him to a gay club, drank liquor, and grabbed men's crotches. He says, "I thought that was what it was all about."

He went home with a model on one night and was injected with cocaine. He had a severe reaction and the model helped him walk it off. He prayed he'd come out of it and the experience frightened him badly.

On another evening he accompanied a man to his apartment. He asked the man, "What is your fantasy?" The man answered, "Mine is dogs' dicks." Marlone said, "How about another fantasy? You must have another one." The reply was, "I have a crush on my father. We've been having sex for two years. It's fabulous." Marlone says, "I left. I decided I didn't want to be gay. I didn't like dogs. I didn't like my father. I was going to try something else."

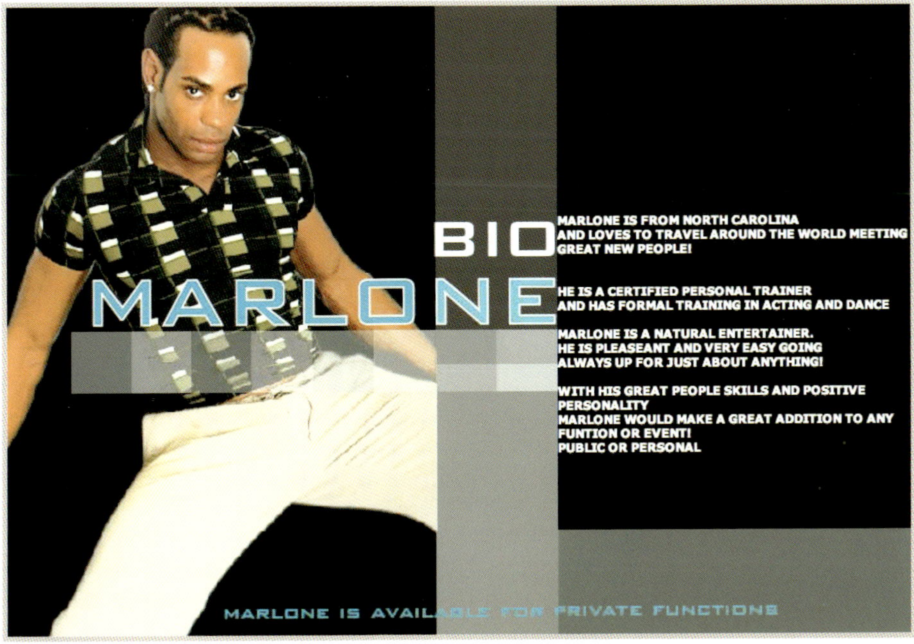

After leaving the Army and dancing in North Carolina Marlone moved to New York where he worked for a private investigation company. He says that it was his boss, who felt romantic about him, who suggested, "Let's check out some dancing places." They went to Stella's at 47th Street and 8th Avenue, a large two level club with about 25 dancers a night, and there Marlone began dancing again. This was in 2001.

He then applied to the Gaiety. The tough Greek ladies who owned it told him he had to audition. He danced to a song called "Brown Skin" which they didn't like. They told him "You have to change your song. It's too black. It will make the clients unhappy." But after working a few days they realized it was his best number and told him to go back to it.

At the Gaiety he began to have clients and took them to the St. James hotel, where the other dancers went. His comment on that hotel is, "It's very prehistoric." Marlone would like to make a documentary on his days at the Gaiety, where he says many famous people like Calvin Klein were in the audience. They would frequently attend the Gaiety before moving on to other nightclubs.

As far as the details of his escorting life, Marlone describes his clients as being mostly between 50 and 60, white and successful. Many are married, although most are not. "Frequently they want to be abused mentally or physically." He points out, "Everyone wants a dominant top. Many also claim that they have never been fucked before." He doubts this claim, however, since the sex is never very difficult. He does have some calls for threesomes. He concludes, "Lots of my clients think I'm straight. If there's a girl involved too, I can charge more. That's okay with me." He says of his clients, "I do to them what in my mind would be hot if I were in their place. I experiment with them as guinea pigs. When they show me how they like it I learn more about ways of pleasing them and having mutual fulfillment.

"My fantasy is of having a gang of Aryan men having rough sex with me. Of course, a scene highly organized by me, selecting the hottest guys: shaved heads, verbal aggressive. Most people want a dominant aggressive top. I pound them good but I don't climax. I bring them to a climax. It saps me of my energy if I have a dancing performance afterwards. If they want me to climax it would cost them extra. About $50. A rich man in the fashion business invited me to St. Tropez in France. He wanted me to have a certain look. This may have been a control thing. I gladly accepted his offer to buy me new clothing to wear on that trip."

He maintains a close relationship with his family, particularly his mother. He says that she does not approve of his lifestyle but she loves him and will never distance herself from him. His mother supervises his financial life and they are in very regular contact at all times. He concludes, "We are all stars made out of star stuff. It's up to us to make it happen. We are all made out of hydrogen."

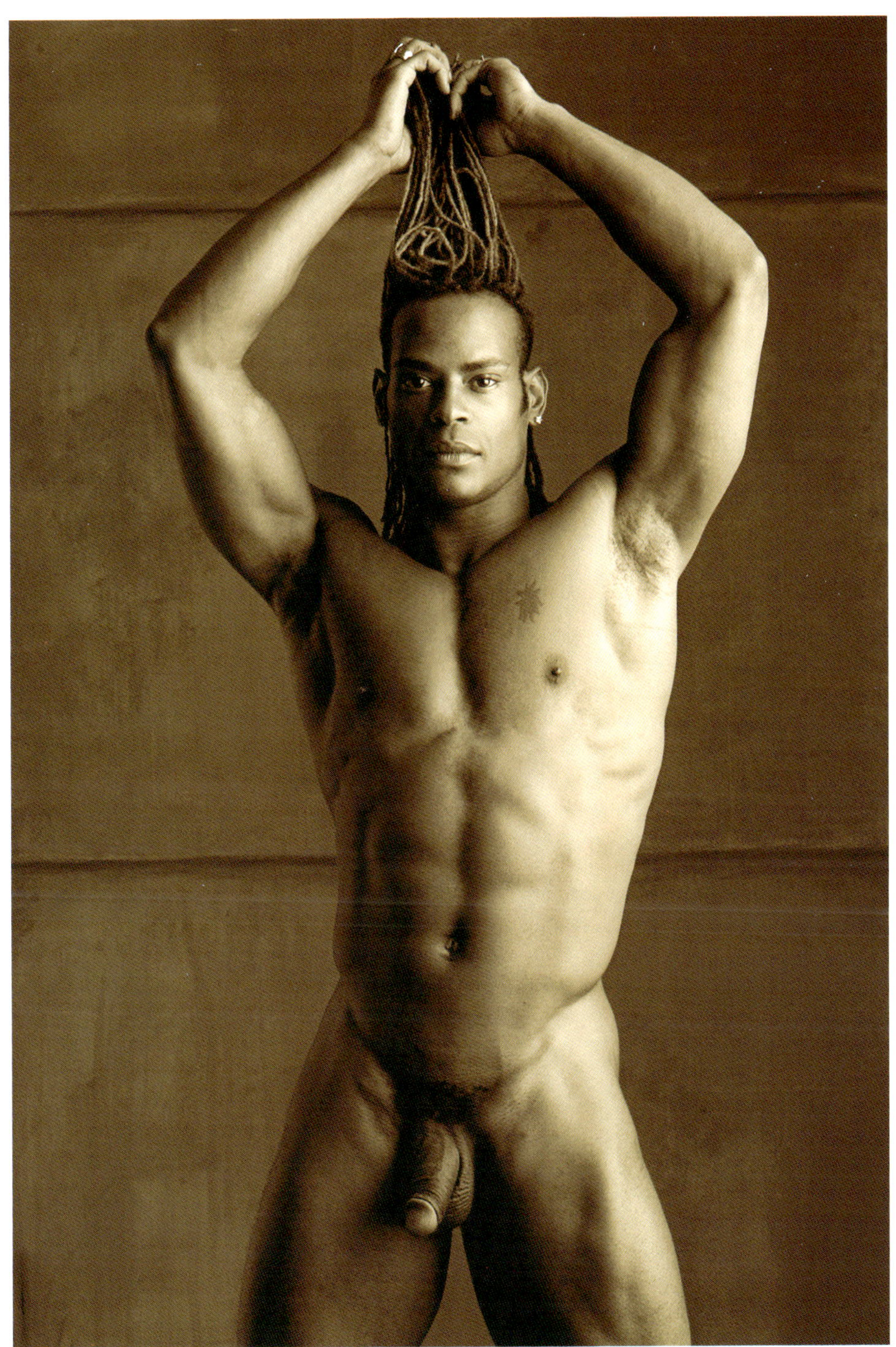

CODY JOHNSON

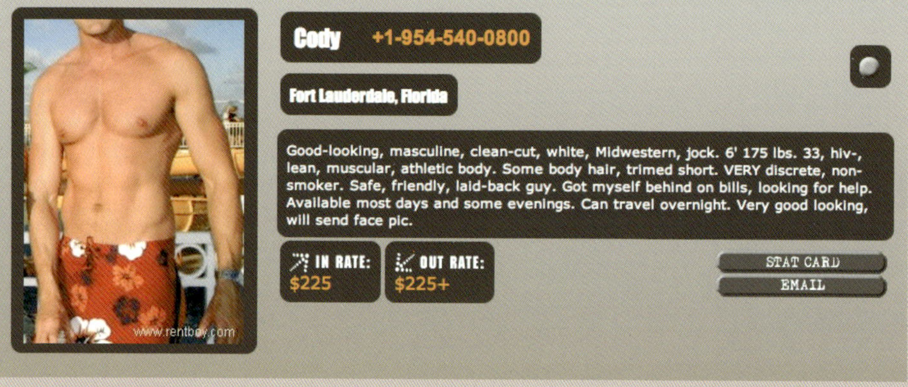

Cody Johnson is so nice, so cute, so polite, and even a little bit shy, that you say to yourself, "This boy can't possibly be an escort." But he is. And he likes the work, too.

Cody is from Michigan, from Dearborn to be precise. His mother worked as a nurse at one time. His father was an engineer for Ford motors. He has an older brother, who is also gay, and a younger sister and brother. His All American looks are a result of Polish, Austrian, Hungarian and German ancestors.

He attended Catholic Central High School in Detroit and studied Graphic Design at the College of Creative Studies there. After college Cody moved to California. In college he had done advertising work for automotive clients. He quickly found a job in Los Angeles and worked as a creative director in an advertising agency. Branching out in this period, he opened a restaurant called Quiznos, which he owned and operated for two years.

Talking about his sexuality he says, "I realized I was gay in Sixth Grade. I realized that I liked boys. I finally had sex with a guy my freshman year in college. It was a drunken episode after a fraternity party in the backseat of Kelly's Camaro."

Cody lived at home during college. He was wearing a Mohawk at the time and says, "I was a little front edge." Seeing him with the same male friend all the time, his parents began to suspect he was gay. His mother sat him down and for some strange reason had his sister listen in on the conversation from the next room. She warned him that he was going to get AIDS and did not speak to him for a year. Cody departed for California with his boyfriend.

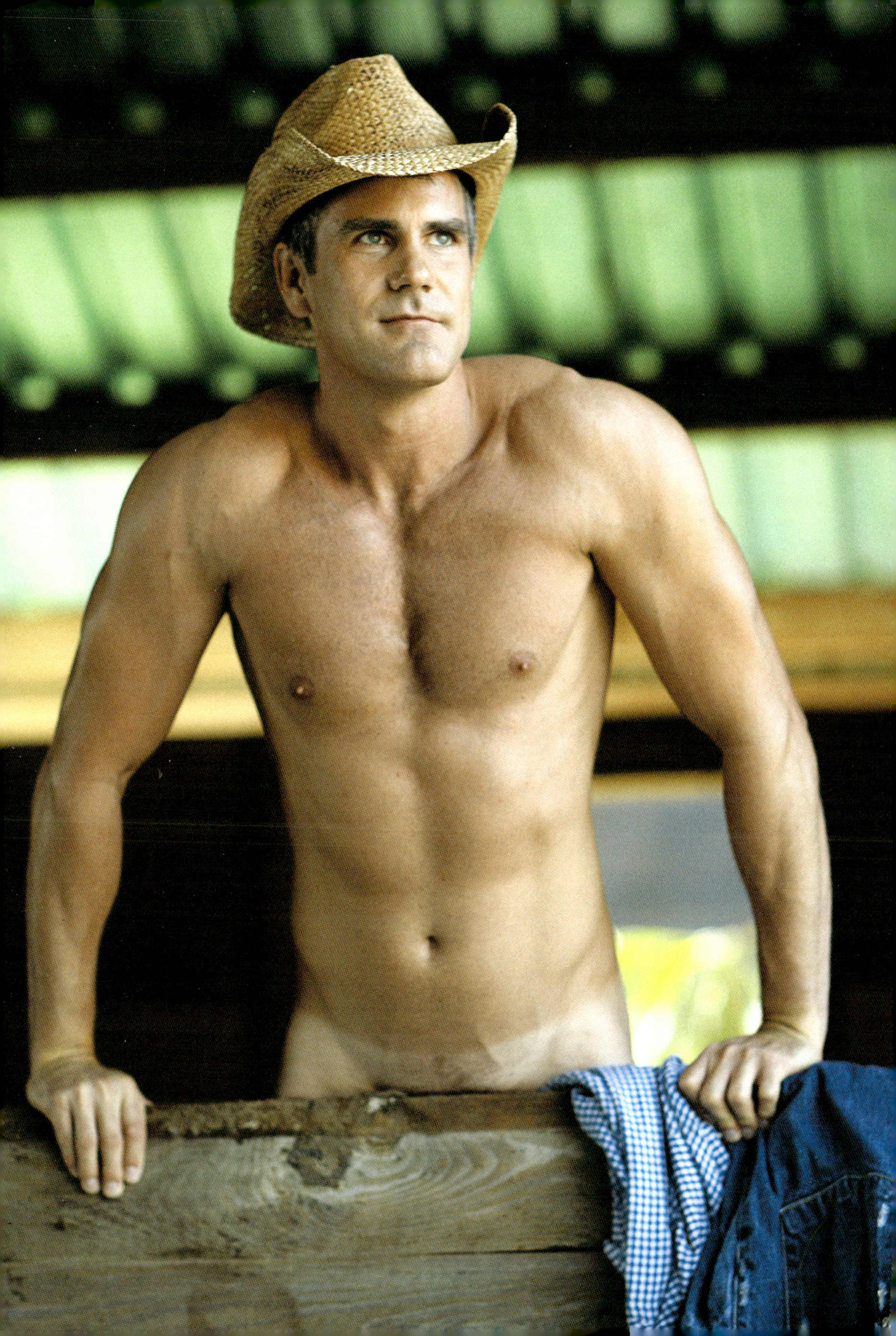

Their relationship fell apart in three months and the boyfriend returned to Detroit. Cody then fell in love with a man named Michael and their relationship lasted for five years. His lover was the music director for a convent and associated college. He says, "Before it was over we had stopped having sex. We tried having sex with someone else in the relationship. We had some three-ways and then Michael started seriously dating the third guy."

Cody entered escorting to solve debt problems. His partner in the restaurant was to sell his condo to help finance the start-up and failed to do so. They were seriously underfinanced. Cody says, "I was on line talking to guys from time to time and one man offered me $60 to suck my dick. I did it and thought 'This isn't so bad'."

A new name was created for his persona on line. He called himself "Bi-Jock" and adds, "That isn't really true but that's what clients want." He discovered he could make contacts on more than one website and his income increased.

Since moving to Fort Lauderdale Cody has been escorting exclusively. "I earned enough money in California to get out of debt and then I moved to Florida. I sometimes work five days a week. I don't do more than two appointments a day. When I go to Detroit to visit my parents I will announce on the Internet that I'm coming and I will work there, too."

The day of the interview Cody had to leave for Orlando, where he has a regular client he sees on a schedule of once a month. Of his clients he reports that they are mostly in their late forties, are probably married and a little overweight. He has had clients as young as 19 and believes his oldest are in their late sixties.

He has done threesomes that include a woman. About 30% of my clients tell me they're married. I charge $200 to $250 for the first hour and $150 for the second hour. An overnight fee is between $900 and $1,000. My Orlando client pays $1,150 for an overnight, as I have to travel there. I don't think this easy money will change me. It's only temporary. A few clients want the 'boyfriend' experience I fill the niche where I'm not a huge muscle-built guy and I'm not a twink either," he explains.

Cody has a lot of callbacks. He has about 80% repeats. He has regulars once a month. Some for every two months. Others every two weeks. "I have to admit that I have worried whether I was becoming sexaholic or not," he says. His unusual experiences include dressing up as Spider-Man for one client. He on one occasion played strip pool with two men. "If you didn't sink your ball on a shot you then had to take something off," he says laughing. Cody will tell you, "I always wear a condom for fucking. And I will take a pill or half a Viagra before I go to an appointment just to guard against being not at all attracted."

Cody plans to return to college in the near future to study advertising. He does date. He concludes, "I have to have some fun on my own. My work makes me appreciate having sex with someone I'm really attracted to." His advice to men considering escorting is, "If you are entering this work big, have an exit strategy. Don't get caught up in it."

ARPAD MIKLOS

Arpad Miklos is a major porn star. One can understand why. Strapping and strong with penetrating brown bedroom eyes, he somehow manages to be sexy and masculine while having a gentle demeanor and soft spoken way about him. If this is being Hungarian he comes from a country one must visit. He was staying at the Raleigh Hotel for a whirlwind visit to Miami Beach when we nabbed him for a photo shoot and an interview.

Arpad was born in Budapest. He makes the point that although many people may think Hungary is part of Eastern Europe it is actually very different from the countries that border it. He feels it is much more like Western Europe. He did his studies in Hungary and graduated with a college degree in chemistry. Upon finishing school he had five different jobs in the pharmaceutical industry, including doing research before coming to the U.S.

The porn industry beckoned while he was still living in Hungary and it was the industry that brought him indirectly to the United States. He had done nine or ten films in his home country, including a few that were done for Kristen Bjorn and distributed in the U.S. He fell in love with a fellow performer and moved to Miami Beach to be with him.

Through his movies he became well known internationally and a few years ago was approached by a friend who asked him if he would like to take a trip through Thailand and Singapore with a man from Australia for a fee. "This was the bait that got me

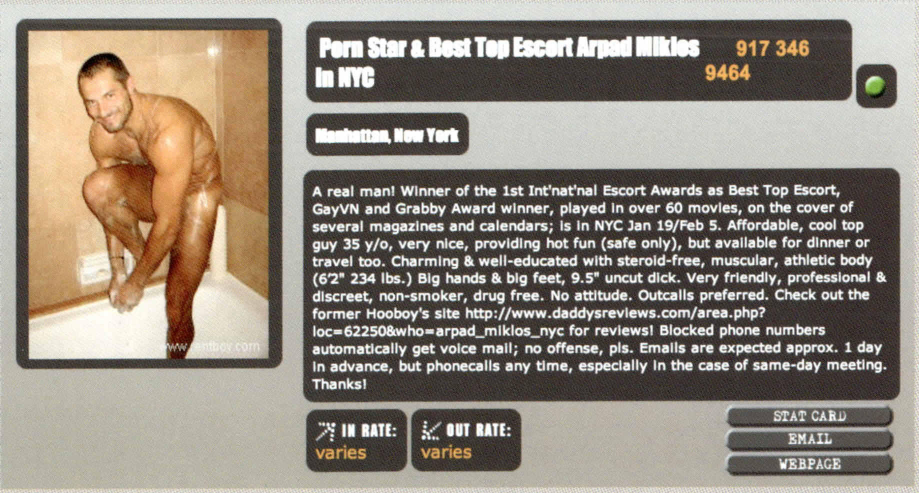

into escorting. Escorting pays more bills than other jobs," he says. He adds, "We had a great time together and we've stayed in touch, although he lives in Australia." Arpad has now been escorting for two and a half years.

Arpad explains that his rates are $300 an hour, $1,000 an evening and $1,600 overnight. He occasionally does an in-call but mostly does out-calls with clients.

About his clients, Arpad reports that they do not fall in an age range but are actually between the ages of 18 and 80. However most clients are in their 40s and most of them are gay. This varies in the Midwest, however, where he finds that most clients consider themselves straight and are married with a family. In the larger cities on the East and West coasts, his clientele is primarily gay. He guesses that in New York, 15 to 20 per cent are married, whereas in Dallas it ranges up to 50 to 70 per cent.

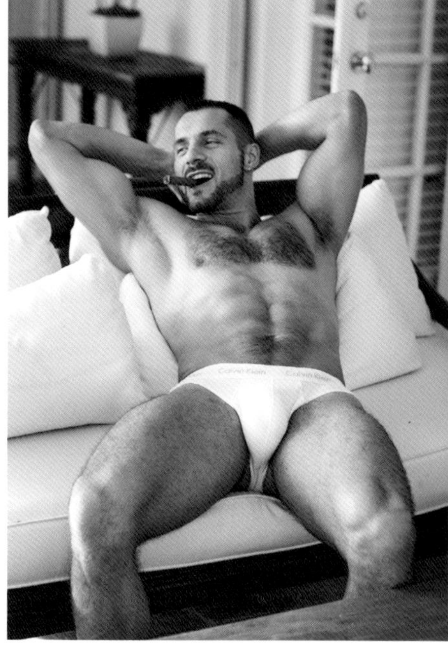

He remembers that one of his best escorting experiences was with a client visiting New York and with whom he went to museums and eleven bars in two days. They stayed at the Four Seasons and Arpad felt like a tourist in his own hometown. "I'm a romantic guy so I enjoyed the company. It was a nice experience. It was what a real escort does."

His worst experience was an overnight where his client had done crystal meth and was busy cleaning his house. He kept Arpad awake and was more "drug bitter than drug happy" Arpad says. When he calmed down he became nasty and out of control. As for his own sexuality, he remembers that he always had an interest in the male body even as a child. Although there was no sexual activity at that time, he always felt attracted to men. When asked if his parents know of his livelihood, he says, "I doubt that they knew about my escorting when they were alive. If the belief in an afterlife is true, then perhaps they can see me from above."

As to what makes him special as an escort he says, "Everybody is an individual and nobody is irreplaceable. I think most people realize that how you look and what you're like inside are quite different. In my case some people suppose that I'm rough, arrogant, even rude, but when they talk to me and realize that I am quite the opposite, it's a surprise and a twist for them.

Asked how he deals with escorting and his personal life he says he does not allow the two areas to overlap and enjoys sex outside of the workplace. "I'm able to separate escorting from my private life. Fun is fun; business is business."

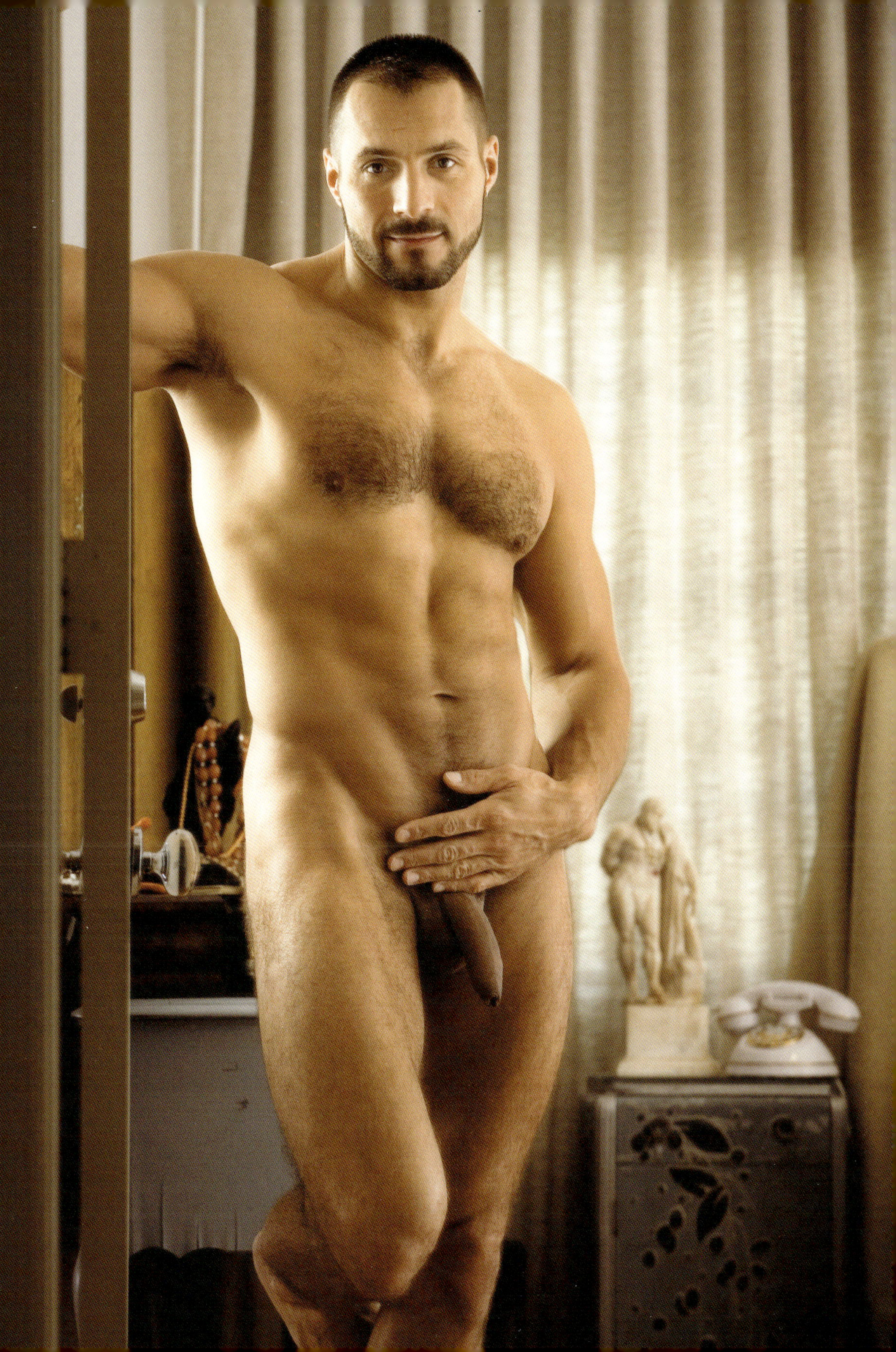

SETH SEGARRA

Seth Segarra has both of those qualities that seem to work well for someone in the escort business. One is a very outgoing personality. He's a lot of fun to be with. Which has to count for a great deal with clients who want to see the same escort repeatedly. And he is sexy.

Seth was born and raised in Miami, Florida for most of his early years. His childhood was that of many young people of his age. He was primarily in the care of his mother, his father having disappeared from the scene early on. In Seth's case when he was only two months old. His mother and grandmother "bathed me in affection" he says. The family was originally from Shreveport, La. where they had been fishermen. In Miami Seth dreamed of being a mailman when he grew up and attended the Hebrew Academy in Coral Gables.

At four he found himself with a new father when his mother remarried. As a computer salesman his father was transferred to Alpharetta, Ga. when Seth was 15 and difficult years followed. His stepfather treated him roughly and knocked him about. At school he was an outsider and accented it by dressing in a Goth rock manner. "Rednecks kicked my ass every day," he remembers.

A girl from the senior class came to his rescue. He says, "She was very upper class, from a wealthy family, on the Honor Roll. I guess I was everything she wasn't." They dated and when he was with her at a club called Illusions he met his first male lover. He was a construction worker who was 21. Seth was on his way to being eighteen at that time. Seth says, "He was dedicated to our relationship. He had an old 1979 Ford Mustang, one of those cars you have to change the oil five times a day, but he came to see me from Marietta all the time." He adds, "A great love affair is always tough on your underwear. I kept leaving it behind in his car."

By the time Seth was in junior college studying broadcasting their relationship began to sour. They began to fight a lot. "Physically. I didn't feel I deserved better. My stepfather had always been tough with me. He'd punish me by making me kneel on rice in the corner. Stuff like that. It hurt," Seth says.

"I had had a lot of molesting when I was younger from relatives and from camp counselors when I went to camp. When I was about ten I had an African-American friend named Darryl. I admired his butch qualities. He came home with me from school one day and he climbed on top of me. I was shocked, intrigued, aroused. That's when my mother walked into my bedroom and caught us. That is a painful memory for me. My mother has suppressed it and says she remembers nothing of it. There was a lot of that sort of

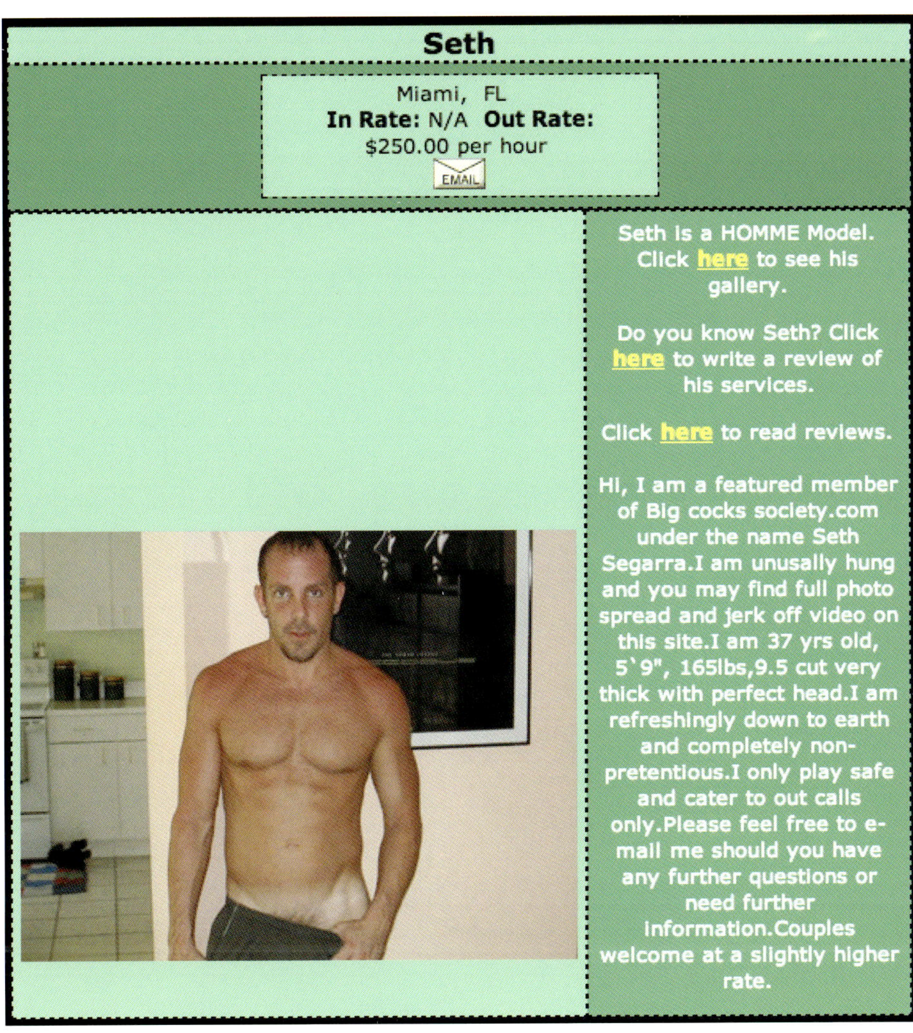

thing. My masturbation fantasy was Rod Stewart. He had a great ass. That should tell you something."

Seth tried moving to Scottsdale, Arizona at this time but that didn't take and he soon returned. He had a telephone relationship with a disc jockey and that inspired him to start his own business. He admits, "I started experimenting with drugs. I had to have a new Camaro. I transcended into another world. Perhaps too much. But music saved me. It surrounded me in the street, in school, in bars, while I was studying, while I was asleep. My disc jockey business was successful because of that."

In 1987 Seth moved back to Miami. His parents were living there again and he wanted to be with his family. And to take care of his Aunt Ruby, his grandmother's sister. When she died she left her estate to Seth and he says of that period, "That was my all time low because I had the money to do it. Drugs, sex. I hung out with people who weren't even close to the top of the food chain."

He began escorting when he noticed on the Internet that the *bigcocksociety.com* website was offering a $500 prize and a round trip to Miami. Entrants were supposed to send in four photos, two of their face, two of their penis. Seth only sent in one of his penis. There was an immediate response. The response was so rapid he says, "It made me apprehensive. I was excited and pleased and apprehensive all at once. I actually loved all of it. The society offered $300 for still photos. I told them I thought my penis was worth more than $300. So finally I did a masturbation film for them for $700."

He goes on, "My mother found out about it. How? Probably because I wasn't trying to borrow money from her." He adds, "So then I went on the website. Photographs were done of me by Warren at the *bigcocksociety.com* organization. I was curious. I wanted to see if people would be interested in me or my big penis. At least I had no responses. But now I work about two times a week."

In a review of Seth on the website a client reports, "His sexual aura is unparalleled." Seth says this is true. "I'm very sexual but it's not a 'Let's do it all night' kind of thing. Sex appeal has nothing to do with your body or your face. Sexiness involves insecurity, humility, and arrogance. Lots of things. You have to be vulnerable and honest.

"The majority of my clients are regulars. Originally I thought I would provide a service, they would pay and that would be it. But it's not. My first client was a man named Michael and it wasn't that at all. It became more personal. The sexual part became a back-burner thing. I never thought I'd do it, enjoy it and get paid for it. I rarely do anal sex but he wanted to and he's not wildly attractive physically, but I had an orgasm. And that is one of the few times that has happened.

"My sex interests have changed entirely. I can arrive at an erection completely without touching myself. I can tell clients the right words to say. The real sex is the conversation. They're not there to get laid. They are there because they're lonely. Who is it wrote, 'Hope is a false sense of security?' Perhaps that's what I'm offering.

"I can smell a bad client and I avoid them. And now I work exclusively out. I'm in a relationship that means a lot to me and we have our home. I don't want to invade that with a client. My lover doesn't approve of my work and we've worked together for a client very occasionally. But that part of my life is separate. "I don't like role-playing with clients. I had a bad experience with one client who had done drugs. Ropes and that kind of thing. Now role-playing is definitely not an option.

"I have a good life. My lover and I have two dogs that are really our children. The dogs are large, and sometimes we just let them have the bed and go sleep on the foldout. My dreams? I'd like a recording contract. I want to keep my family together. I think I'd rather have an emotional affair with a woman. I've never had a relationship with a woman. And very recently I realized that I've never had an emotional affair with a man."

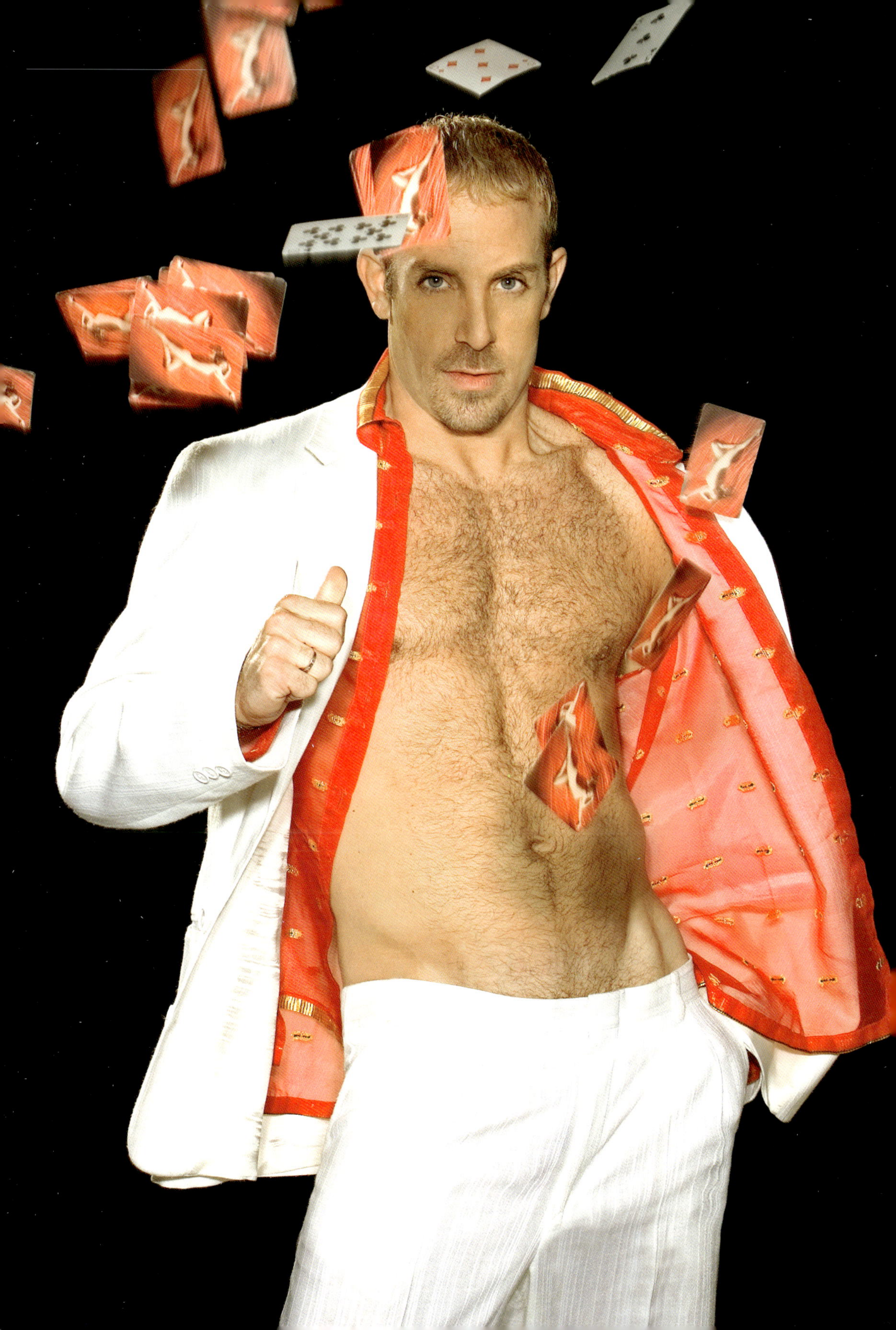

Chris

Miami Beach, FL

Phone: 305 793-2536
In Rate: N/A **Out Rate:** N/A

EMAIL

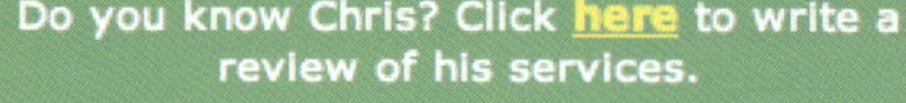
Do you know Chris? Click here to write a review of his services.

Click here to read reviews.

Hi, I'm Chris! I'm 31 years old and American, of Irish Germen decent. I'm 5'10", 195 lbs, with 8" cut! I'm 100% respectful and discreet. I love to fulfill fetishes and fantasy's or maybe just a massage / body rub is what you're in need of. My female friend can help if you would like. Available for private, party or club dancing.I'm also available to model for photo shoots.

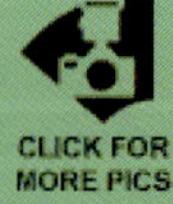

Chris is surprising. In a restaurant in Miami he resembles any number of the other young businessmen lunching there. Clean cut, a neat haircut, handsome features, good but unassuming clothes. There is nothing in his demeanor to suggest that he is particularly aware that he is attractive.

Yet he has had a beautiful Argentinean girlfriend who was a Madame supplying girls to clients. He himself has answered calls when one of the girls needed a man to complete a threesome with a male client. His picture naked with an erection is on a website.

He is listed on the website *bigcocksociety.com*. He seems not at all the type, which is certainly his appeal.

Chris sees this kind of money-making activity as just an adjunct to his real career as a photographer. Although he considers himself a bisexual, it is in a very limited way. On a spectrum of gay as a "1" and completely heterosexual as a "10" he says that he is an "8" or "9". His great interest is in photographing women and he has done a lot of this work among the women he has met in the escort business. Now he is ready to make his bid to break out into a wider world.

He is from a white collar background. His family knows that he has worked as a dancer in bars and that he is pursuing a career as a photographer. He doesn't see a lot of them. His parents divorced when he was a teenager and his very fit body is largely a result, he explains of his mother being a personal trainer. He began working out in his teen years because of her influence.

He went to college to study work as a private investigator but his life headed off in a new direction when he was approached on a nude beach by an agent who offered him a lucrative stint on a cruise, dancing in the ship's bar. He had to work naked on this his first job and he says, "I had to drink a lot to get through it. I probably spent more on drinks than I earned." But through this job he met other dancers working in clubs like the Warsaw in Miami Beach and the 1235 in Fort Lauderdale.

He remembers, "I got paid $150 for working three sets. I was paid in cash. And if I wanted to stay and work more sets I could and earn even more money."

He adds, "I also danced for women at Le Bear's in North Miami Beach. The dancers were very competitive. If they didn't like someone they might key his car and once one of the guys had his leather jacket burned.

"I also worked at the Gaiety in New York but that business was ruined by the Canadian dancers, who would work for less money. The difference between the Canadian dollar and the American one meant they could work for less and go home where it was worth more.

"The whole field has changed completely since then. Now in the clubs where the girls work they pay to work there. I worked for two years only dancing and not escorting and did very well, but that's impossible now."

He concludes, "Even though I am a very sexual person I wouldn't have as much sex as I do if I wasn't in the industry. I'd rather be in a relationship. I prefer things to be more romantic, more intimate. The first time I have sex with anyone is a little awkward for me."

He would like to finally be involved with someone and working as a photographer but finishes, "There are some couples I would probably continue to see. Some I've been seeing for eight years. We're really a happy little family."

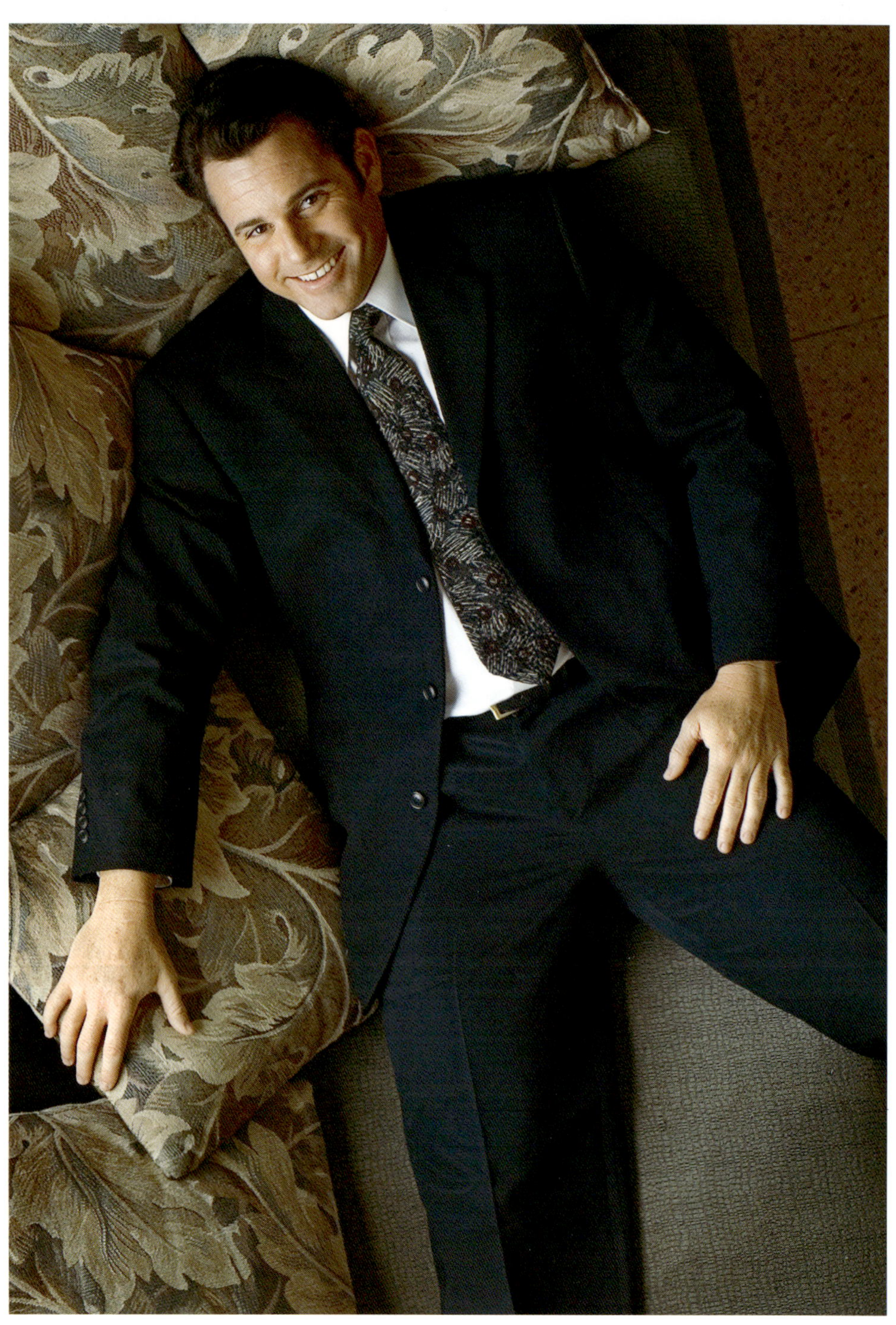

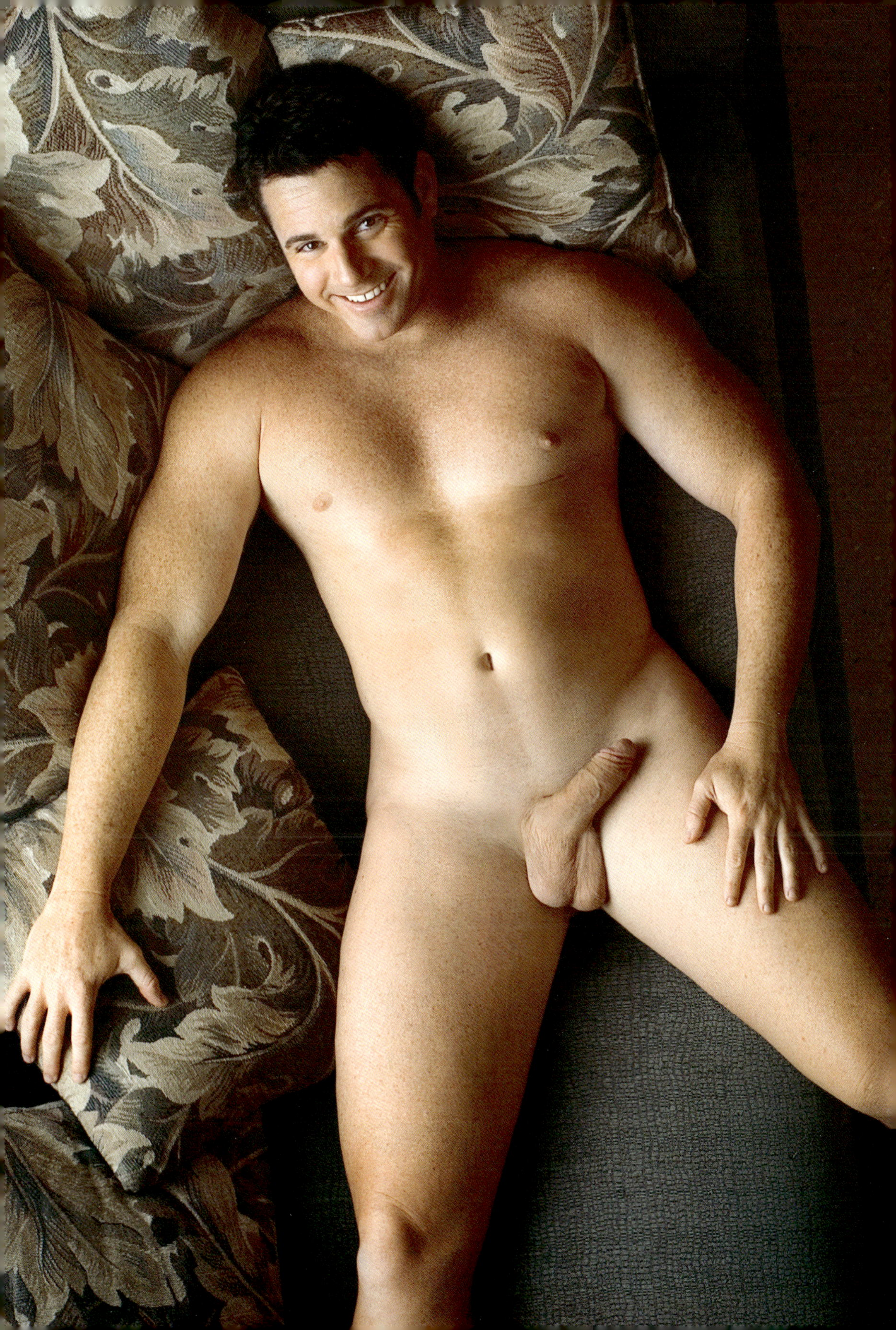

DOUG MASTERS

Doug Masters

Fort Lauderdale, FL
In Rate: $150.00 per hour **Out Rate:** $200.00 per hour

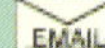

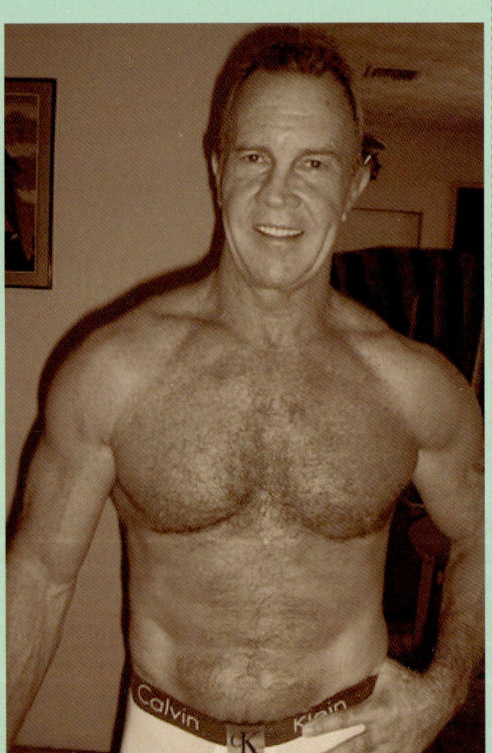

Doug Masters is a HOMME Model. Click **here** to see his gallery.

Do you know Doug Masters? Click **here** to write a review of his services.

I am a 47 year old white male who is muscular and hits the gym everyday. I am 6'2" and 205 lbs. I have salt/pepper hair, clean shaven, a hairy, muscular chest, and have been told numerous times that "I have a beautiful cock"!! I sport a true 8 1/2" long by 6" around cock fully erect. I am uncut, BUT have the appearance of cut. I have very little foreskin and NOT an "ant eater"....I sometimes go to the nude beach here at Haulover beach. I like to rub oil on my cock and get excited.

Doug Masters is the thorough professional. He has the look and the relaxed manner of a Hollywood star who has seen much, survived much and is very definitely still here.

Doug caters to a female or couple clientele, many of them relatively longtime acquaintances, as well as single men. When asked how he gains contact with women clients he explains that the local Miami newspaper, The New Times, offers an ideal place to advertise. He offers massage and more and finds women feel comfortable contacting him in this way. He also advertises in the Broward Entertainment Guide, a publication specifically for Broward County which will reach Fort Lauderdale clients. He also places ads in Hotspots and Concierge magazines.

He is represented on several internet sites and finds that older4me.com provides good results. In his late forties, Doug Masters is extremely fit, well tanned and socially at ease.

Born and brought up in New Jersey, he has family there as well as in Florida and explains that he is the South because he really likes the weather. He has worked as a private investigator and a bodyguard, as well as a lifeguard. He's done personal training also.

In his private life he has had long term relationships with women, although he is single now. He confesses to having a roving eye and after a certain period of time finding it difficult not to pursue women outside a relationship.

He remembers that in his early years he had sex for the first time when he was fifteen. "We were standing up, my pants were around my ankles. It lasted for about twenty minutes." His masturbation fantasies were of "I Dream of Jeannie."

He has been working as an escort only for the last three years. He says that for the prior three years he did a lot of "swinging", meeting couples in bars or on the internet for threesomes and foursomes.

One day an artist friend told him that he had a very great asset. As he says, "I have a beautiful cock." And the artist friend told him he should be doing more with it that he was and helped him prepare an ad and pictures for a website. He explains, "I had never looked at a gay publication so I needed help.

"I tell clients I'm a massage therapist and I am in many, many ways." Doug recounts stories of some very unusual clients. "I have one guy who will make a date with me and say 'Take care of me if I get very drunk.' Which he does. And I make sure he gets home all right. And that's it. No sex. No nothing." He has had some male clients and he can be a top when the situation calls for it. He has had one client who greets him dressed and made up as a woman and he admits that he can be turned on occasionally by a feminine guy. "I get a lot of acting out roles with clients," he says.

Doug adds "I grew up homophobic. But as an adult I've changed a lot. And in the Florida market 80% of the clients are gay. So you have to adapt. You get guys who say, "I've never gone down on a guy and I want to see what it's like.' And I'm thinking that this is much too good for someone's first time.

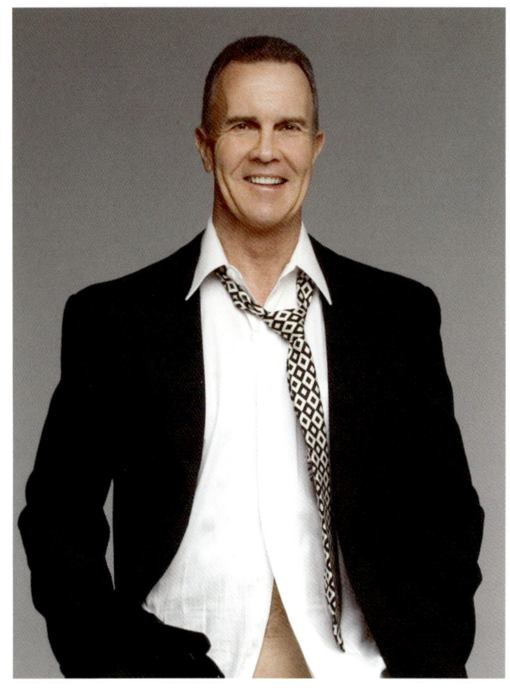

"I don't do drugs and won't be involved with them. Some gay clients will use poppers. And I've had a client who was really soused. I saw the vodka bottle sitting there. He said, 'I just want you to lay here with me awhile.' And sometimes a client will say 'I want to be slapped around.' But I don't like to do that. But when he says 'I'll pay you.' I will."

Most of Doug Masters' clients come to his home, which is in a discreet cul-de-sac where no one is going to see the client's car on the street. When it was suggested that women clients are more likely to want to have a "date" with dinner, perhaps flowers, or the theater, Doug says that is not the case. Women make appointments and he says, "They have their fun, they pay, they're out the door. It's over. Some of them are married. They have to get home and fix dinner."

He tells this story. "I have a call to meet with a man in Fort Lauderdale. He's quite a well known owner of a number of restaurants. I go to one of his restaurants and wait there. My price is $180 an hour out of my own house and the clock is ticking. He approaches me and asks me to go to another restaurant of his, which I do. There he asks me to go into the men's room and go into a stall. He said, 'I saw your ad. I had to see how big your cock was. I'll come in and peek through a crack.' Which he did. He paid me and I left. On the way home I get another call. It's him. He asks me to go to another restaurant. A third one. He says, 'I have to suck your cock.' He takes me into a back room where they store cleaning equipment. It's next door to a laundromat. You can smell the soap and hear the washing machines turning. He's down there for 15 seconds. He says, 'That's good. That's good.' And he has to pay another $400."

He has a number of couples he sees and frequently the husband will watch him have sex with the wife. And at other times the couple want him to watch them. Doug says, "I'm an exhibitionist. And I'm a voyeur. With some of these scenes it's hard to know what the fee should be so I let the client decide what the service is worth."

He has been in love five or six times and concludes by saying, "I've been called a lone wolf."

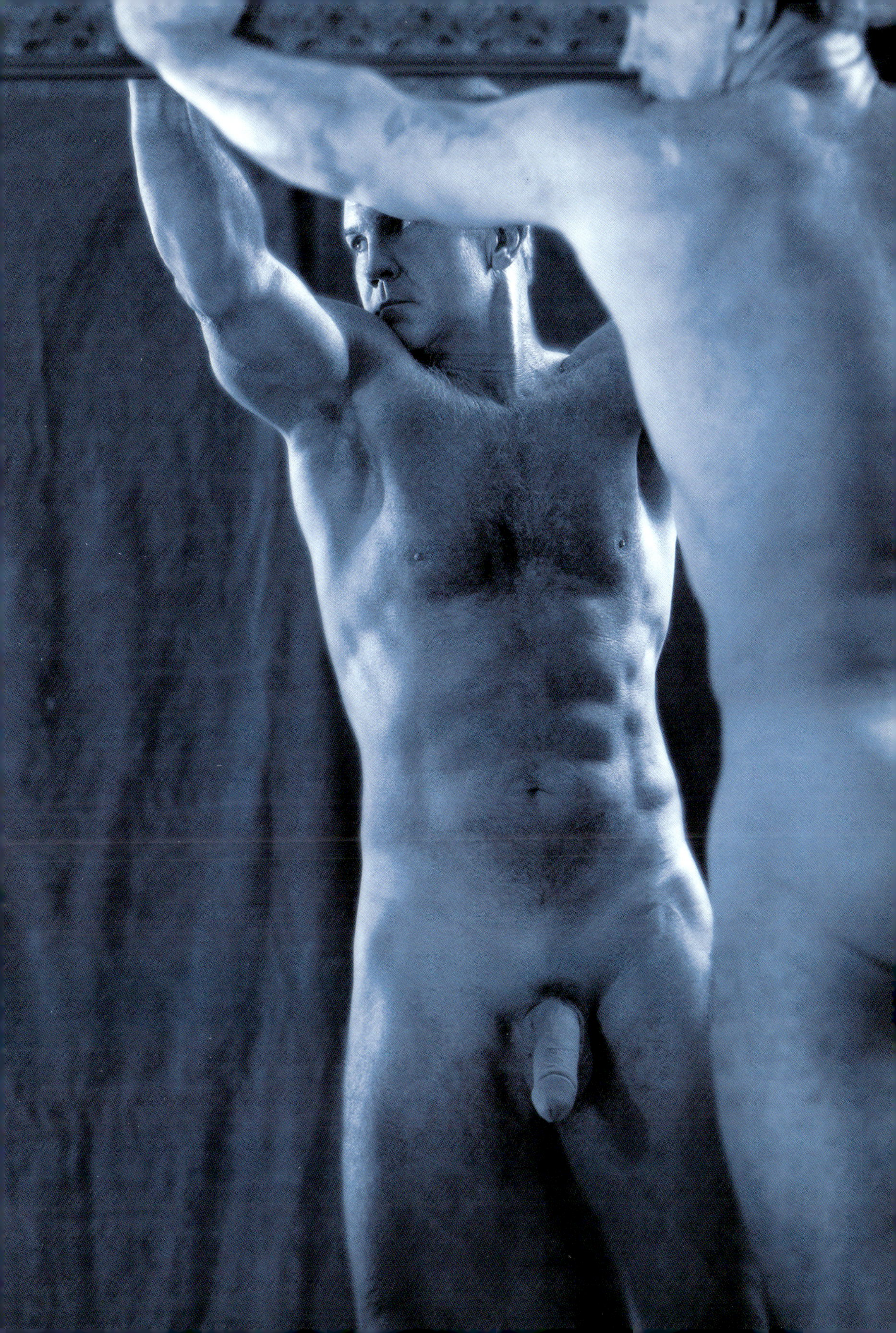

FRANCO

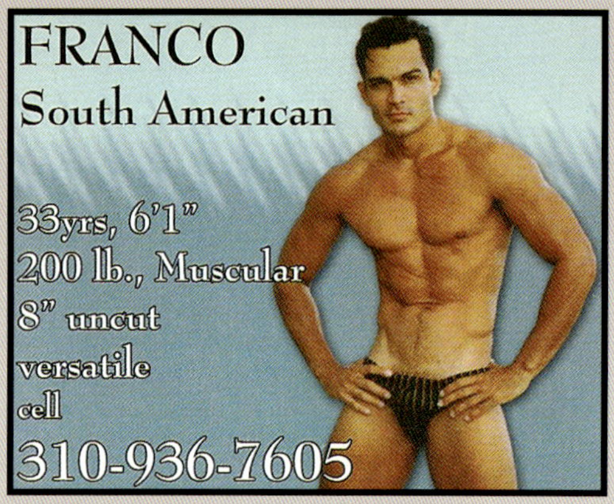

Handsome Franco has waves of dark hair and sultry eyes and sensuous lips. He is in every way what one would expect of a Latin lover. Entering the restaurant for his interview his skimpy t-shirt and jeans made many eyes turn as he came to the table.

Despite his appearance, Franco is not spoiled and petulant at all. He is very well educated and can talk seriously on a wide variety of subjects. He says immediately, "My looks are the result of a prohibited love." Who wouldn't be interested to hear more? His father is from Ecuador, his mother from Colombia. They met in Colombia when his father went there to study. His social background was no match for Franco's beautiful mother's and her family much frowned upon her interest in the young man from Ecuador. With her brother's help, his mother escaped her home and fled to Ecuador. To Quito. Just a month before Franco was born the couple returned to Cali in Colombia where his father was accepted by his new wife's parents. They then had more children, a brother and a sister for Franco.

He says, "My looks come from my mother. My seriousness from my father. He is half Basque and half Indian. He is fifteen years older than my mother but their marriage was one of great passion."

Franco left Colombia in 1997 and moved to South Beach in Miami. He was en route to New Jersey where there was a job waiting in a restaurant. "I ran into a man in Miami Beach and he asked me if I could dance and strip. And so I started working at a club called The Boardwalk. I also worked at Twist and Score and 825 in Fort Lauderdale.

"I fell in love with a man. We were together for eight months but he wanted to move to New York and I didn't want to go. My real relationship was with dancing. It was between me and the music. But the club scene changed and they paid less and less.

"I worked at the Gaiety in New York. This was a big change for me. I was more stressed and tired. I would have two or three clients a day between shows. People would meet you at the bar and ask if it was possible to be with me. And it was.

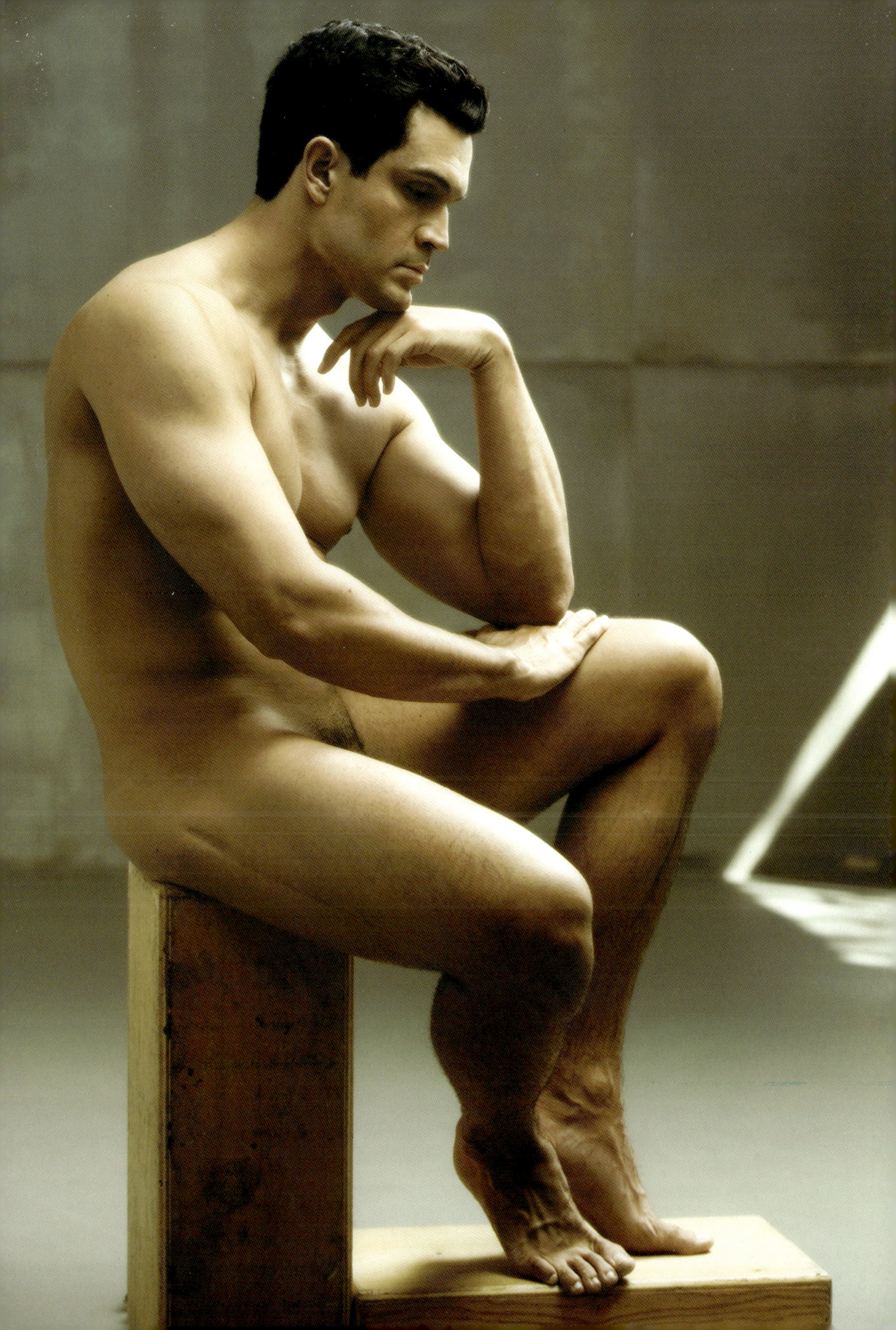

"I moved here to Los Angeles two years ago. I think the clients here are of a higher level and more respectable than the people I saw on the East Coast.

"But I have to remind clients when we meet on the internet that this is a business. They often want to talk and take me to dinner. And I tell them, 'I have a refrigerator full of food. If you're looking for a boyfriend you really need to look on another site'."

Franco says, "I think I was always gay and knew it but didn't want to accept it. I came out of the closet when I was 23 and had a boyfriend for five months when I was 24. He was quite violent."

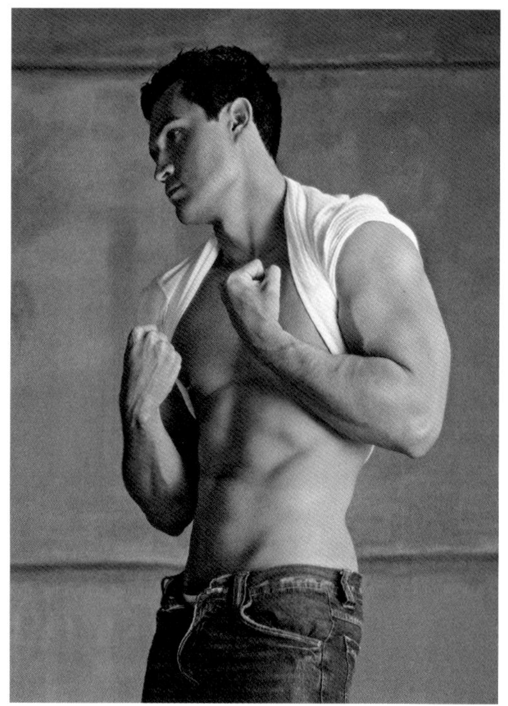

After studying sales in Colombia, Franco explains that he then managed a sportswear store for five years.

Of his present life he says, "Of my clients, 75% are regulars. Some a couple times a month, some once a week. Yes, some clients fall in love and some become obsessive. I think I'm good at this and I say to them, 'Let's just have fun.'

"I find some people hire me because they're lonely. They just want to talk to someone. Very few clients call only because they're horny. Here in Los Angeles many people live in big houses all by themselves. They're all alone with just their dogs and they get lonely."

Franco does not do threesomes with a man and a woman and he reports that although sometimes young women call him he does not accept women as clients.

As far as men go, "I sometimes get someone who wants a top. Rarely. We can always discuss it. "I do get very young clients. So young I have to ask for I.D. Some boys just want to experiment. They're so afraid and so horny."

Franco advertises in Frontiers magazine and is listed with *rentboy.com*.

His advice about the business is, "You can't mix business with drugs and parties. Some escorts try to mix it and it always turns out badly. You have to take it as work. It is not your social life. You cannot date a client. Never."

As for his private life he says, "I have three very close friends. They have the privilege of my friendship. I'm not ready at the moment for a relationship."

MAXIMUS

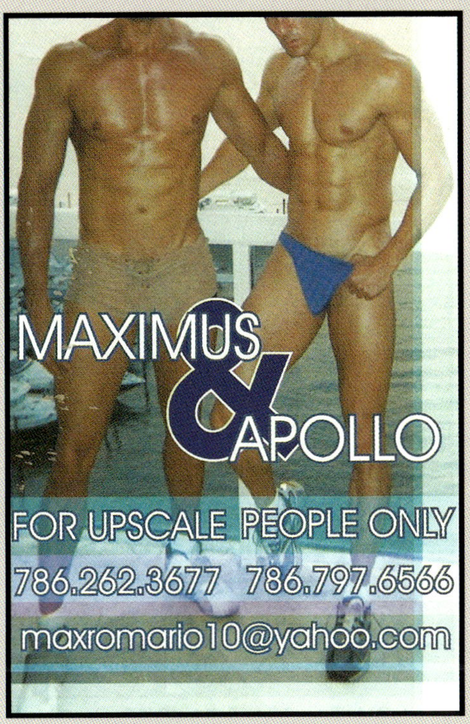

Big and brawny Maximus is a native of Brazil. He was born and brought up in a small town far from the big cities of Rio de Janeiro and Sao Paulo in the little state of Parana. He graduated in 1994 with a degree in Social Studies in Brazil. He also had earned a degree in Hotel Management there. He came to the United States in 1995 to study English. His father, who works in real estate, had lived in the U.S. for ten years and wanted his son to speak the language.

Studying in Boston, Maximus worked part time as a waiter and bar back in clubs around Harvard Square. He found jobs, one at Pizzeria Uno and another at John Harvard's Brewing Co.

He had always been interested in bodybuilding and had had training in Brazil. He says, "I always admired Arnold Schwarzenegger, Sylvester Stallone and Frank Zane. I admired what they achieved with their bodies." While throwing beer cases around in the store room at John Harvard's another waiter saw him and later when they were changing in he dressing room said," You shouldn't be tossing beer cases around, you should be stripping in a gay club." Maximus was offended. "I have a very strict Catholic background and I knew this guy was gay. I didn't speak to him for several weeks but then I began to think about it.

"It took me two weeks to think it over. I had changed shifts so I wouldn't have to speak to that guy, but then I looked for him and decided to give it a try. When you come to the United States you see a different world. There are many options to improve yourself, both economically and as a person."

Through his contact, Maximus got the names of some clubs and found work. He explains, "I couldn't really dance. It was more like posing. I got paid for an hour or an hour and a half of work. At first it paid $100 but then it was lowered to $75. The reason most dancers go to escorting is that you can't make enough money just dancing."

Maximus had a student visa at that time and then married. His new wife was a waitress he had worked with at John Harvard's. He says that it was not a marriage for citizenship reasons. Maximus insists that he is straight and his escorting has definite boundaries. He says of his wife, "She was an evil redhead." He and his wife spent three years together. He says of her, "I needed someone at that time. I have to admit that it was a romantic relationship." His wife was studying to become a dentist and Maximus wanted them to spend six months of the year in Brazil. Because this would seriously interrupt her studies she refused to do this. They were married from 1997 to 2000, which Maximus says was approximately the same period that he was dancing in Boston.

In September 2000 he began escorting. Other dancers had told him "You can make extra cash on the side." He placed ads in several Boston gay papers. Of the responses he says that out of a hundred responses he had perhaps fifteen responses from women, five from couples and the rest were gay men. His ad had specified he was available to men, women and couples. He says, "Only once I had a straight couple." His rate was $200 an hour and for the most part he went out for his engagements.

Maximus came to Miami Beach in 2005 because he wanted to see a new city. He was tired of snowstorms and thought, "If it's not good, I'll go back to Boston." Of his work as an escort in this city he says, "You get a lot of jokers here. People who call and want to waste your time just talking. I thought everybody was a millionaire here, but that's not the case."

He now works with a cousin from Brazil who escorts under the name Apollo. They are available as a team and also work individually. They say they like to work as a team because they feel more secure that way. They both prefer escorting older men whom they refer to as "Sugar Daddies." Maximus says, "Older men look for companionship and conversation. My profile for a client is older, professional, rather than masculine. I'd say that 20% of our clients are married men. Married clients are best, as they prefer to keep a low profile. I'd like to have a 'Sugar Daddy'. I don't have one currently."

Maximus reports that he has had some bizarre experiences. Clients who wanted their nipples burned with a candle. One who wanted him to dress in a German officer's uniform and then abuse him. When asked how heterosexual his cousin and he actually were and how different it really was penetrating a man or a woman Maximus says,

"There is a different human contact, the odor, the skin. My sexual fantasies are of women. Only heterosexual porn do I find exciting." He adds, "I think from my experience that the top fantasy for women, even if they will deny it, is to be the only woman with two men."

When the cousins work together their rate is $150 per hour for each. Maximus explains that eventually he would like to have a fitness center in Brazil. He concludes, "Being an escort isn't bad. What is bad is not being intelligent and not using the money you earn for your own future.

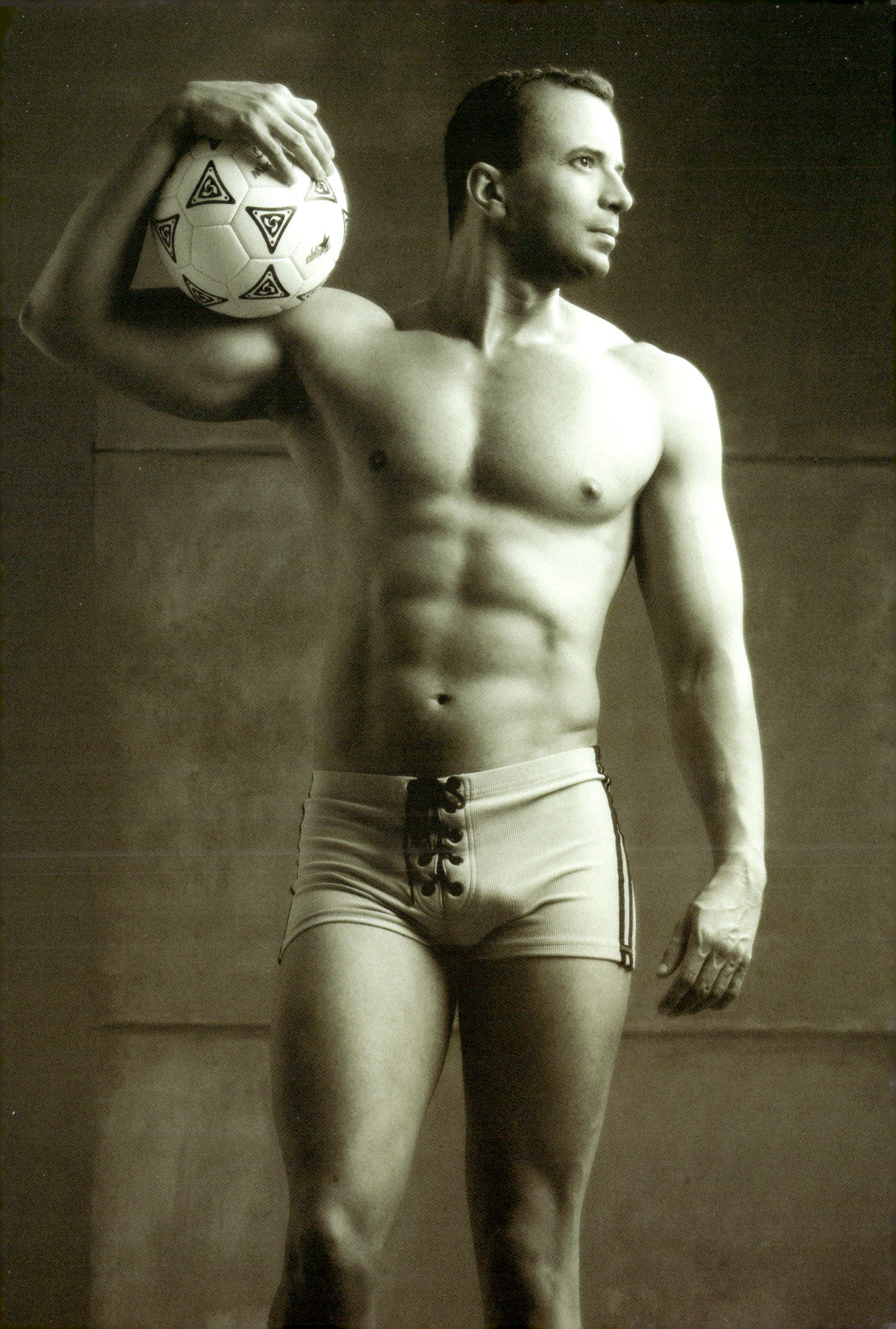

RIDGE

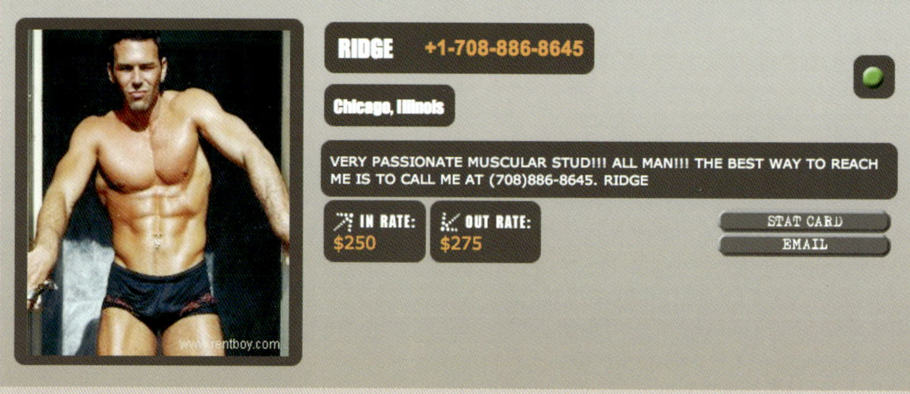

Handsome Ridge. Chicago must be proud of him. Big and strapping, great body, great face, great personality. What more is there to say?

Ridge is from Cicero, which used to have a bad reputation for gangsters way back when. He went through school there and then studied journalism at the University of Indiana. He started bartending while he was in college and says, "Then I became more interested in making money than getting further in debt." He considered studying meteorology, and then left college after two and a half years to start working in Chicago full-time as a bartender at Gatz, which he found to be a celebrity hangout with many sports stars coming by. He is still working as a bartender at Mother's in Chicago and is also part-owner of his own neighborhood sports bar. He was scouted for escort work and an agency called him. He was represented by the agency for a short while in 1998 by this agency. "This was pre-internet," he points out. "The agency wanted me all the time for both male and female clients. About 30% of the clients were socialites spending their husband's money. I would meet them at hotels.

"I had regulars. Some women would fall in love with me. It became a problem. Some escorts can make the move to being kept. That wasn't for me. Then it became too much working for the agency. They charged $350 an hour and kept $100. They said they'd give me more if I would stay but I didn't."

For a man who must spend a lot of his waking hours during the night, Ridge is very bronzed and fit. He explains that he has a gym in his own home and works out every day except Monday. Monday is very likely his night off, too.

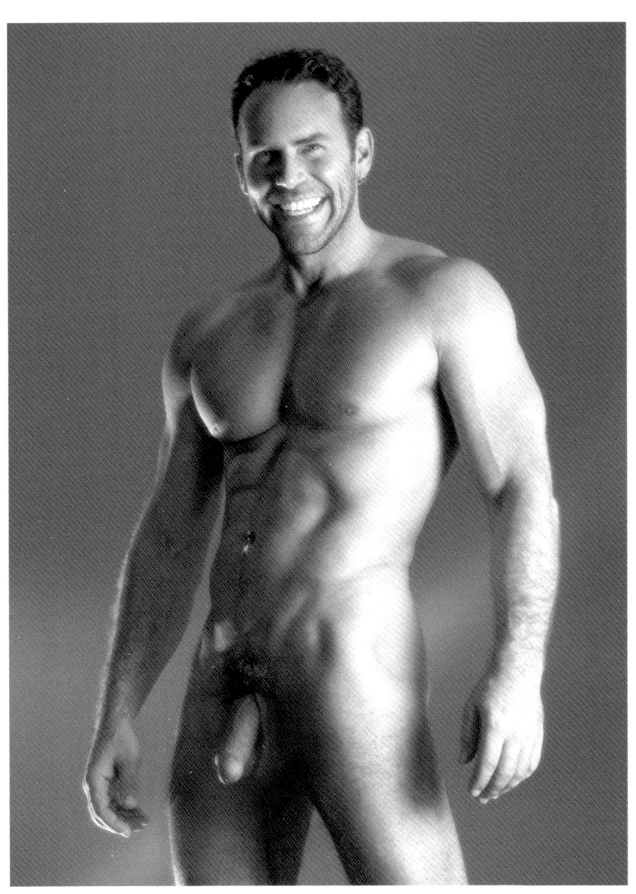

He says, "I started working out at fourteen. I was on the football team and wanted the advantage of being heavier. I was pretty full grown by that age."

His family of parents and one brother and one sister do not know of his work as an escort. Nor do his partners in the sports bar he owns.

Of his escort history he goes on, "I was out of the business for six months and ran into a friend who was escorting. He encouraged me to run an ad in Gay Chicago, a local magazine, which I did for four weeks. I got so much business I didn't have to run an ad again for several years.

"I was introduced to Trey Rexx when he visited Chicago and he really was my entry into the escort world I know now. But I never stopped bartending from 10 PM to 5 AM, which I still do.

"About that time someone told me there was a website called *muscleservice.com* which was kind of a forum where men exchanged information about other men. I checked it out. You know in this business you can be the new hot piece of meat. People wanted pictures of me. Pictures, pictures, pictures. Reading about all these accolades made me gun-shy. I thought, "I'll never live up to it.'

"There was a muscle photo contest on this site. Some 500 guys sent in pictures from all over the world. I sent in a picture and won it. I then became Man of the Year. The photographer, Richard Morris, called me and I agreed to do nudes for magazines. This was 2000.

"The next two years were a whirlwind. A lot of traveling all over the world, a lot of money, a lot of fun. I was flown all over the world. I did three day minimums. And finally it began to taper off.

"Partially because I didn't want to and partially because the business became larger. There were many more men available. At that time, Colt offered me a contract but I decided against it. I've never done movies. Even in all the magazines I have worked for. I always posed alone."

When asked if he thinks that escorts begin to require all the attention they get, Ridge says, "I really don't need that kind of attention. I get plenty of attention at the bar and I certainly don't need porn movies to get more attention."

Ridge defines himself as bisexual. He remembers, "In high school I realized that I admired athletes. I would think, "I'd like to see him naked.' Then at 23 I had a brother who was killed in an automobile accident by a drunk driver and I thought 'Whatever I want to do I'm going to do.'

"I had a girlfriend at that time and the following Fourth of July we ran into a former school friend who was home on vacation. He was an aspiring model and actor and was openly gay. Always had been. We went out together and then had to drop my girlfriend off because she was working the next day. I stayed over at his place and a little massage led to more and before you knew it we were full-fledged fucking. It didn't lead to any kind of relationship. We slept together a few more times and that was it. I wasn't ready for more. I wasn't mentally ready. I stayed in the relationship with my girlfriend and began to see men when we would have one of those "break-up" periods.

"I've always been a top. I bottomed once for that first guy I slept with. And when I was in a real relationship with a man after we have been together for two years I bottomed just to keep the relationship together. But I hated it. And I thought, 'If our relationship depends on my bottoming, there's the door.'

"With my clients a blow job is okay but I don't reciprocate." When asked how important the attractiveness of the client is, Ridge says, "I can find something attractive in most people. Sometimes it isn't even physical. Working in this business is not a problem for me. If I cam make someone happy for one hour, two hours, three hours, I am very pleased to do it. I'm half-Italian, half-English. Maybe that has something to do with it."

How escorting relates to relationships is not a problem for Ridge either. "When I'm really in love I stay in love and don't want to cheat. Fifteen minutes of animal sex isn't enough to warrant destroying something important between two people."

When Ridge broke up finally with his girlfriend it was 1996. He began a relationship with a paramedic he met at work which lasted for nine years, until 2004. His partner didn't like his escort work at first, then began to accompany him when a third person was asked for and then later began to have clients of his own.

At the moment Ridge's partner is a dancer who also works as an escort.

Ridge has never experienced problems with a client. He has never had a client with whom he might fall in love, although he has had clients who would have liked to fall in love with him. Now he sees the end of his work as an escort is hovering into view.

He says, "I never did drugs or drank a lot. I've always put my foot down about things I saw as not being good for me. Now I have enough. I've earned a good bit of money. I have a business I own. I'm still working. I have a man in my life I love. It really is enough."

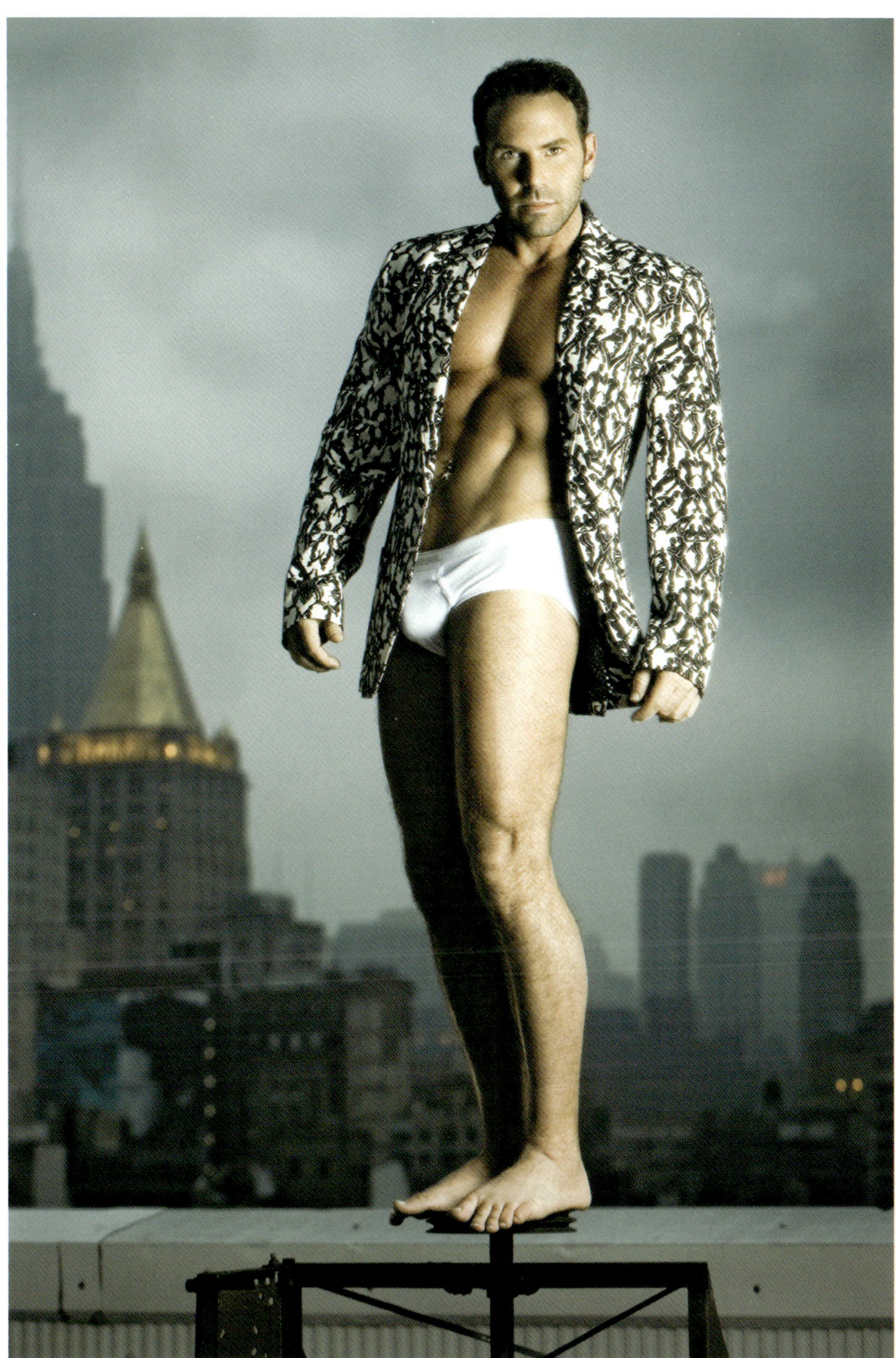

ELI DURAN

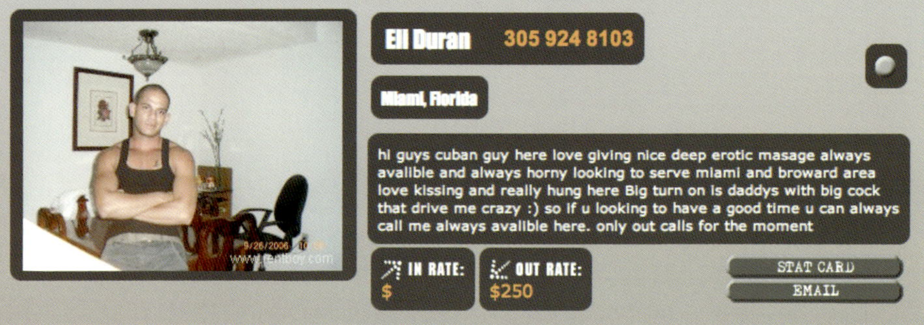

Eli Duran is pretty adorable. Especially on roller blades, which he arrived wearing for his interview. He is 25 years old but his tight little physique and shy manner suggests a young man perhaps five to seven years younger. Eli came to Miami from Cuba about ten years ago with his mother and sister. His grandfather had preceded the family by many years, coming to southern Florida in the 1970s. He had been a political figure in Cuba and was allowed to leave, as was his family in the mid-1990s.

When Eli first arrived in Miami the family lived with his uncle. He spoke no English and was enrolled in studies created for students with English as a second language. His English now is completely fluent. Upon finishing high school he remained out of school for a year and is now a sophomore at Miami-Dade College. He is studying Interior Design.

About a year ago he met a Miami Beach personality named Paolo online. He visited him and became part of the escort service offered by Paolo. The escort Geronimo also worked with Paolo, who frequently offers the services of more than one escort at a time. Now Eli can be found on *rentboy.com*, and *men4rentnow.com*. He says that he works about four times a week. He has one regular client who likes to go clubbing on Sunday evenings and get drunk. Eli says, "I am only going to be escorting while I am going to school. I don't plan to do it after I graduate."

Eli explains, "I realized I was gay when I was 17. I had slept with girls before that. I had a boyfriend for eight months. I met him at a nightclub. We talked on line. We met; we fucked. Then we went on a date. I was really in love with him but he wanted an open relationship. He was a personal trainer and a graphic designer and he didn't think in terms of relationships." Eli looks very unhappy when he tells this story and it is evident

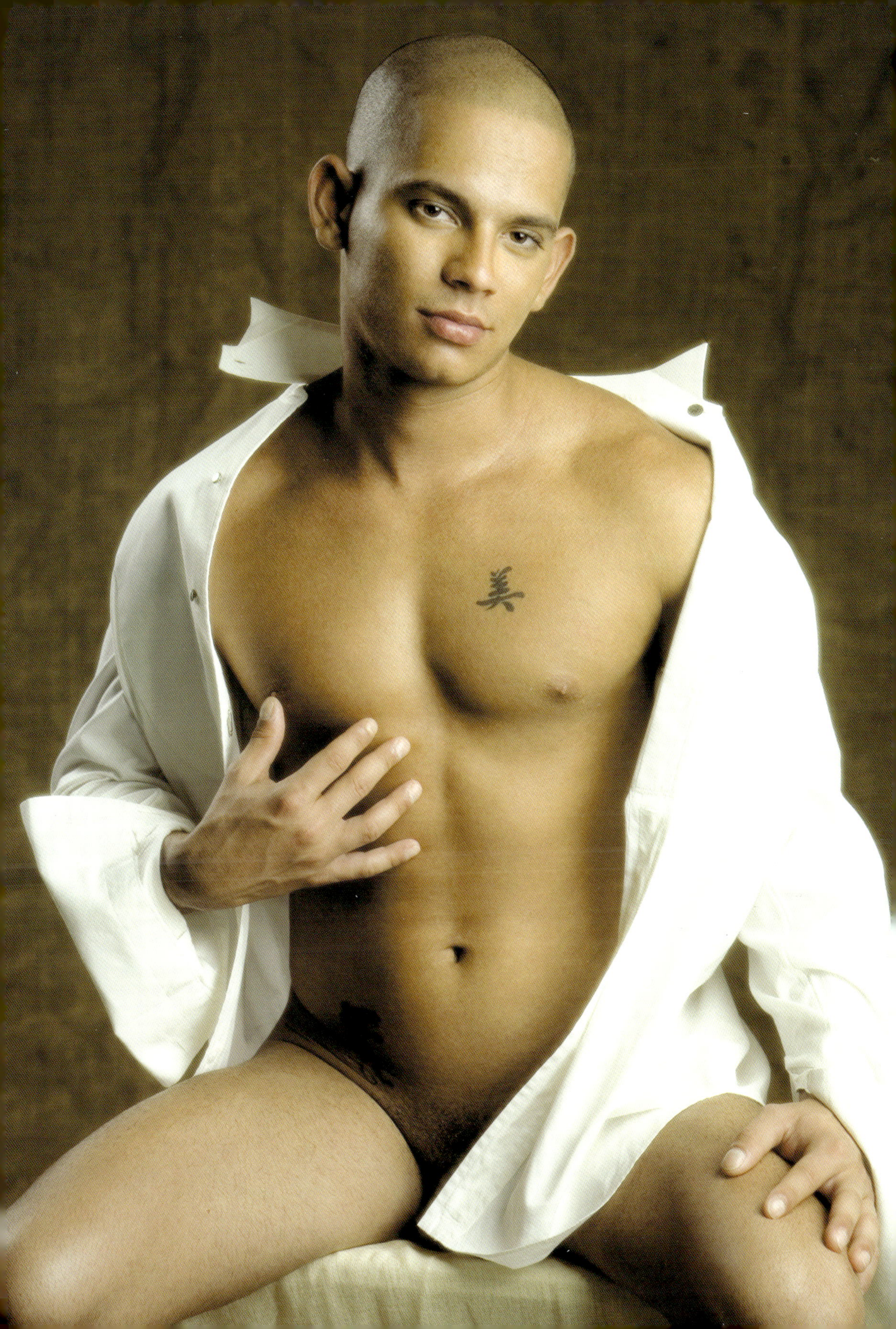

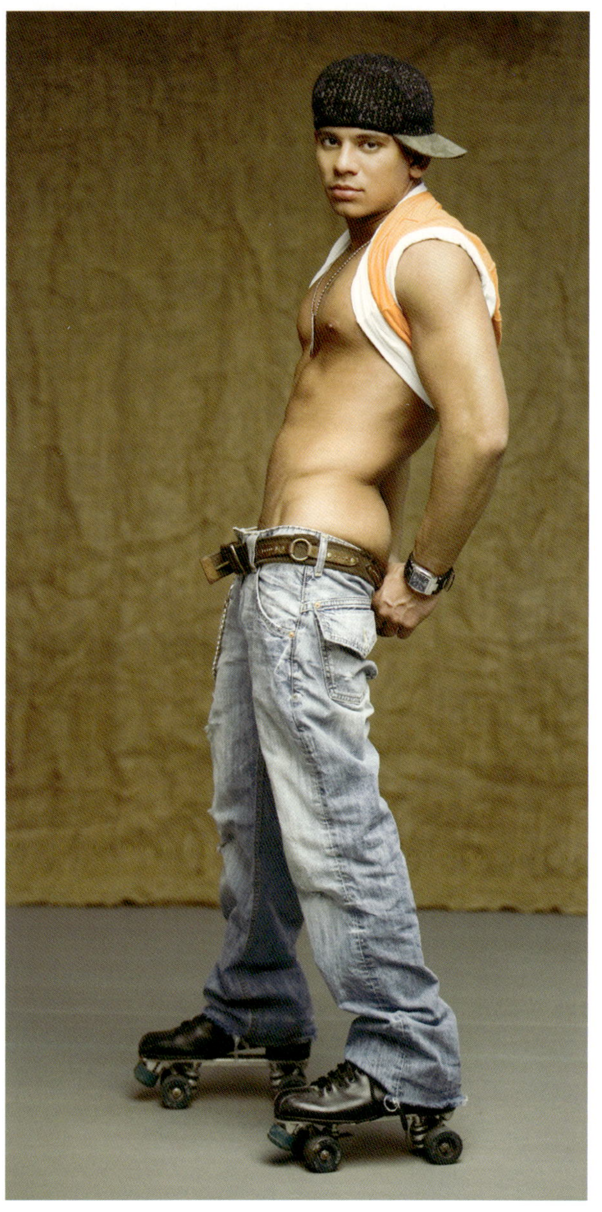

that he had been hurt by the failure of this love affair. When asked how he accommodated his escorting in the relationship he says, "That's not at all the same thing as an open relationship. That's work."

His rate in Miami is $250 an hour, $300 an hour elsewhere in Florida. He does travel and his overnight rate is $900 plus the client must pay for the travel. He says, "I have to be careful with payments as a guy here in Miami Beach paid with a check and then made a stop payment. A client wants me to come to Canada soon and the fee will be $1,500. I have required that I have the check to deposit in the bank three days before departure."

Eli has done a number of porn films for a company called Pride as well as the website, *poppy.com.* He says that most of his clients are over forty. His mother knows that he is gay and working as an escort. His father, who is still in Cuba but planning to come to Florida, does not know he is gay. Of his father he says, "He is so handsome." And he is obviously uneasy about the prospect of discussing his gayness and his employment with his father, even though his parents are long estranged.

His clients he estimates are 25% married, over 40 years old about 99%. He recently had a 21-year-old client. He says, "He was very cute and I said, 'Why are you paying me?' and he replied, 'Because you're an escort'."

When asked if he is concerned about AIDS he replies, "I use protection but I'm not really scared." Then he corrects himself. "I am and I'm not."

RAFAEL ALENCAR

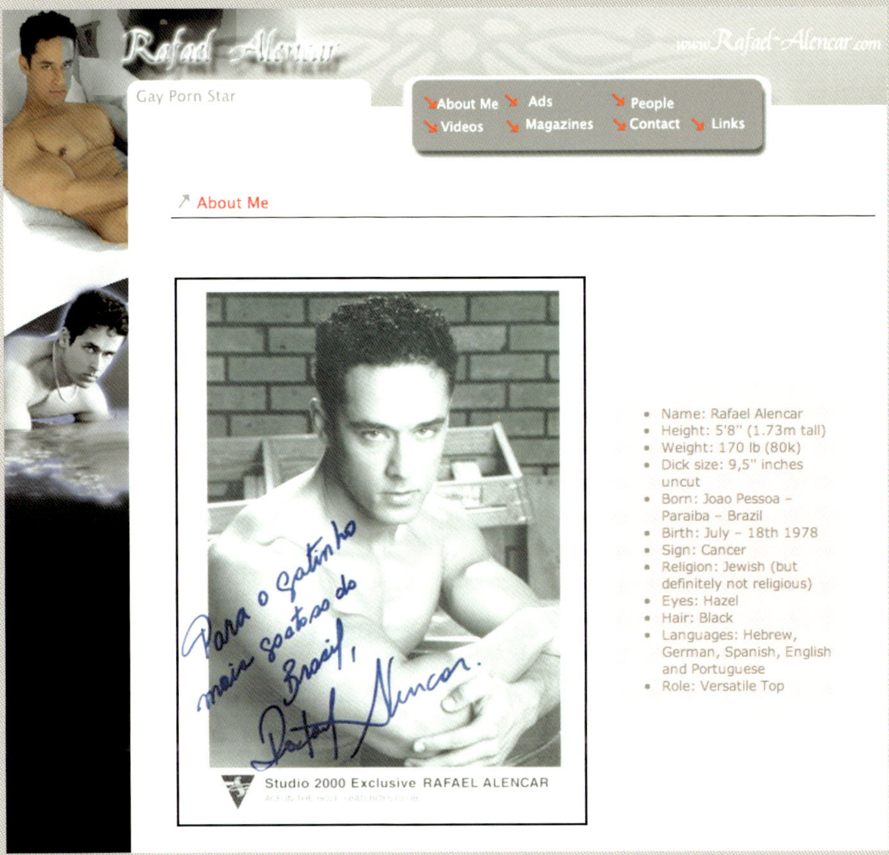

Oh, Rafael, Rafael, Rafael. How much more gorgeous could one human being be? Rafael Alencar is quite a beauty. He is from Brazil and has broad shoulders, a narrow waist, a bountiful butt and the face of a 1920s movie star. His tanned face is lightened by pale, gray eyes and he has an intelligent, thoughtful look. Really. His success in the escort business after one year in New York is highly understandable.

Surprisingly, Rafael Alencar has a degree in dentistry. He is from Joao Pessoa in the state of Paraiba in Brazil. His father, who is a doctor, is separated from his mother. She is now living in Israel. Rafael has two brothers and a sister.

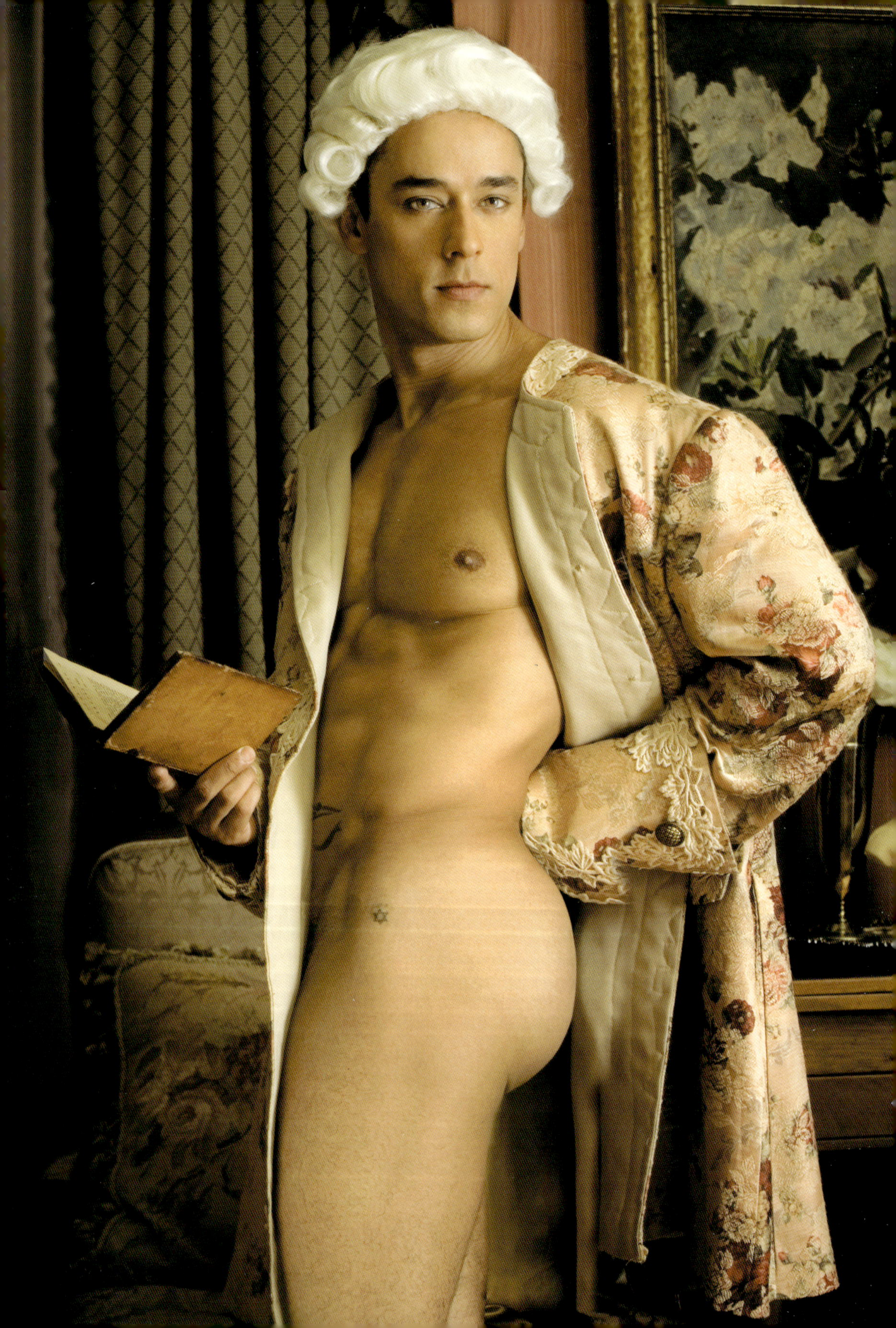

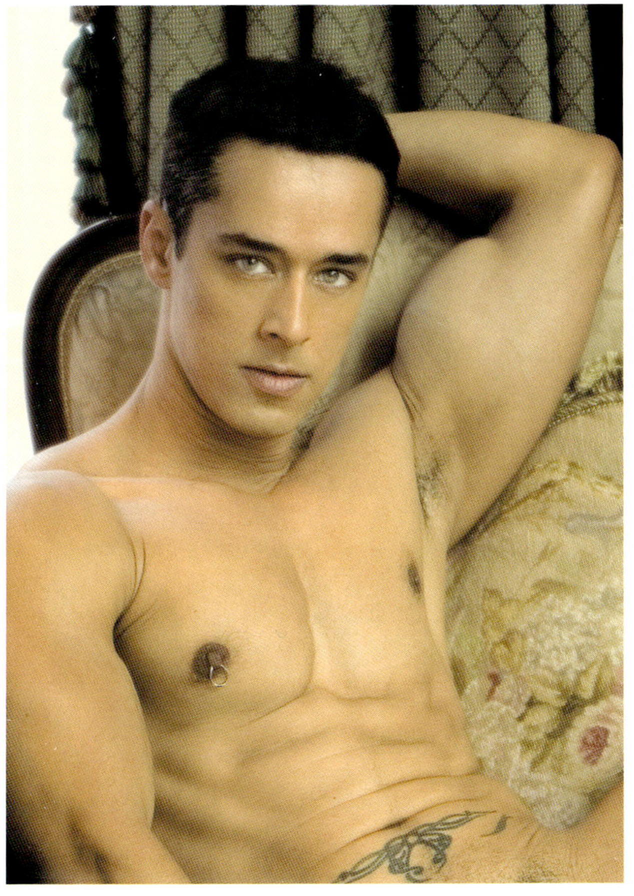

After receiving his dental degree, he lived in Sao Paulo where he also did some modeling. He spent two years there and then was invited to come to Germany to work by some German agents, who saw his model pictures. This work not only involved modeling but work as an escort and photographs for male nude magazines.

He came to the United States a year ago. He discovered that to have his degree in dentistry honored in the U.S. it would cost $80,000 in tuition fees at New York University. He decided against this and did some porn films instead, which he had originally been invited to this country to do.

Rafael has been very successful as an escort and no longer needs to advertise. He says, "I began by being on *rentboy.com* but now word of mouth is enough. I charge between $250 to $300 an hour, depending on the number of hours."

He does not do overnights or travel because "it really cuts into my time too much. I keep a chart on my kitchen wall of my booking and it is always full. I earn about $2,000 a day just by being available in New York."

As far as love is concerned, Rafael says, "I was in love with a man in Germany but he couldn't handle the escort business. So we parted and I don't plan to fall in love again anytime soon."

He does plan to use his savings to buy an apartment in New York and hopes to have a studio for making adult films.

His advice to anyone thinking of entering the business is, "I do everything very safe and I don't do drugs. Anyone in this business should do the same."

MARCOS DAVID

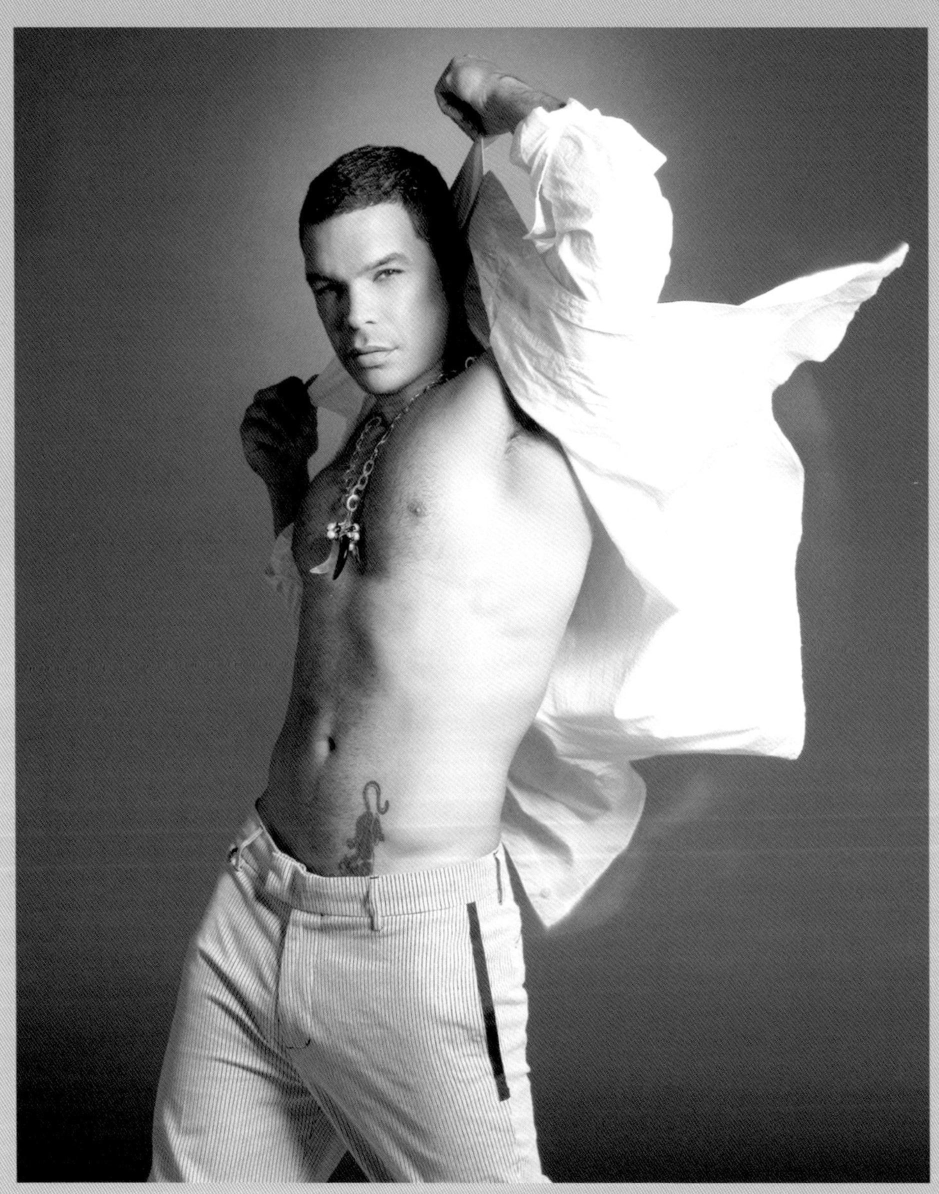

In addition to a very handsome physical presence, Marcos David has a lot of charm, too. His porn movies do not capture that high-voltage smile in a one-on-one conversation. It is no surprise in his escort work that he has a lot of repeat clients. Even in an interview he projects a lot of warmth and personal interest.

Marcos is originally from Cuba. He was trained there as a dancer and worked in

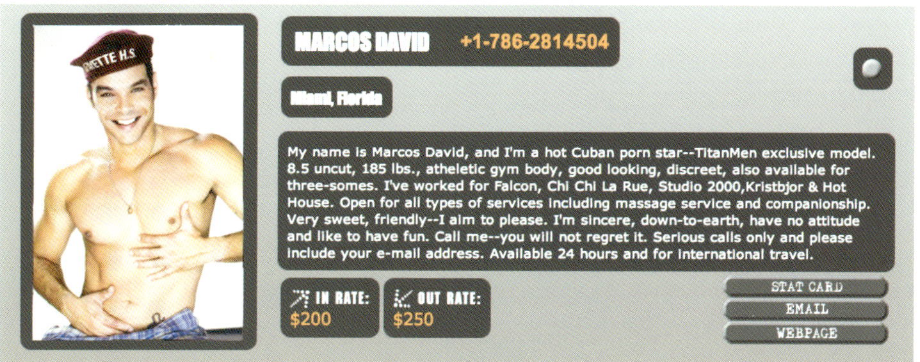

nightclubs and musical revues. In 1998 Marcos went to Barcelona. He had been seen in Cuba on stage and had been invited there to work in porn movies. He did 22 to 25 films. He was able to move to Spain and leave Cuba by marrying a Spanish dancer whom he had seen at the Riviera hotel where he was working in Cuba.

His marriage lasted for five years, and during that time he also worked as a male escort in Barcelona. He began escorting about two years ago when he heard friends talking about needing "a third boy."

Marcos David says that he knew he was interested in men when he was 20. He had relationships with girls before then, but realized that he felt something for men and acted upon by going home with someone he met in the street in Havana.

He fell in love with a dancer/singer at the Tropicana, where he was working. He says, "This was my first love. My first passion. Then my first disillusion." His English is excellent. He had another romance in Cuba about which he says, "Was beautiful but only lasted six months." And he has had a third romantic episode in Miami that lasted for a year. Of his work life he reports that in Barcelona he worked three or four times a week and his fee was 150 Euros at home, 200 Euros to meet someone outside his home. That was the hourly rate. He had three or four regular clients there.

Of his clients he says, "I prefer my American clients because they are less demanding. They do not demand a full hour, as most European clients do." For his future he would like to have a store in the Miami area as he is very interested in fashion.

Thanks to Base, Miami Beach, for wardrobe.

TREY REXX

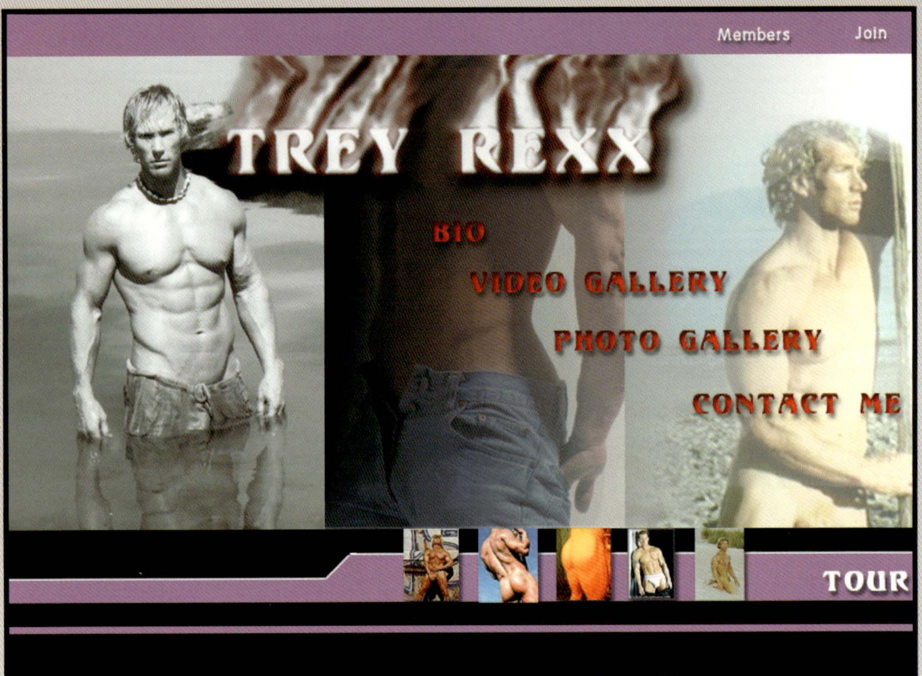

Trey says, "I'm an amazing dancer for a white boy." He certainly has a body that suggests it would be fairly amazing in motion, particularly topped with his mass of curly blond hair.

Trey has a very unusual story. He says, "When I came out I had been married for fifteen years." Born in California and living in Washington state as a child, his parents moved to Salt Lake City when he was an early teenager. He says, "All my friends were Mormons but we still drank and had fun." His father and mother had married at 17 and 16 and Trey followed in their path. He married his high school sweetheart, who was a Mormon, when he was 16 before finishing school and was a father when he was 17.

"When I was 19 I was working in a warehouse and came up with the idea of a company with a partner called "Document Destruction." We collected documents from companies and shredded and destroyed them. Through it all I found time to go to the gym and I stayed in good shape. I never drank or smoked," he recounts.

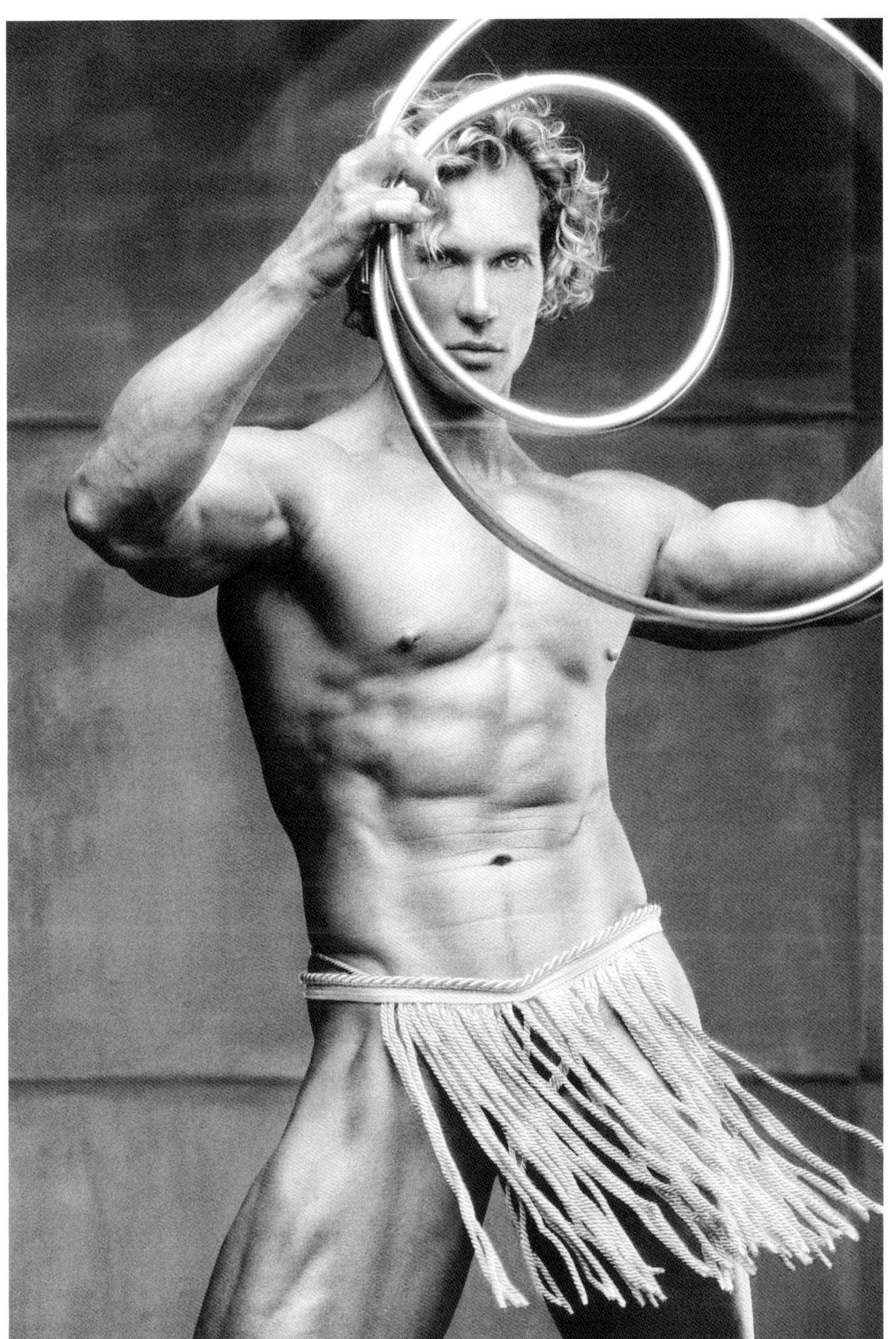

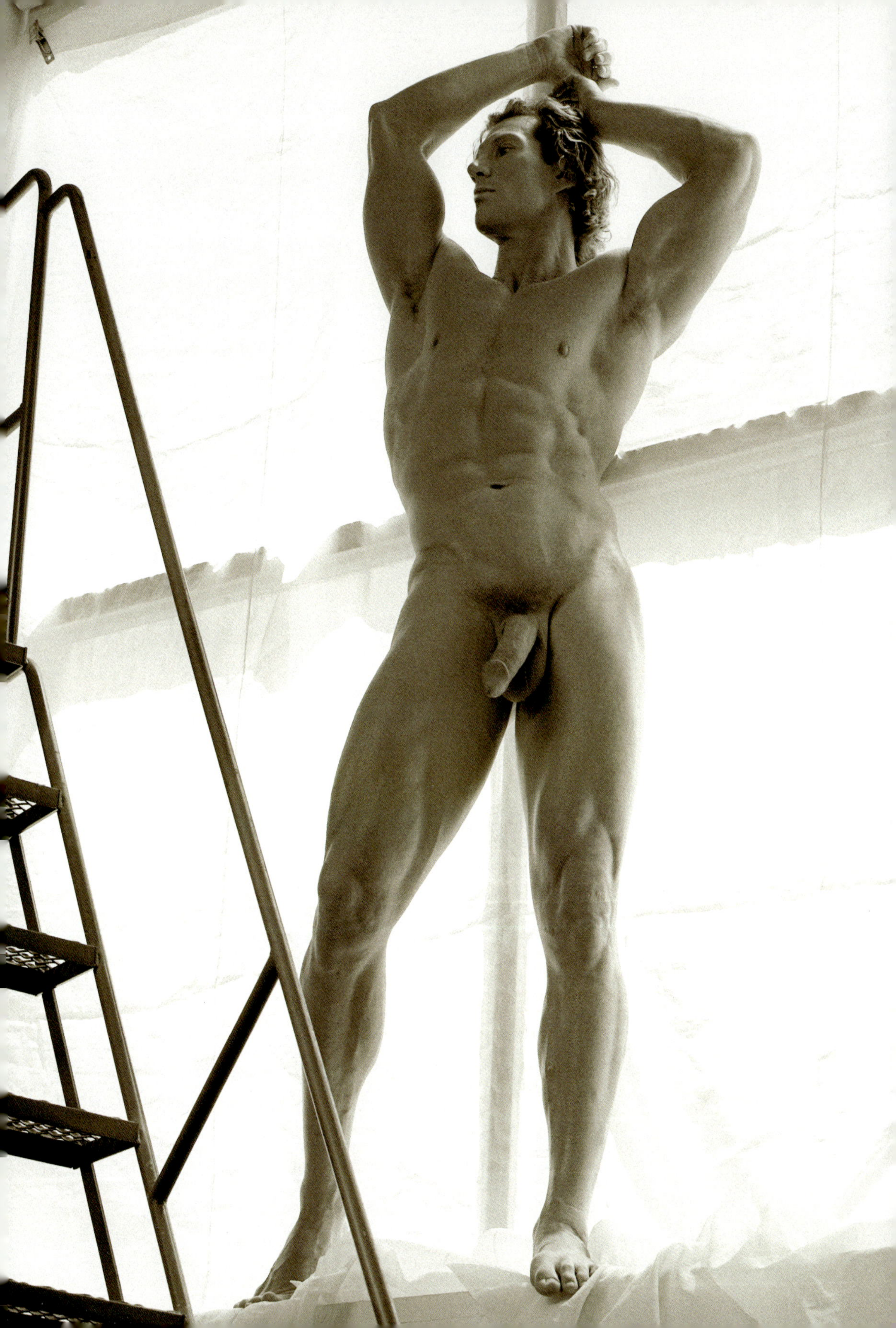

He goes on, "Our marriage was running into problems as we had no time together. We had children. I was working two jobs. My wife was working, too. We had to take turns staying home with the kids. It was tough.

"Then when I was 25 I went to a strip contest. It had a good cash prize. My wife went with me and I won. So I entered other contests and won them, too. In Salt Lake City there were a number of these clubs and each had their own strippers. They were very competitive. I was working three nights a week as well as my day job and I earned one hundred dollars a night plus tips. We suddenly had enough money to get along pretty well. Then the internet killed the dance scene, but that was after I had worked for ten years dancing at night and working days."

Trey also entered contests. There was one for Mr. Tight-Filled Jeans, a national contest that had finals in Las Vegas. He was Mr. Utah on a motorcycle and won the contest. Then, he says, "I started messing around. When I was dancing most of the other dancers were straight. But when I got involved with bodybuilding contests many of those men came on to me. And finally one day I gave in. I thought, 'Oh, God, I didn't do that.' And a couple of years would go by. And then I'd slip again. I was doing fitness modeling and that world was gay and they talked. I couldn't slip away in Salt Lake City. Everyone knew who I was. And I have to admit that I got off on other men getting off on me. I got into that. I was digging all this stuff that guys were doing to impress me, to know me. I'd go home and try to sleep well. It wasn't working great.

"My wife was working as an airline attendant at this time and she had gay friends who were also attendants. They repeated gossip they had heard and she asked. I denied it. We still had a great sex life at that time, so I just denied everything. I wanted her to have a life of her own, also. That way I wouldn't have to feel so guilty. She finally did have an affair with another man. A real affair. My daughter found out and told my mother. There was a big, big scandal.

"I was hurt because I had never betrayed our relationship. What she had done was very different in my eyes. And I continued denying everything. I lived in a kind of limbo for two years and then I started spending a lot of time with another man. A slightly older, professional guy. My wife found out about it and went to an attorney. She didn't really have the money to hire him but she managed to transfer travel mileage to him, paid him in that way and she got a divorce. "I was living in Bountiful, outside Salt Lake, with this older man. He had been married and had three children. They often came and spent the weekends with us. I was working full time as a dancer and started a business training dancers. I worked under the name of Austin Wells at that time.

"My lover was a real mentor. He was falling more in love with me all the time and I was actually looking for someone more like myself. Sometimes he would hire a younger man to join us for sex and then he saw the difference for me between having sex with him and sex with someone young. He wanted me to be happy but I knew I had to walk away.

"I had met an escort named Ridge in Chicago and he invited me to come to New York and go to a big party with him. I realized that my relationship with Daniel was over so I went and there I saw the photographer David Morgan. I had met him in Montreal before and he was very eager to photograph me. I also met Leo Bramm at this party and that was instant fireworks. We went to Fire Island together and I spent all the rest of my time in New York with him.

"I had been supporting myself in Salt Lake City doing interior painting, faux finishes, that kind of thing. Leo decided that he would move back there with me and we moved all of his things. Everything. Immediately. "Leo had made a porn film for Chi Chi LaRue in Los Angeles. One of four he was under contract to make. Leo agreed to come to L.A. and make the others if all his scenes could be with me. And that is how I started making videos for Falcon.

"Leo and I were beginning to have trouble. Finally I came out to my family, sent Leo back to New York and suddenly I was a hot commodity. Leo wouldn't allow me to travel. Now I could and I began to make lots of money. I started dancing in New Orleans. I met a man in Austin when I was dancing there and moved to San Diego to be with him. He was Swiss and a trust fund baby. "He was very much opposed to my escorting and didn't understand that I am a very erotic, sexual person. 'How is what your doing any different from what you do with me?' he asked me. I tried to explain that I have never asked anyone out, ever. It has always been others who were interested in me. All I do is cooperate. That's quite different from pursuing someone".

"But when I did I wound up making quite a few porn films. I have to say that I was railroaded many times by directors into doing things I didn't want to do. You'd get on the set and they'd say, 'So-and-so didn't show up and we need someone to do this or that.' You have to do it. And you do it or you know you're never going to get paid.

"As far as escorting goes, a good client is someone who can become a friend. Most of the clients who become friends are married. No one knows and no one ever suspects. I've never been in love with someone like that but I'm happy to do it for them.

"A bad client? I have had one from Indianapolis. He thinks he's God's gift. Thinks he can buy you and anyone he wants. "Bizarre requests? When I worked in New York through Chelsea Boys I used to have up to six clients an evening. One guy wanted me to walk on him with boots. I didn't mind because you can't have all-out sex six times in one evening. You have to save something for when you go home".

Rate-wise Trey has normally charged $200 an hour. As a porn star in New York he has been able to charge $500 an hour. Now in Florida he has a standard rate of $250 an hour. He is presently living in Miami Beach and sees his children regularly, who come to visit.

His plans for the future included finding a soul mate, creating a website for myself that has "...cool, erotic images that can live forever like Jeff Stryker."

ALEXANDER

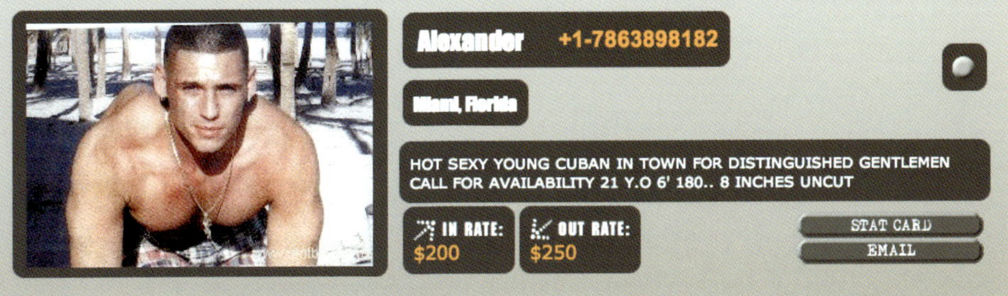

Alexander was born and brought up in Miami Beach. Which is almost as much of a rarity as meeting a native New Yorker born in Manhattan. As he says, “I was brought up right across the street from Flamingo Park. Which is a famous gay cruising area in Miami Beach.”

Alexander’s mother is from Spain and as an adventurous young woman left there to go to work in England, then passed through New York and came to Miami. His father arrived in Miami in the Marielito boatlift. He has five older brothers and one sister. He is the youngest.

Alexander attended local schools in Miami Beach near his home and says, “I always worked a lot. I worked as a waiter in a restaurant, I worked in construction, I was a teaching assistant, I’ve clerked in clothing stores, and I’ve styled videos.” At the moment he has been spotted by a scout for a model agency and may begin that career also.

He remembers as a young teenager seeing two men kiss on the street and thinking, “Oh my God, they’re queers.” He adds, “But it was a lesson for me.” His escorting career had actually begun at an early stage when he was 15. His parents had separated, money was short, and he went out into Flamingo Park to meet men and to be paid in exchange for sex. He says that he has always made contacts and accepted payment, even though he has held regular jobs also. “I’m always up front. Why should I play around with someone’s heart?” he says.

He admits having gone to jail last year, but it was only a two-day stay in the local jail. He had been stopped on Collins Avenue and taken in for suspicion of having drugs on his person. Alexander says it was very unpleasant; one large room filled with men who were forced to sleep on the floor and the food was terrible so he didn’t eat. For him the most embarrassing part was that he had gone to high school with one of the policemen on duty, and they talked about school and people they knew in South Beach.

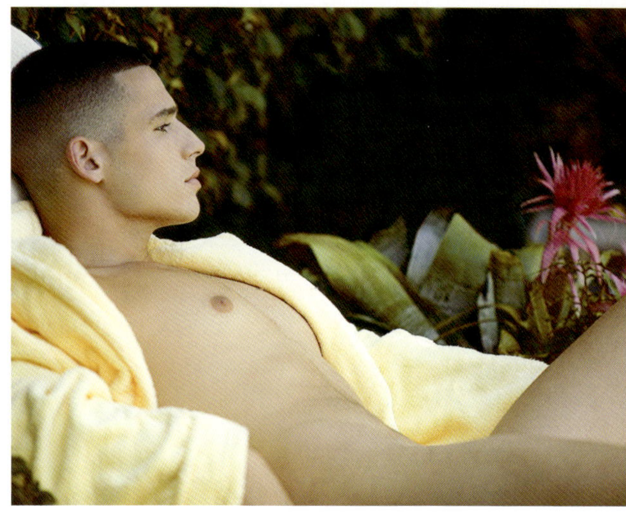

Of his escorting career, Alexander explains, "I had an ad in the local magazine, Hotspots, when I was 19. I worked a lot immediately. I traveled a lot, too. I went to Mexico. I went to France. In a year, I probably had 500 calls." He thinks that his clients are more tourists than local. And although he both tops and bottoms, he says, laughing, "Everything you thought he wanted to do to you, you wind up doing to him."

When asked about bad clients, he says there's nothing he likes less than a client who opens the door and says, "Get naked." For the most part he has liked his clients and only had one frightening experience with a client who was driving him to a motel and he realized he was on drugs. He says, "I could have left as he was checking us into the motel but I didn't have any money with me and we were way out of Miami Beach. So I waited until he had paid me and we had had sex, and then while he was in the bathroom I dashed. Luckily for me, the motel was right by a metro rail station and I was able to grab a train and get out of there quickly. He was hallucinating and had a knife. It was really scary."

Of good clients, Alexander remembers, "I had amazing clients. So good-looking I couldn't believe they had hired an escort. My very best was a green-eyed guy from Egypt who had a cock-ring vibrator. He was one of those clients where you just have to say, 'Wow!'."

"You know, I wanted to go to college but my parents didn't have the money and I had to use my money for them." When asked if his parents knew what he did for a living he says, "They took the money. They have to." He adds, "I've always covered for them. They've never covered for me. It's because of me that my parents got back together again. My sister became a Jehovah's Witness and wouldn't speak to me for a year. My mother wanted me to have psychological help and I told her, 'Mom, don't spend the money'."

Now Alexander is living with his mother and sister and says, "I need to separate from my family. But they aren't happy to see me go." Of his immediate life he finishes, "I treat my clients the way I want to be treated. I don't run into disrespect." And finally says, "Hiding from the world is not my way of life. I am spiritual. I have been the head of the household since I was very young. I am ready for wherever my life will take me."

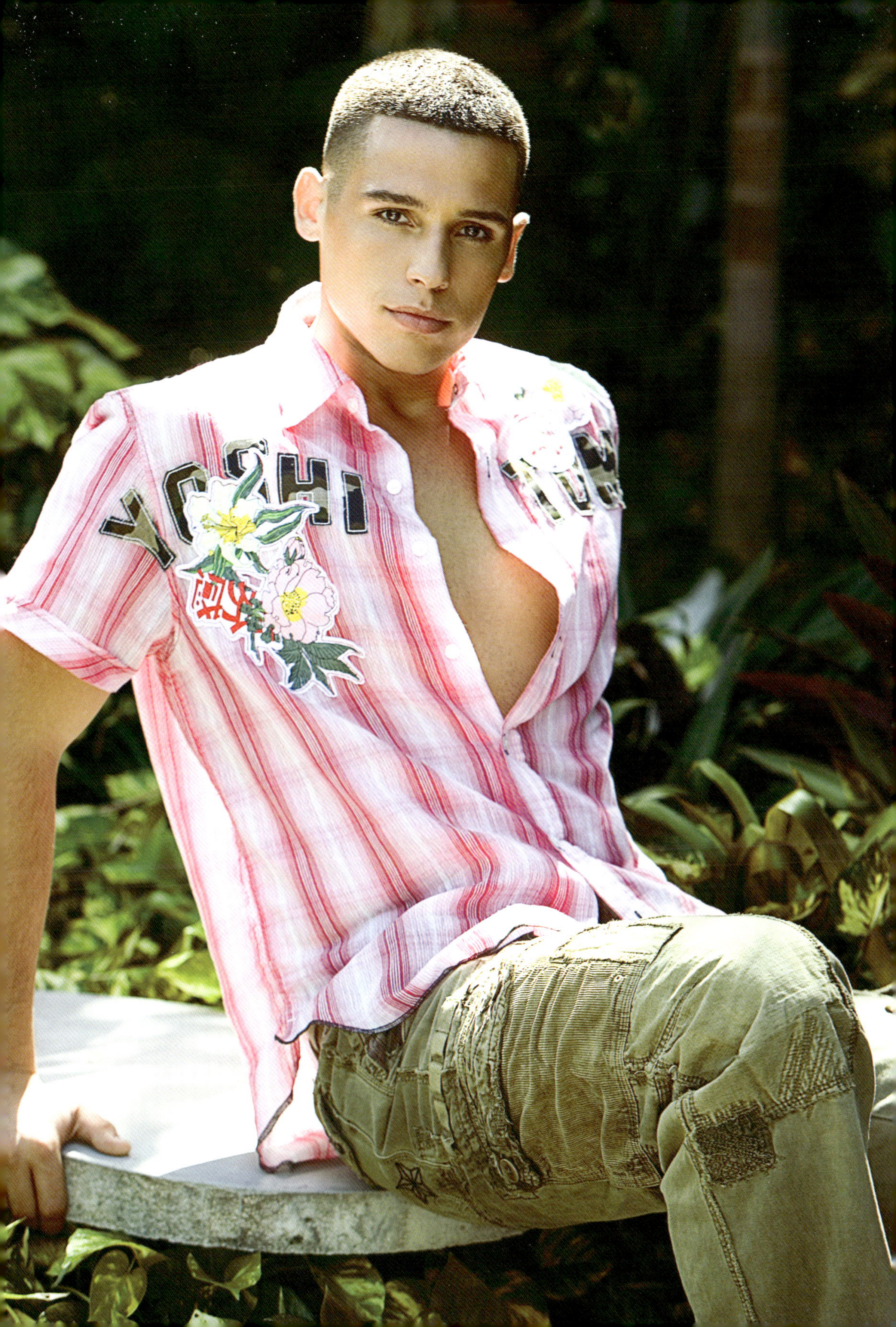

EDUARDO

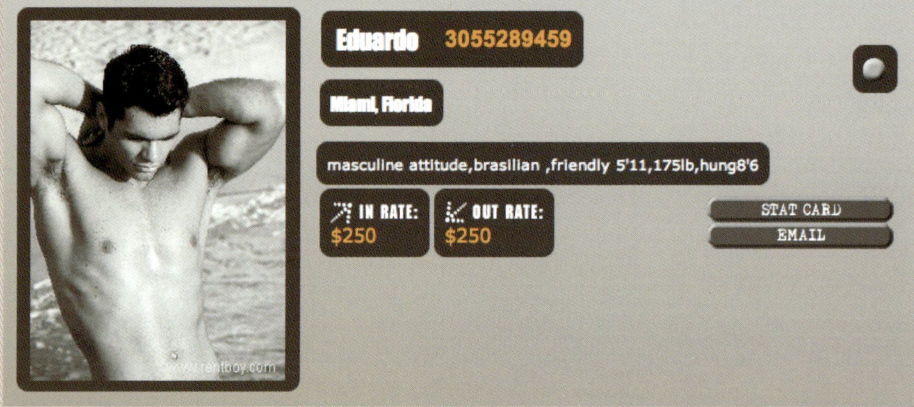

Eduardo is a beautiful young man from near Bahia in Brazil. From Fortaleza to be exact, which is a seaside resort. His history is unusual. His father is a banker. He was a happily married young man with two children when a baby was dropped off on his doorstep in the night. That baby was Eduardo. In the basket with him was a note, written in a literate hand, saying that the mother was sure that he would have a happier life with his new family than she could give him. Very recently Eduardo asked his parents if he could have that note and it is now in his possession.

In a curious twist, his new parents at first decided that they could not take him and they found a foster mother for him. But within a few days they had second thoughts, his mother woke his father in the night and said, "We must take him back." Which they did, but only after a good deal of wrangling with the other foster mother whom also loved him and wanted to keep him. They had to buy him back finally.

Eduardo attended school in Fortaleza and studied Business Administration in college there also. His family remains there. His older brother is a computer designer and his sister is married to a dentist with two children.

Eduardo loves his parents very much and he says that after his mother by adoption died when he was eleven, he said to his father when the funeral was over, "This is why I was dropped off at the door, so that I could be with you."

He remembers being discovered in the streets of Fortaleza by a model agency talent scout when he was a teenager. "I was a long-haired heavy-metal fan." Both Ford and Elite model agencies had scouts there at the time and he was seen by both and was signed by Ford. He remained in Fortaleza until he was 18 and then moved to Sao Paulo.

In Brazil the competition for Mr. Universe is important and Eduardo represented the state of Bahia in these Contests for two consecutive years.

In Sao Paulo Eduardo was with Boss Models, as well as Wilhelmina, and after working as a model in Sao Paulo Eduardo went to Paris to further his career and was there for seven months. The long, gray Parisian winter was not appealing and he moved on to Miami Beach in 2002 when he was 22. In Miami Beach he worked for Boss Models as well as Wilhelmina and Michelle Pommier agencies.

Concerning his sexuality, Eduardo says, "I think you always know you're gay but I had my first relationship with a man in Miami Beach when I was 22." He adds that he had had girlfriends in Brazil before that time.

"My first boyfriend was 20 years older than I was. He was a flight attendant. We met at the Laundry Bar. I invited him to a birthday party a few days after that. He arrived late but we started to talk. And we became boyfriends. I wasn't in love with him. I don't think I've ever been in love. I like him a lot and anyone who gets him is lucky. He wanted to settle down. I wasn't ready for that."

Strangely, Eduardo was being interviewed on his last day as an escort. He explained, "I have a very good friend who works as an escort and other friends look down on him. I wanted to try it just to prove that you can be an okay person and still work as an escort. I took out an ad on *rentboy.com.* for one month and I forgot to cancel it so it ran a second month. This is the last day of the second month. I haven't actually worked for the last three weeks as an escort. I've started painting."

For the brief period he was working Eduardo charged $250 an hour and lowered the rate if it was for more than five hours. All night was $1,500 to $2,000. He did not travel but had the opportunity to go to New York and Los Angeles. He also had a curious invitation to come to Nigeria but shied away from it, although it was supposedly for a prominent person in that country. Because of all the fraud schemes emanating from Nigeria at this time Eduardo thought it was wiser to decline. It was for the prominent person's birthday and the plane ticket had been purchased for him, but he declined even so.

When asked about his average clients, Eduardo said they were about 40 years old for the most part. He did not have any married men to his knowledge and he only had one call from a straight heterosexual couple that wanted to experiment.

Eduardo does not bottom, which he says probably eliminated a certain part of potential clientele. He feels his best clients were those who did not hire him for sex only, but also for companionship. His worst clients were those "who open the door and touch you down there."

He had his share of bizarre requests, some of which he accepted, some of which he turned down. Turned down were requests to be urinated on (water sports), to be spit upon and to be treated like a slave. He also demurred at the request to be walked like a

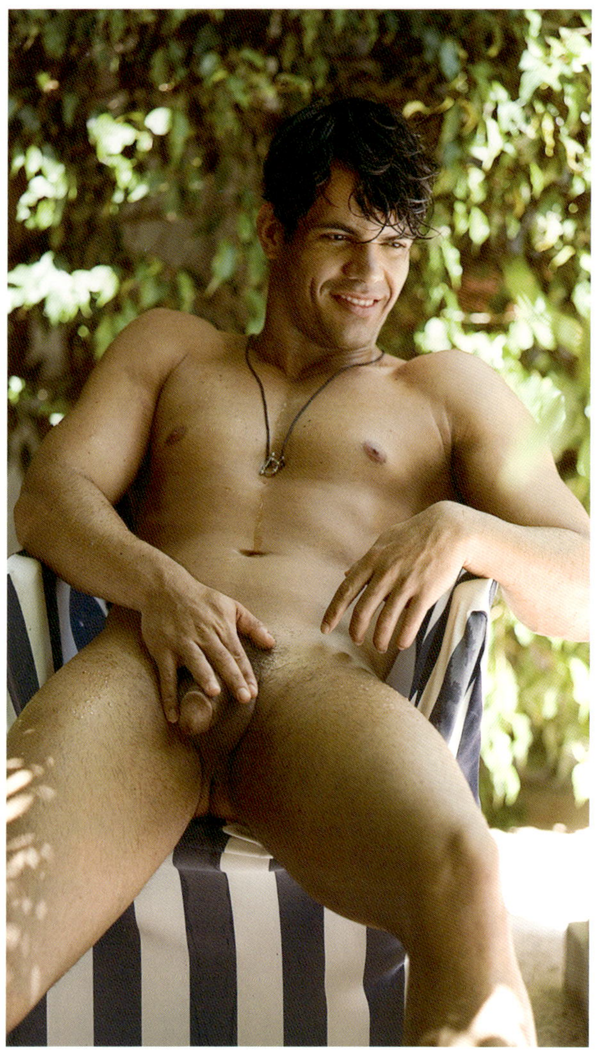

dog with collar and leash. Requests to kiss his feet he felt were acceptable. His most unusual client only wished him to model a collection of ten swimsuits that the client had collected.

He has had some clients so undemanding that he had to ask, "Why did you contact me?" He adds, "Just hugging someone for an hour can be a long time." And interestingly, his first client was someone who answered his ad whom he already knew from the gym that they both patronized. Eduardo has turned down many client calls, left many others unanswered and says his selections were made based on the personality of the client as it was projected over the telephone.

At the moment he is studying singing with an 82-year-old Cuban diva who sang formerly at the Metropolitan Opera in New York. A very demanding lady, when she first heard his voice she asked, "Did you have a horse in your house? You sound like one." Now she is pushing him to the edge of having an operatic voice and recently told him, "Now you are my best case. If I can make you sing I can make anyone sing."

For the future Eduardo hopes for a career as a singer and music producer. He has already had small roles on programs with Univision and Telemundo, and considering his great charm, affability and looks, it seems entirely possible. He does not think his brief career as an escort will make any negative difference.

In conclusion Eduardo says, "I had just moved and I needed the supplemental income. And I also wanted to show people that you don't have to be a fucked up person to work as an escort. But it really isn't for me. I'm not so much a sexual person. I'm much more a romantic person."

Thanks to Base, Miami Beach, for wardrobe.

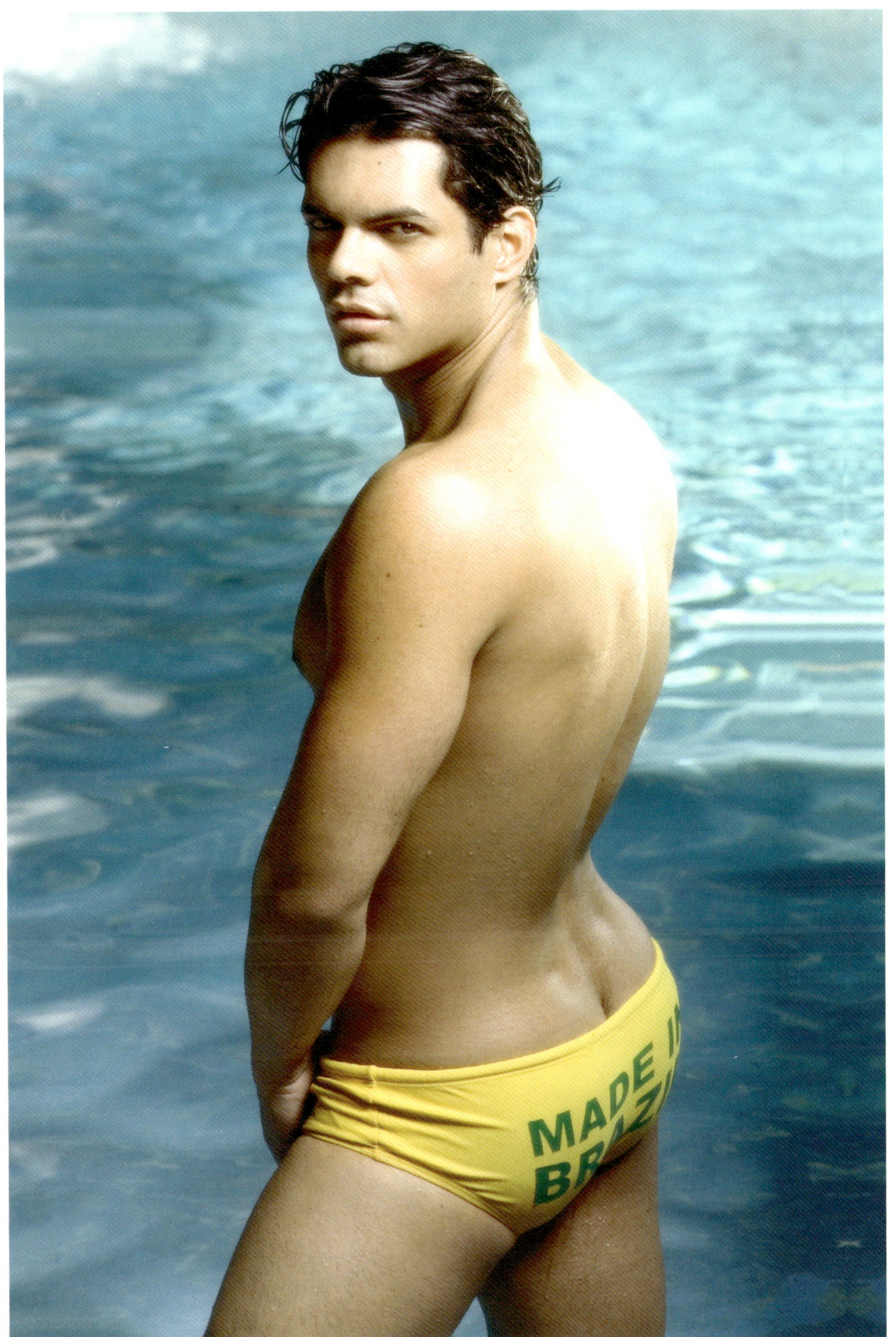
MADE
BRAZ

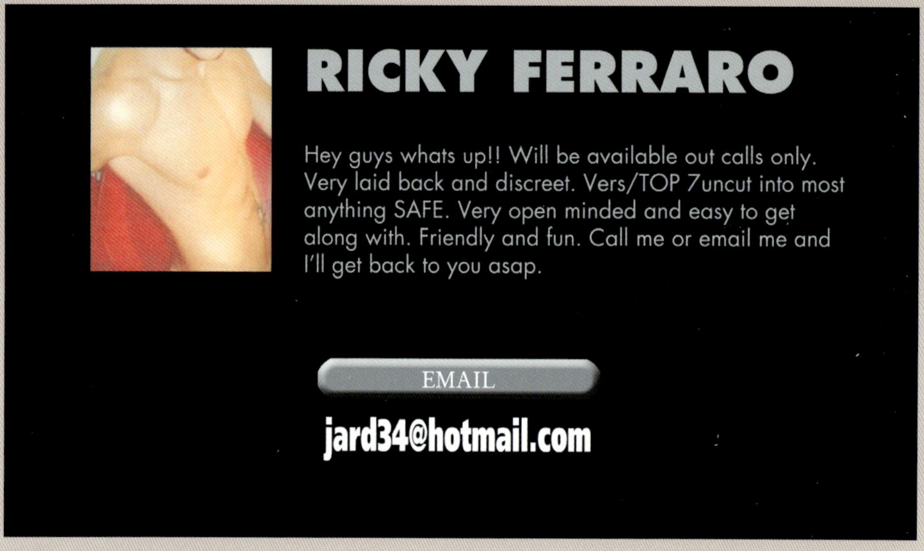

Ricky Ferraro came to Miami Beach from Venezuela in 2002. He says, "I came to improve my life. In my country it isn't easy for gay people."

His best friend from Caracas had already moved to Miami Beach. He had already finished high school and done two years of college in Management and Tourism when he left his home country. He has left behind his parents and an older sister and a younger brother.

He explains, "When I first came to the United States I traveled for six months to see this country. Then I worked as a waiter. In that same time period I started dating a porn star I had met in a bar. I don't want to tell you his name. He's major. He wanted me to work with him so I did five movies. Then I started working by myself. Now I'm taking a break."

"I've been in the porn movie business about two years and I like doing the movies. I really enjoy it. But I do get embarrassed when people recognize me and ask if they haven't seen me in a film.

"I started escorting when I met another porn star and he became my boyfriend. I started making a lot of money very easily. I still love that guy but he's in Los Angeles and he loves me too, but we can't be together. It just doesn't work.

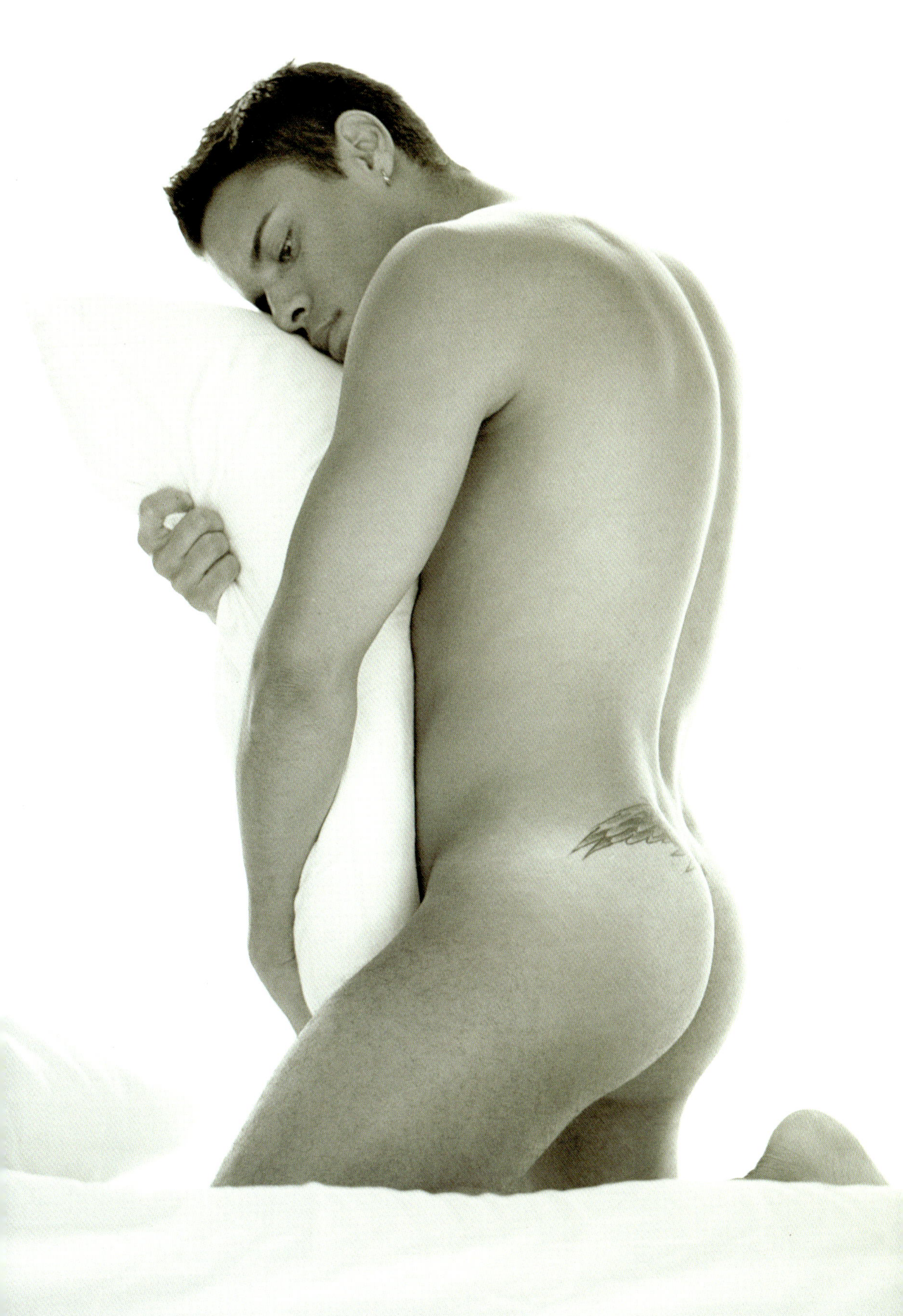

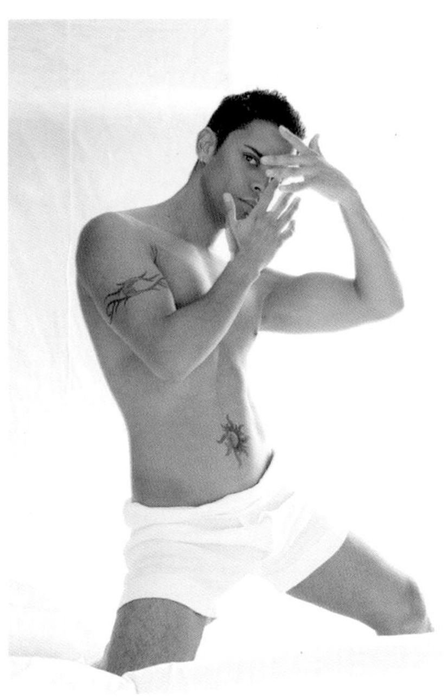

"I have someone in my life right now but he's not my boyfriend. I don't want him to be my boyfriend right away. I've done that a lot and I want to know who the person is before I get involved again."

Of his work he says, "In movies I only topped and I didn't do oral sex. Now even if a client wants to give me a blowjob I insist on a condom. I am very concerned about AIDS. I've been escorting for about five months and my ad is on *rentboy.com*. I charge $250 an hour, $1,500 for overnight. I regularly have two clients a day, sometimes three or four if I am in Los Angeles. New York is crazy. I could have six clients a day there.

He adds, "Some of my clients are very young. In their mid-twenties. It is their first gay experience and they hire an escort for it. You know, many clients only want body contact. I've had clients who want to go to dinner and then the theater and then have drinks and after watch some TV and just hold me. I have one regular who is only 27 who does that."

When asked if he makes any kind of reduced tariff considerations for such undemanding clients he replies, "I never give anyone a financial break." Ricky has only had one client who said he was married. A New Yorker, he made very precise arrangements to meet in New York when his wife was out of town. He told Ricky that he had found out he was gay after he had married and had children and he did not wish to change his life in any way. The client was 42.

Ricky defines a good customer as someone who is sweet and just wants rubbing, not real sex. He says, "Many clients don't want real sex. That's how it's possible to do it a number of times a day.

For him a bad client is "Some guy who wants a 'golden shower.' I don't do that. There are many people who want it. And I don't like weird stuff like leather.

"I had one client who only wanted to see me change underwear. We were at my place and I have lots of different kinds of underwear so I was able to do that. That's all he wanted." The client sounds as though he may have been a client of at least one other escort interviewed for the book.

Ricky concludes, "I just told my mother a month ago that I was gay. Our relationship is much better now. You know, my father has a taxi company. My sister works as an accountant. They still think I'm working as a waiter at that Japanese restaurant. They're just average, normal people. I'm happy if my family's happy. Now I want to take a break. I'm dating someone and I want to take a break from escorting. I want to go to school and get on with my life."

A.G.

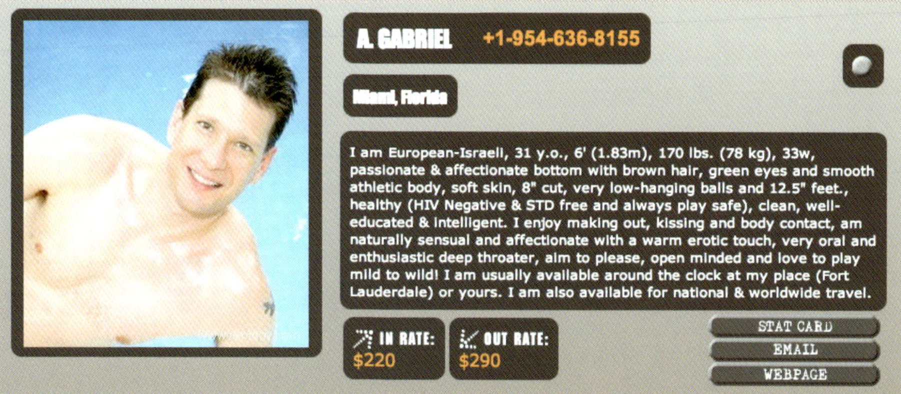

The man known as A.G. is a fascinating guy. Genial, charming and very sociable he has a one-of-a-kind life story. Born and brought up in Israel, his family lived in Tel Aviv. As a sixteen-year-old, his parents had left him at home one summer while they took a vacation visiting Europe. At home alone, A.G. was leafing through a magazine that had ads concerning lost and found animals. He loved pets and was interested in their welfare. Turning the next page he fell upon advertisements for men who wanted to meet men. Reading them he flashed on something. "I'm gay," he told himself and immediately called one.

This man was a bus driver who picked him up at a bus stop and took him to the end of the line. A.G. was somewhat disappointed but answered a few more ads before he encountered a man who was serving in the Israeli army at the time. "With him I began to understand what being gay was all about and I liked it," he says. He then called an escort service and was able to earn a little money before his parents returned from vacation.

He says of Israel, "Being gay and working as an escort is not a particularly scandalous thing in my homeland. People can understand it and you are not scorned for doing that kind of work." Which was good, as he worked his way through college doing exactly that kind of work. He remembers, "At first I had a bedroom in an apartment with other students and some of them saw I was earning good money so they wanted to do it too. Finally everyone in the apartment was working as escorts." He had to move his group to a larger apartment. Then a house. He was making a lot of money but closed it down upon graduation. "It was too much with all those difficult personalities. I wasn't enjoying it."

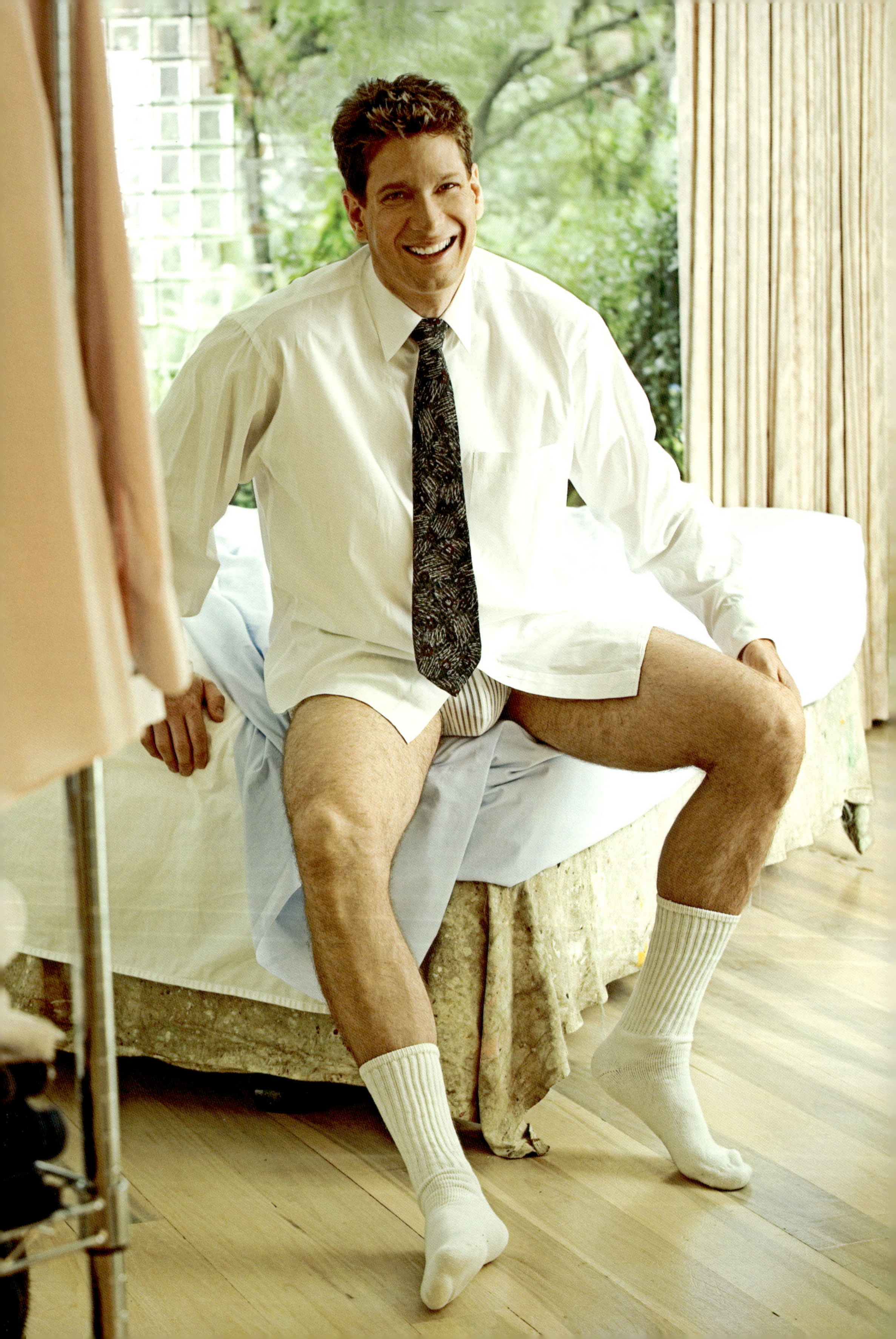

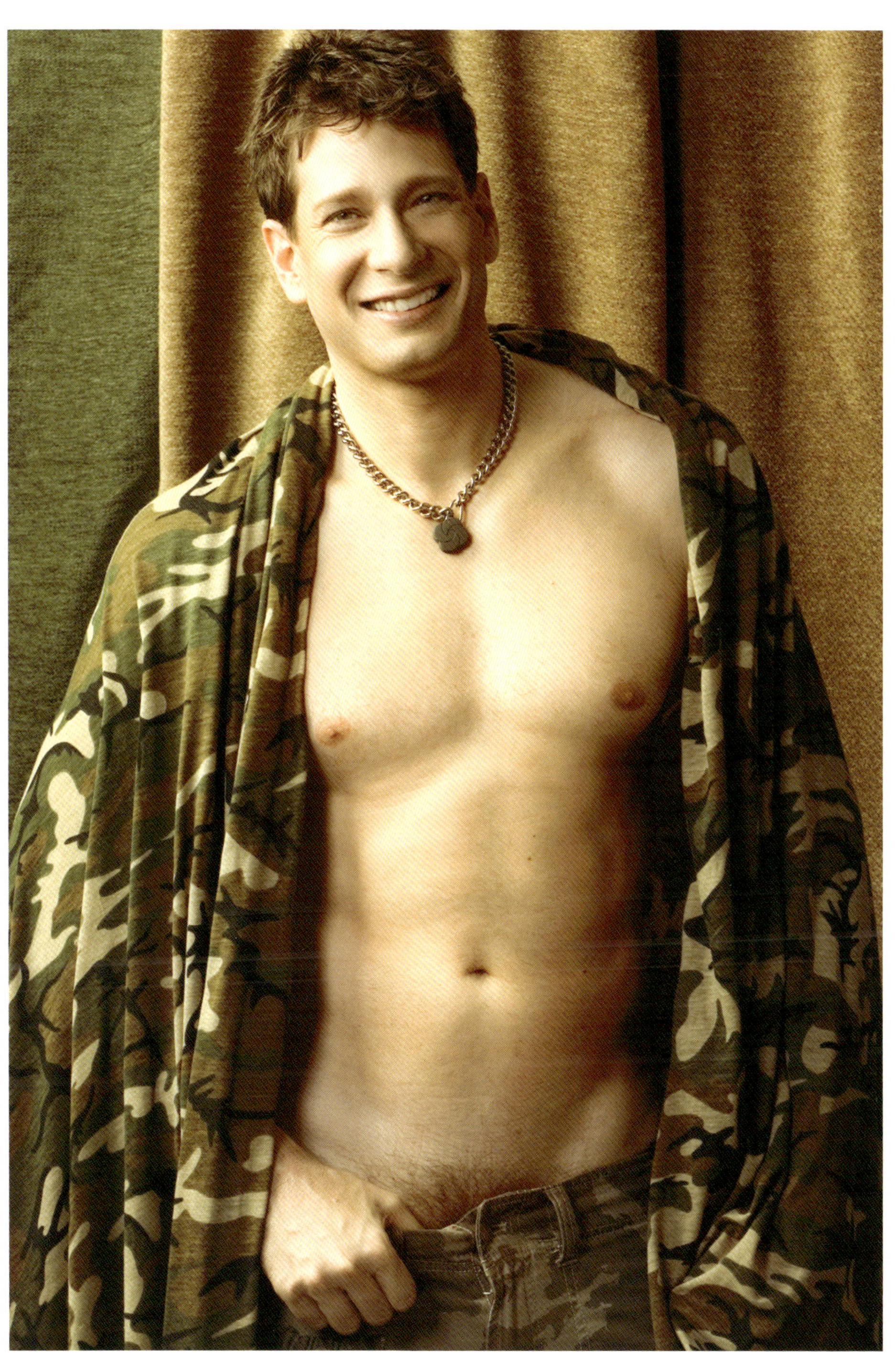

When asked how he explained to his parents why they did not have to pay anything for his college expenses, he says, "They didn't really ask too much about it. They accepted that I was working and paying my own way and we left it at that."

After college he had to serve in the Israeli army and as things were frequently slow on guard duty out in the desert he decided to return to doing some escort work. One can imagine A.G. on the phone saying, "Yes, I'm just 7.5 miles out in the Negev desert on Highway 101. I'm in the guard booth on the left."

"I was studying at the same time I was finishing my military requirements and also doing quite a lot of escorting with gays and bi's and even one a prisoner who was on vacation or what the prison would call 'leave of absence.' That's Israel for you."

He had pursued an advanced degree after college, so he was able to secure a job in the United States in Washington working for an accounting firm. After an apprenticeship with the company there he was assigned to a new office they had just opened in New York. He says, "Things were pretty slow in the office so I thought I might as well do some escorting in my spare time.

From that office, A.G. then relocated to Los Angeles and continued his parallel careers of working as an accountant and also escorting. He says he has done a few films but mostly for private clients. But living in Los Angeles where most porn films are shot gave him the idea of creating a website where live sex is available several times a week and then those films are recycled on the web and made available for sale.

Now he is relocated again to Fort Lauderdale where his start up of the website is occupying most of his time. He continues to escort and reports that many of his clients are regulars and have become friends. He frequently travels with them and does not charge the kind of rates that he might for first-time clients. He tells his interviewer, "Twenty minutes of sex in the morning. Twenty minutes of sex at the end of the day. What does that amount to? It's nothing and there you are having a wonderful trip in Italy or France or Portugal." A.G. has told his mother and his aunt of his work and he says, "They do not have religious affiliations so that is not a problem for them. They don't like what I do but they love me and respect my decisions."

At the moment he reports that he bottoms for less than 50% of his clients. Other clients just want body contact, touching, affection and some oral. His rates are $220 at his own apartment and he is able to accept credit cards through his connected tax services. The rate is $230 out and $850 a day for travel.

Among his unusual experiences was being with a client who was the manager of a synagogue and having sex with him in the synagogue. He also has a high-ranking church official client in the U.S., not Catholic he points out. As for married clientele, he estimates in Florida it is 20%, New York 30% and in Israel 50%.

He also has made tax accounting clients of many of his regulars, providing a dual service. Free of repression and Puritanism, A.G. is and original.

SLOAN CHRISTIAN

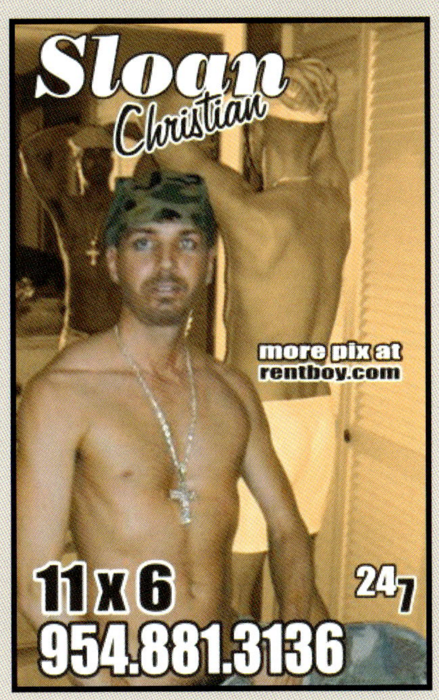

Sloan Christian is a hoot. Tall and rangy, he has a kind of Gary Cooper appeal and has the sexual equipment that Gary Cooper was always rumored to have. He has the look of someone who has only recently emerged from his teen years although he admits to being a fair distance from that time. He is something of a non-stop talker and an interviewer does not have to drag a story out of him. Quite the contrary.

Sloan Christian says, "I come from a long line of people who were something of sexual renegades. One of my great-grandmothers had a baby and didn't get married way back in the early 1920s. My sister and I both worked as escorts and my family knows about this. I don't know to what degree they accept it but it doesn't seem to bother them a lot. We keep in very good touch."

He has worked as an airline steward for some years and also has held office jobs but he believes that he suffers somewhat from attention deficit disorder and nine-to-five occupations are really not for him. Sloan earned some fifty thousand a year with the airlines but upon retirement found himself working for an advertising agency for much less. He resented all the deductions and says, comparing work in an agency to work as an escort, "They're not giving half of the blowjob so why should they take half of the money?"

Of his family, he recounts that his sister had overdosed at one point, had spent some time in jail, had then been living with an aunt but felt she was being too closely supervised and wanted to live with Sloan. He did not agree. He says, " In my family everyone is addicted to something. I am addicted to sex. I can come fifteen times in one day. My father is addicted to alcohol and my mother to shopping.

"I have been working as an escort for five years." He goes on. "I have an 11 inch cock and size 13 foot. I have clients who are into foot fetish. I send pictures after a pedicure. One man complained that my toes are short. But another dipped my feet in

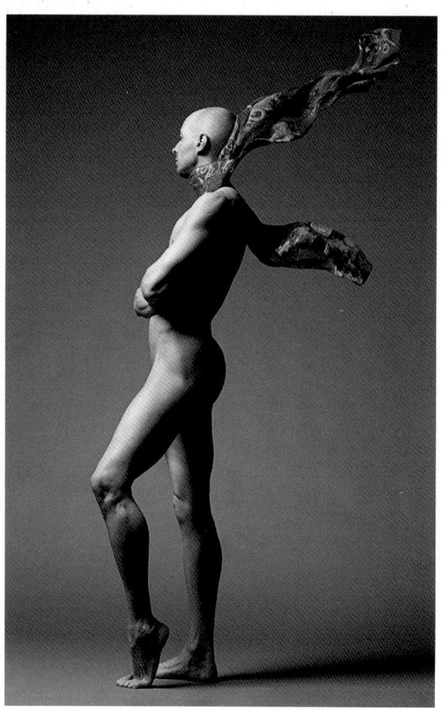

chocolate sauce and licked it off. I have also had someone who liked blue-cheese dressing. Those clients jerk off lying on the floor licking my feet."

He lives in Fort Lauderdale and works a good deal. His average work week involves six clients and he does not work when he is tired. He advises other escorts, "In your ad never say you are in Miami or Fort Lauderdale. Say Dania or some town in between. Then they never think that you're too far."

Of other escorts he also says, "I dislike St. Tropez escorts because they advertise escorts that they don't have. They block the faces and you order up a six-footer with big muscles and they send a twink. Sebastian de Winter, who heads up St. Tropez, runs false ads as far as I'm concerned."

His rates are $190 in Fort Lauderdale either in or out. $225 in Miami He says, "When a client is really good-looking I charge less and then I want to do it again. As a sex addict when it stops I get really depressed. But I never let anyone know that I think they are really hot. You have to keep the upper hand.

"I have only had one call from a couple. She whined a lot and he stopped me when she screamed. I am really big. I don't travel with clients. I don't do what I don't want to. Never. I am not a whore. I do what others won't do because I like it. I do not cuddle. I really am not affectionate. Maybe kissing.

About love he says, "It's not going to last. And if it does last, I'm going to end it. I am unlovable because I won't let someone love me. When you think that you are a one-half and you get into a couple, you find out you've become a one-fourth instead of part of a one. I used to want to be in a relationship for the wrong reasons. Now I don't want to be in one for the right reason."

He is an amazing man and one can imagine that his clients enjoy his company as much as his physical presence.

Sloan says, "I think money can buy happiness. If I had more money I would be happier now. " He adds, "If I never meet anyone or fall in love I'm fine. I used to cry over it but not anymore."

Sloan Christian has no plans to change his present occupation in the near future. He saves his money, has bought a condo, and his youthful body and energetic personality will probably allow him to continue for some time on his escort trajectory.

Of his work, he says of other escorts, "The ones who claim that they are 'versatile' and then don't want to get fucked, that's stealing."

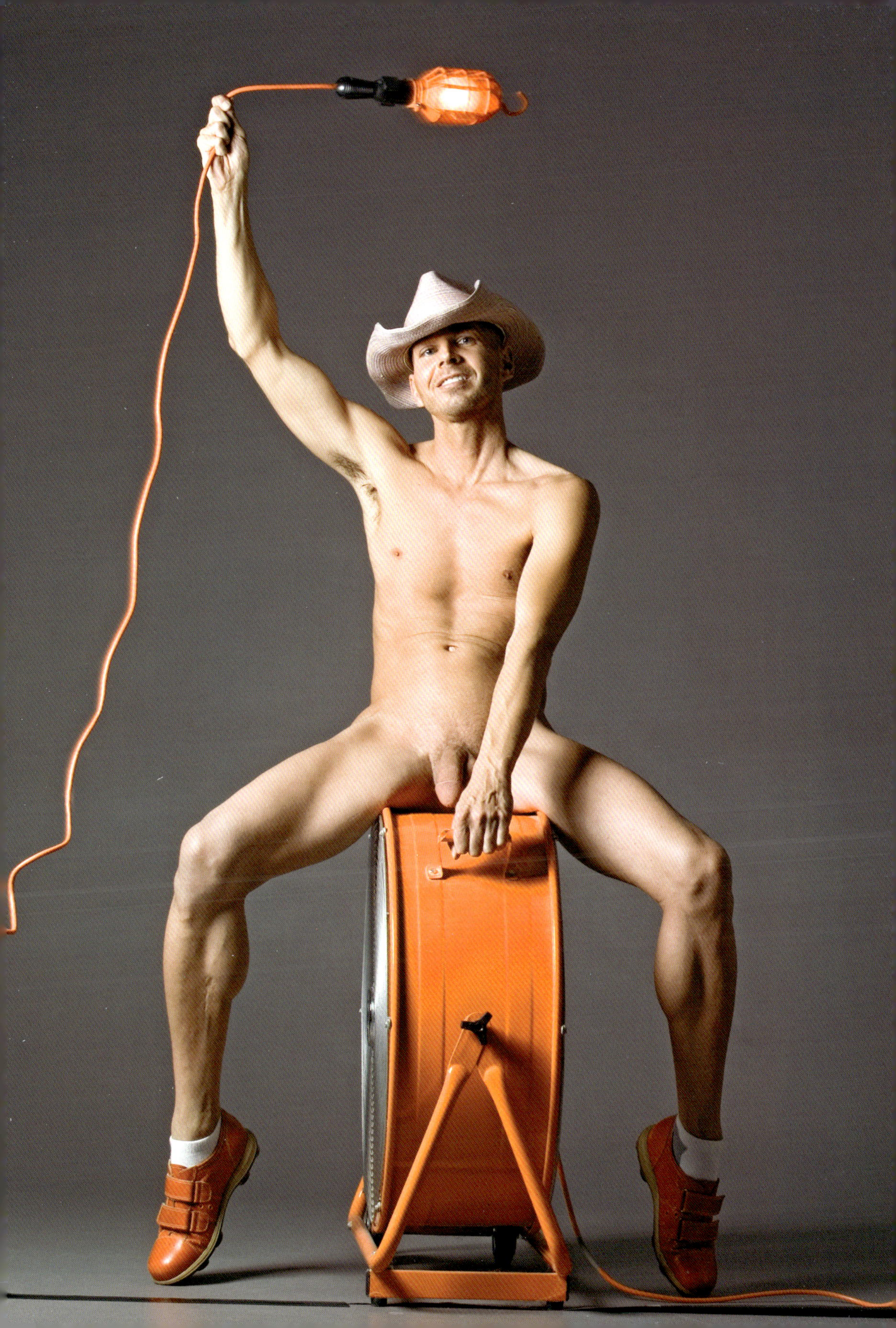

BOBBY BROCK

whitedudechillen

Hot 26year Old Whiteboy Available!

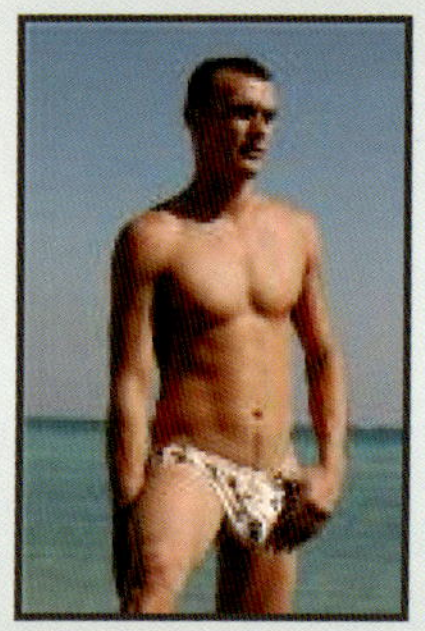

Click here for more pics

Hey boys! I'm 6' 1" 160lbs. toned and smooth.9"cut. Available for outcalls only. Very easy going and friendly. Safe, reliable, and discreet. If you want to know more call me on my cell! Peace! Bobby

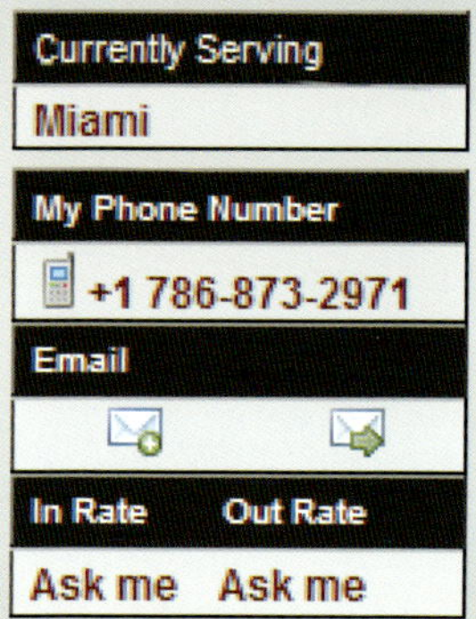

Lanky, tanned Bobby Brock is an escort who will frankly admit that he has entered the field because of the economic recession. He says, "I was working as a head waiter in an upscale Italian restaurant and I was earning between $1,200 and $1,500 a week. Suddenly I'm only earning $500 to $600 as people have stopped spending money. I am used to having a larger income with my rent and other responsibilities so I need the extra money."

He then surprised his interviewers by adding that he had only been working as an escort for three weeks. Though he thought he would probably be doing it for some time. At 28 years old, he has had close to a decade of working in the restaurant and food service business and continues to do so at this time. But because of the recession he only has a four day work week. "My clients are in the evening and on the week ends anyway so it really isn't a problem." he adds.

Bobby Brock is a native of Miami. His parents separated when he was quite young but he remains in regular touch with them and his two sisters. His family has accepted his being gay and he says, "I have had enjoyable sex with women but my preference is men.

"My mother prefers honesty and asks for details. She knows about my escorting and porn work. Her only concern is my safety. My father drives trains. We love each other but I don't give him details. Also, with the recession my mother has been having financial problems with her business and I have been helping her. So she pretty well has to know where the money is coming from."

When asked how he began working as an escort Bobby explains, "I was already doing porn films here in Florida. And also in Atlanta. I had a friend who made these movies and I talked to his agent and decided to do it, too."

The friend who introduced him got a finder's fee. He reports that he worked with many straight men in the gay male porn world and heard one man talking on the phone with his wife and telling her he was about to receive major anal sex. For a porn film his usual pay is a flat fee of $3,000.

Bobby tells his interviewers, "With my money problems the agent suggested I start escort work so I went on *rentboy.com* and have been working frequently since." He discusses his clients and explains they are mostly out-of-towners on business and are largely in their forties and white or Hispanic. He says, "I have had young clients who may have had a fantasy about paying for sex." Although he doesn't take clients to his own home he has an apartment he can use. "Only about ten to twenty per cent of my clients want to come to me. For the most part I go to hotels." He explains, "Meeting a client for the first time is not easy. Both of us are a little nervous. For me, it is easier to skip the socializing and getting to know one another partly because it can be a turn off. Knowing personalities may make it more difficult to get a boner. I find it's better to just discuss what the client wants sexually and move to those activities right away. I say, for example, 'What do you want to do?' And he'll say, 'Let's play.' and we get right into it.

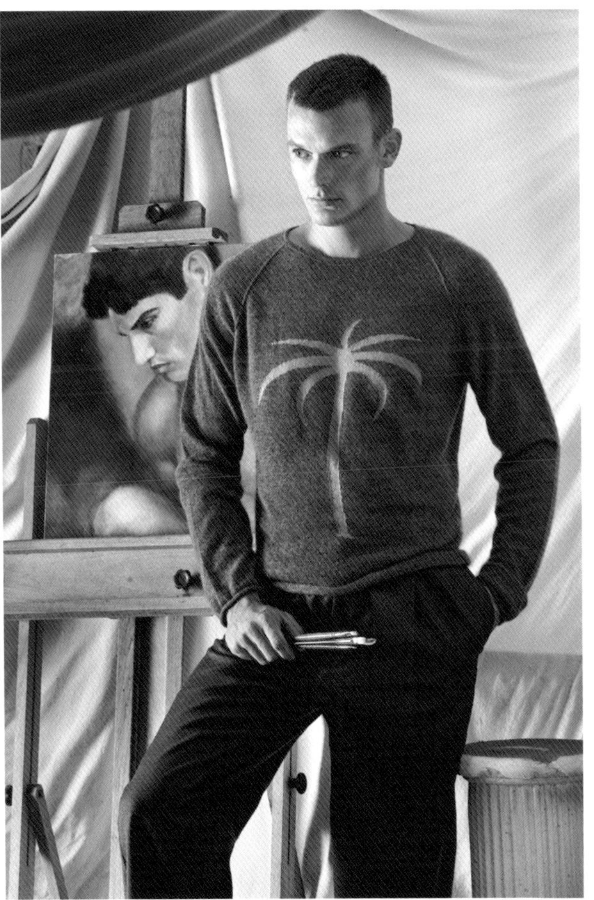

"My only difficult experiences, and they aren't really difficult, are cancellations at the last minute. "My best experience was quite by chance. I got on a bus, looked out the window and there was this guy rubbing his crotch and rubbing his fingers together to indicate that he had money. I got off the bus and the next thing we were partying, watching porn and masturbating. I got paid four times my normal fee."

As far as dealing with the "sex with strangers" aspect of his work Bobby says, "My philosophy is if I

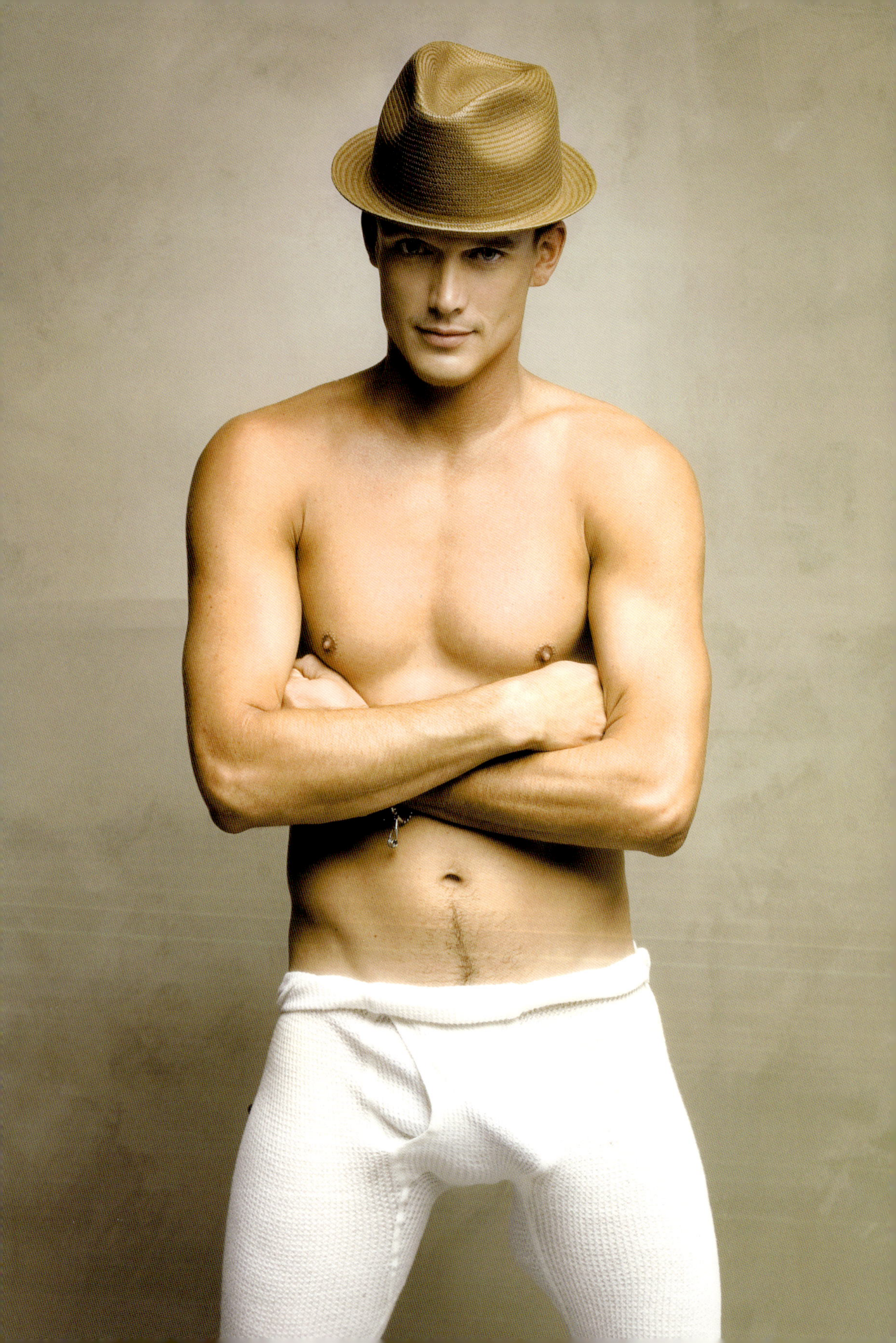

can get paid for it and enjoy it, why not? When I was younger I could only involve myself with sex in the context of a relationship, but now it's not a problem even if it is a business transaction."

Bobby has spent a brief period in jail when picked up for drug selling. He didn't have drugs on him, he says, but was sentenced anyway. He reports, "In prison, everyone is homosexual. You either have a boy or you are a boy. I was lucky enough to meet someone there close to my own age and I don't know which of us would have been considered the 'boy.' He was a sweet kid. I don't know what happened to him. I saw a lot of very bad stuff in there. You saw young guys being raped really brutally and it changes you. I also played basketball in high school and played in prison, too, so that made me more acceptable to a lot of the prisoners."

"And that' s another aspect of escorting. Once you have a prison record a lot of jobs aren't available to you. And you begin to see escorting more as a business. There's an expression 'Trick or get tricked' in the business. When you begin you don't know what anything is worth and clients try to get as much as they can for their money. Then you begin to know what the prices are. Basically for an escort it's $150 in and $250 out per hour. My clients are about 20% in and 80% out. But if the client wants certain kinds of activities you can charge more."

In his personal life, Bobby Brock had a two year relationship starting when he was 19 with a 27 year old man. But he says, "I got tired of the arguing, the sneakiness, the jealousy. I wasn't in love with him." More recently he was involved with a man of his own age. When asked if he had ever been in love Bobby Brock thinks that he had strong feelings for this man but isn't sure that he would call it love. The man was a twin and they spent much of their time with the twin brother also. "When we were alone together it was great but it just didn't work out."

He concludes the interview by saying, "I don't look on escorting as a career. It is just additional income. I just want enough money to pay the phone bill, give my mother some money, buy groceries. I'm not like some escorts who will be paid $250 and walk down the street and spend it on a pair of shoes. For now I have certain financial needs and I have to meet them. That's why I work as an escort."

Bobby Brock's advice to an aspiring escort is, "Use your dick, not your ass. My ass is not on the menu. Young guys may not realize that they can refuse to do things. Make sure you are comfortable with what you can do casually. Don't have your first time when you try something new be during a client assignment. You want to be able to say you don't want to do it.

"I've seen so many young gay boys lose themselves on street corners. There's no way to sugarcoat being an escort. Even at it's best, I'm a whore." When asked if he's concerned about catching STDs/ AIDS/HIV, he states, "I use protection and this is non-negotiable. I'm tested every 30 days as required by the porn producers or else they will not hire me."

THE HORSECOCK

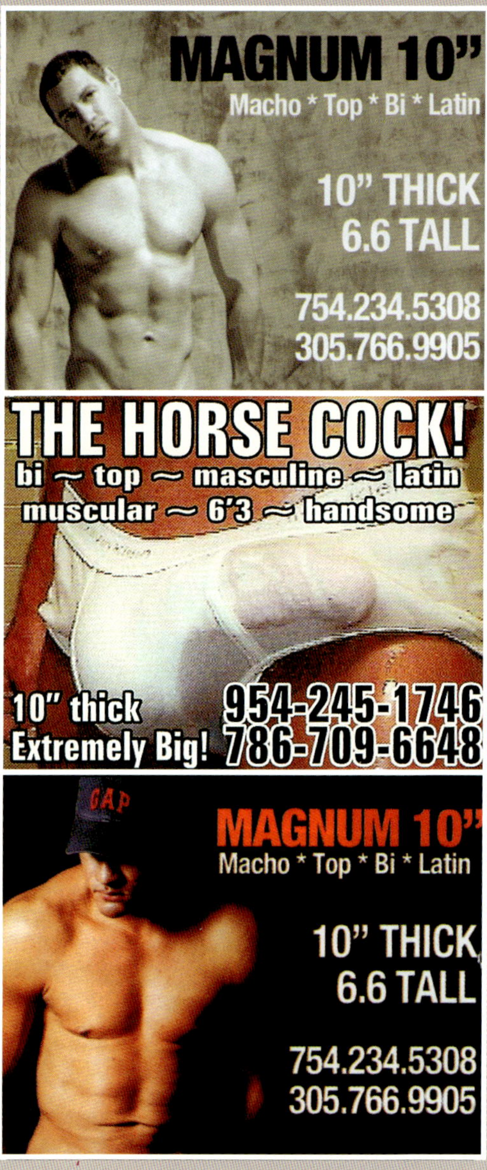

The man who advertises under the name "Horsecock" is in fact a tall, affable fellow from the Dominican Republic who is a bit shy. There is a lot more to him than his advertised appendage.

H.C. came to Miami from his home country in 1990 when he was 19 to join his father. His father had come to the United States to find work, leaving H.C. at home with his younger two brothers and two sisters. He immediately went to school upon his arrival. Somewhat to his discomfiture he was put in tenth grade, despite the fact he already stood six feet, three inches. He graduated in 1993 and was already working part-time in a store to cover expenses. He hoped to work with computers, but after working for a time for Winn Dixie, moved to Fort Lauderdale for a better paying job as a security guard.

At the hotel where he worked as a security guard, he made friends with a pizza delivery boy. This young man decided to move to Chicago and suggested H.C. take his job, which paid $100 a day, a big step up from his work as a guard. Delivering pizza in the Fort Lauderdale area, he found himself regularly propositioned by male clients, who would pay $20 or $25 extra for some sexual hanky-panky. One day he made a delivery to a photographer, who took some pictures and he was ready to place some ads in Hotspots, a local gay magazine, and started carrying a beeper.

He says, "I was playing around for free all the time. Going to The Eagle and The Ramrod, local clubs, and visiting parks and the internet. I thought, 'Why not?' I was brought up in a religious household, even if my parents did work together organizing cock fights. I was a Jehovah's Witness. I had a girlfriend. But in this country when I was out of school I was living in Hialeah. I had lots of proposals for sex from men and I was masturbating a lot at home. Then one night I decided 'No more' and I went out and met a Cuban guy and we did all the things I had been thinking about.

"When I was younger I had played around with boys, from about the age of eight to thirteen. But I was studying the Bible and stopped until that night I went out and met that guy. We broke every religious commandment. I then broke away from religion at that point. I was in love with a Puerto Rican guy shortly after that and he found a job with the Post Office in Fort Lauderdale so I moved there to be with him. We actually broke up because he didn't want to have sex as often as I felt I had to. After I started escorting I stopped working as a pizza delivery boy two weeks later. And I haven't held a regular job since."

H.C. says he works six or seven times a week and can work more if he advertises more. He has made tours of New York, Dallas, Houston, San Antonio, as well as San Francisco and Los Angeles. He reports that in the West, many clients are eager to hire Latin Americans but want a change of pace from the many Mexican men in the business there. He also works regularly in Atlanta and in Washington, D.C. Many customers will fly him into their hometown for one night. His regular work area is Fort Lauderdale, Miami and West Palm Beach, which he says he knows very well, having driven to many addresses in these cities. He adds that his regulars are very important to his business.

He initially found he wasn't making enough money, since his delivery boy work was already bringing in $100 a day. So he advertised his services at a rate of $50 per hour. He says, "Then the phone was ringing off the hook. I had a war with the other escorts who called me and said I was ruining their business. I found most clients paid more, usually $100. And in a few months, I had enough regulars that I could go back up to the $100 fee. Now the fees are routinely $200 and $250. I charge $250 for a couple. I usually fuck the guy and they love it. Sometimes I have sex with the woman. I had one couple that called me to a very discreet hotel near the Miami airport. The man started sucking me and the woman shouted, 'What are you doing, you fucking faggot?' I decided to get out of there."

When asked if he could sometimes lose a fee that way, H.C. points out that because he begins each contact with the request "Do you have the fee?" or "Do you have a contribution?" he is always paid first. His overnight fee is $1,000. He adds, "I use condoms for everything. Even for a million dollars would I not use a condom. I always top. Bottoming never comes up. People who call me are looking for a man, who feels like a man, who smells like a man. Some of my clients are effeminate, but all of my clients want a man."

He laughs and continues, "I was at an orgy on Star Island in Miami where a client had hired ten escorts who were supposed to fuck him. I wound up fucking every escort. Escorts are supposed to do many things but when they see a big club they change completely. I fucked the client, too. I told him, 'You have to pay me double. I'm doing all the fucking here.' Clients want a big cock. Big cocks are more successful than others. And of course, I cover both markets, gay and heterosexual."

H.C. tells the interviewer that he doesn't do porn films. "They don't pay enough." He can make up to $600 a day but he doesn't have an orgasm with every client, he points out. He has learned to exercise mind control and also there are herbs that help him. He says, "There are herbs that help create sperm. I need a lot of sperm daily. The herbs help with the circulation of the blood, too."

Discussing his clients, H.C. says, "Some clients I don't like a lot and then I imagine I am fucking a woman. But usually I really like them and I enjoy the guy and making money at the same time." He says he has many clients between 27 and 30 but more are in the 27 to 45 range. About ten percent are older and he estimates that 90 percent are married or have girlfriends. Continuing about his clients, H.C. adds, "I have between ten and eleven inches and it's thick. Clients love it when it's time to get fucked, but it can be very painful. I had a married client who made an appointment to meet me in a hotel in Hialeah. He said, 'Fuck me hard,' and he's screaming and bleeding. And then he said it was the first time he got fucked. I said, 'You picked the wrong guy for the first time.'

"I have clients who want to drink urine. Who want to lick my feet and my hands. And some clients don't want you to fuck them. Overall I would guess that ten percent

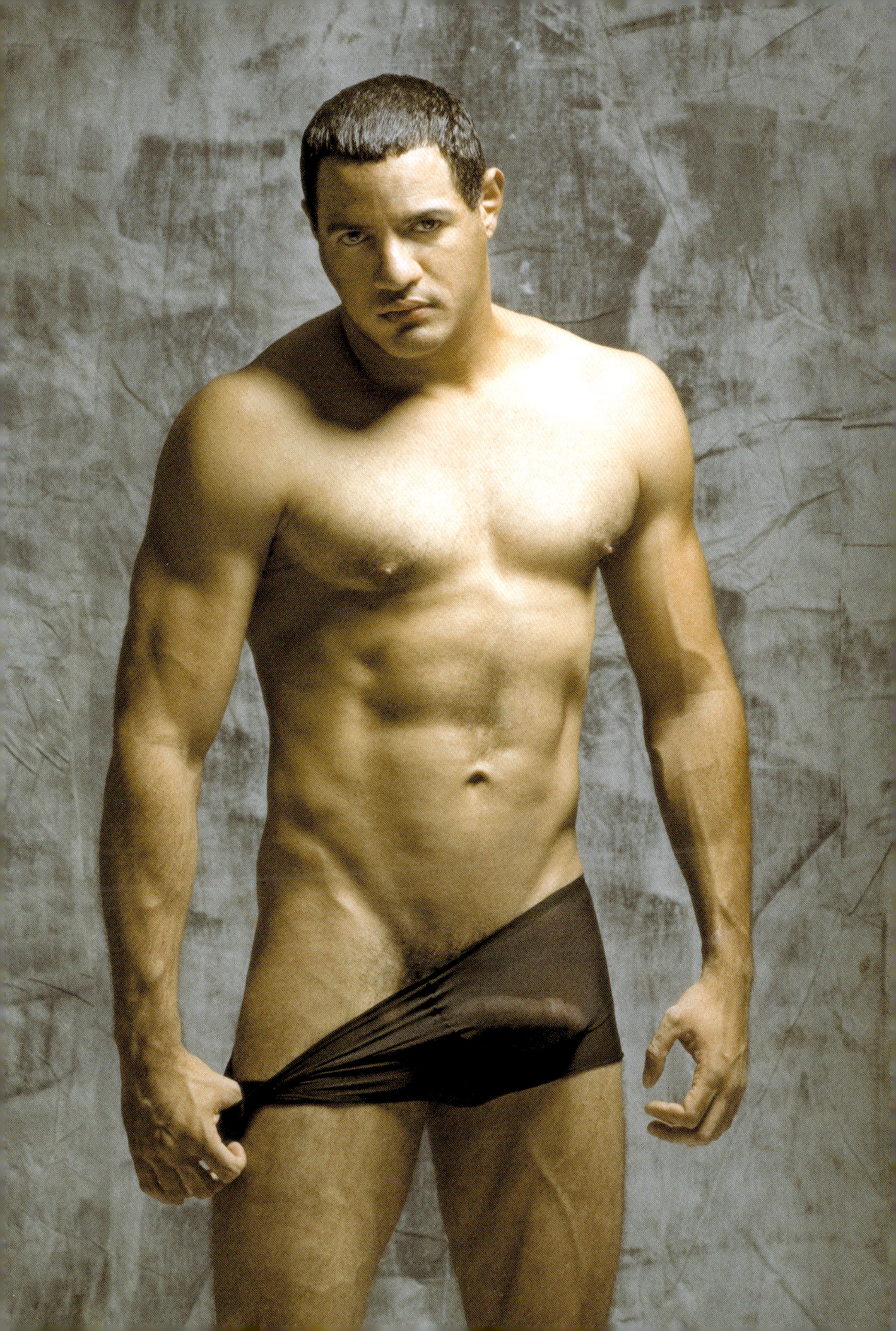

of my clients are women, twenty-five percent couples and the rest men. I have just one major rule: Never accept two people together in your own home. Somehow, it makes for trouble."

Although tall, H.C. is strongly built, if not overly so. He says he goes to the gym every day and watches what he eats. He feels that his profession requires an escort to be an actor. Every client requires a slightly different kind of acting.

He says his clients include policemen, a famous singer, judges, lawyers, football players, a congressman and local politicians will call him because someone has recommended him. He has answered calls from priests and has a priest for a client whose apartment is in the church. He says, "I think he pays me with money that has been collected in the church. I didn't like that a lot. And once in Texas I was in the balcony of a Catholic church fucking a priest. I was in shock, looking at all the statues and paintings. I know I was paid out of the collection there.

"Three weeks ago I went to a Marc Anthony concert and the guy behind me was complaining and complaining he was behind a big guy. That's all I heard all night long was 'I'm behind a big guy.' A few days later I had a call. It was from the same guy from behind me at the concert. I had him in doggie position and I thought 'You're the guy who was so rude. Take this. And that.' And he says, 'You're so rough'."

Asked about bad client experiences, H.C. remembers a call in Miami from a client who when he arrived revealed he had about 50 cats. He says, "It smelled terrible. I ran out." And he had a client in New York that was lying on the bed when he arrived. The client weighed about 400 pounds and completely covered the bed. H.C. declined that one, too. The worst he says are "...drugged up clients. They call again and again. They have their own fantasies and don't want sex." He also includes a client who was very unpleasant. "He said, 'I can't tell you what I want you to do but I'll show you a video.' In the video someone defecated on a man who then ate it. I told him 'No.' That was definitely my worst experience." H.C. will accept leather and bondage clients but says, "I have to change my mind around completely and get into another mindset with them."

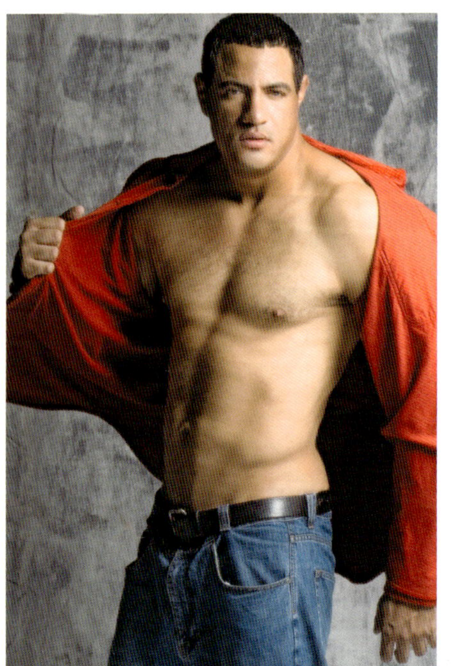

H.C. feels that in a few years he won't be escorting. "I save my money and I have bought houses and apartments in the Dominican Republic." He finds that many clients want a massage and a few years ago he took a massage course. He points out, "Even then, clients want to have sex. But most of my family and friends think I am a massage therapist."

MARTIN

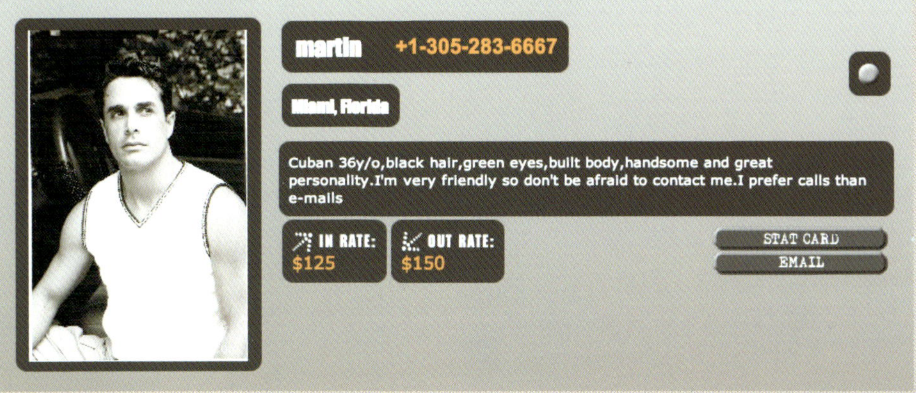

Oh, Martin, you are so very handsome. Martin not only looks like a movie star he has a lot of skills that led him to his present occupation as a male escort. Coming to the United States from Cuba in his mid-twenties, he began to cut hair in his own home and found a clientele among male strippers, dancers and escorts. Evidently expert at this work, his clients suggested that he add body waxing to his services. It would save time for them and he could double the fees that he was earning. Martin found clients asking for some even more personal services from their handsome barber. Services that they were willing to pay for.

Martin recounts, "I continued for some time in that way, and then I began to realized that I could earn a good bit more money just doing the escorting. Which I now do exclusively." He remembers that he realized he was gay when he was 13 and had his first boyfriend when he was 15. "In Cuba everyone is hot and people are having sex in cars and buses and stairways. They're married or not, young or old, it's everyone."

Martin left Cuba when he was 27 with his sister via the Dominican Republic. His parents had already gone to the United States. He and his sister had to remain in the Dominican Republic a number of years.

After arrival Martin worked as a hairdresser, in hotels and for an eyewear company. Then his hairdressing slowly orbited into other services that began to include escorting. He adds, "As of 1999 my rates for doing hair included being dressed or naked during the haircut. I suggested a $10 tip. It was $50 for masturbation release. It was $100 additional to have sex. If they're not clean or don't have good energy I just do hair service. I have worked full time as an escort for the last three years because I need the extra income.

"As soon as I lower my rates I get more clients but I prefer quality clients, just one or two a week. I have regular clients; one I see almost every week. I also get a lot of visitors, business travelers, and people here on business. Most clients in hotels are 29 to 45 and have a nice appearance. I have fewer in-calls and I charge $150 to $160. My out-calls are $175 to $180. I do give discounts to repeat clients. I love threesomes and playing with different guys at the same time. I rarely do women because usually they have issues if I play with one more than the other and get jealous. With gay couples I try to be neutral.

About bizarre experiences he remembers having a small man from New York wearing a yarmulke who did not want to be affectionate but wanted to be tied up and slapped. Martin did not enjoy doing this to a man he felt was hiding from wife and children and wanted to be treated like a slave. He has a client who is an employee of the Miami Archdiocese who is involved with swallowing, both sperm and urine. He was so demanding that Martin took another man with him and even after drinking four bottles of water to prepare for the encounter they both found it wasn't enough.

His most difficult client was a man who had recently had a tummy-tuck and still had a drain in his stomach that was leaking blood. Martin had to deal with blood on the bed and a mess in the bathroom, plus concerns about HIV contagion. It was an in-call so he had to clean up with Clorox after the client left. When asked about a particularly disgusting over-age and overweight client who required anal sex, Martin laughs and says he did it, "... because I'm a dirty whore!"

When asked about escorting as it might conflict with personal relationships, Martin says, "I never talk about what I do. My lovers and I haven't lived together." As a Cuban he admits to being very passionate. But then adds, "Whores can not fall in love. If they get depressed or lose clients, they go bankrupt."

He struggles with the effect of his work upon his spiritual growth. He feels many clients bring bad energy into his life and "There is a stifling factor that one has to consider."

Martin does not travel, finding that he has better opportunities for income earning in Miami. What he does report is that he finds himself frequently employed for parties by visiting clients, who hire a number of escorts. "There is a lot more of that going on than people realize when clients come in from out of town. I like doing that so I get hired quite a lot for it."

Martin has been in love and now in his thirties believes that he will be again. But he admits, "My favorite kind of sex is threesomes but I realize that when you are in love that is out of the question." He works full time in a manufacturing concern and sees his future as continuing in that line of work. But he also plans to continue escorting as long as there is a demand. With his brooding, mature Latin looks and his fondness for his escort employment, that should be for some time to come.

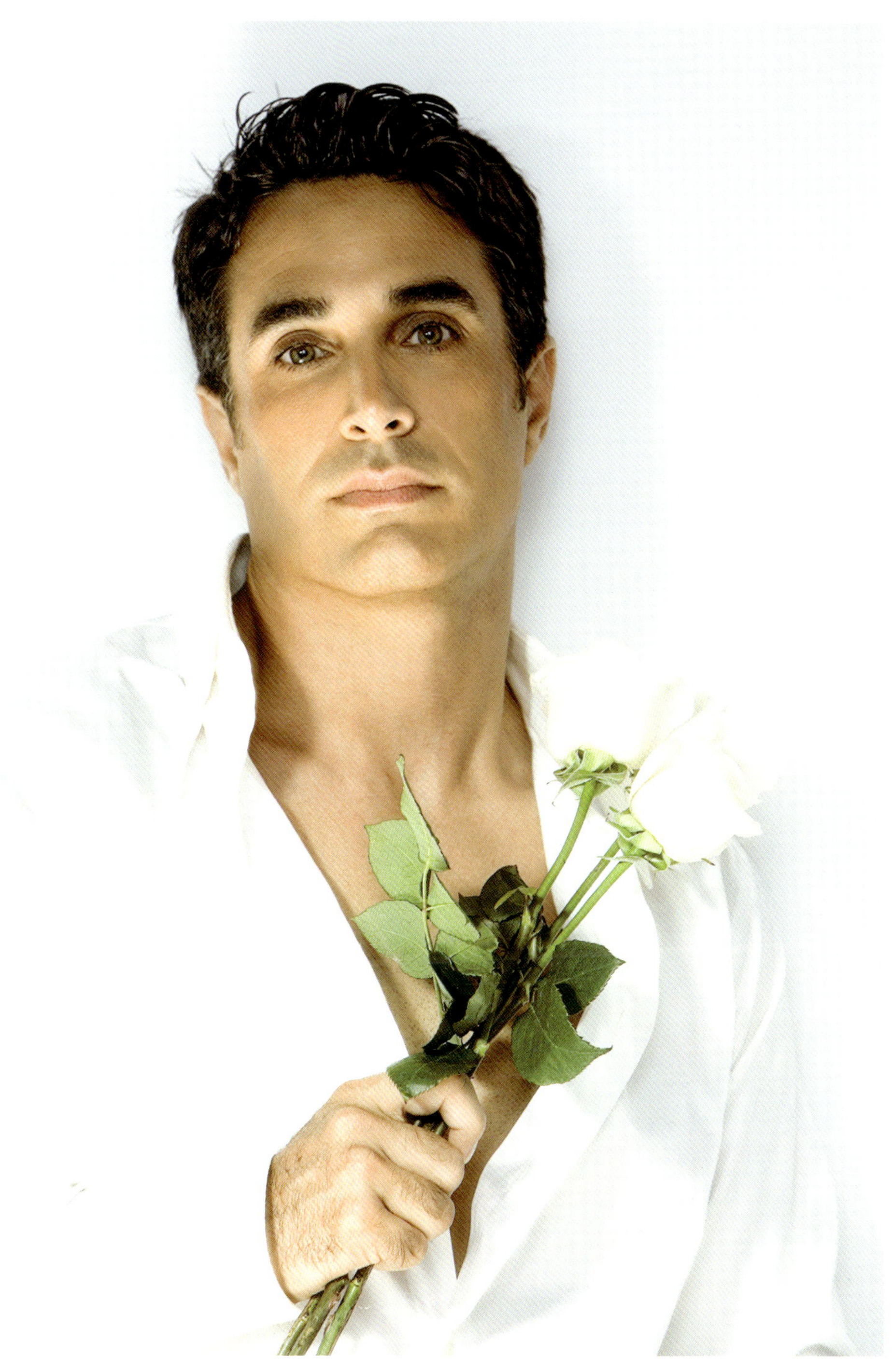

THE GERMAN MASTER DIETER

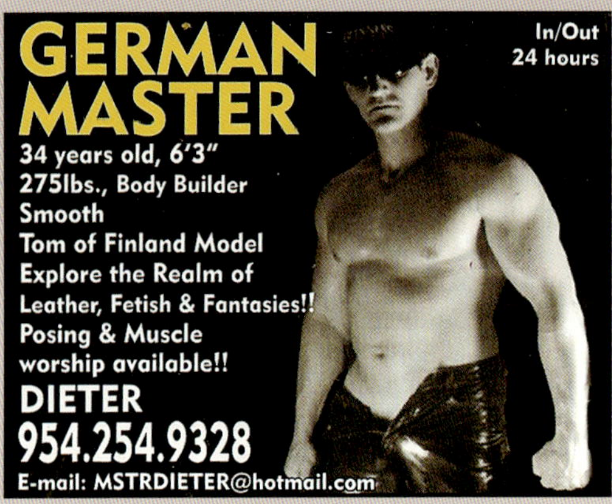

"I was born in Hamburg on July 1, 1972," says the German Master Dieter. "My father was a car salesman. I have a sister and two brothers. We lived comfortably." In his ad, the German Master Dieter is a formidable mass of muscle, somewhat forbidding. In person he is still pretty formidable, over six feet tall and plenty of muscles, but he also has a very cute smile and is slightly shy.

Seated across from his interviewers in a crowded restaurant, he is well mannered and his English is excellent. He goes on to tell about himself. "I studied Psychology at the University of Hamburg and then spent three years with the German Armed Forces in Yugoslavia. I was actually an officer in the Navy.

"After I left the service, I worked for my father for awhile as a car salesman and then worked for a bank, which I am now doing in Fort Lauderdale. "As far as my family is concerned, my parents are divorced. My father's new wife is about my age. Probably our only claim to fame is that my mother is a cousin to the famous photographer and film maker Leni Riefenstahl."

When asked if he has ever been in love, he says, "I fell in love for the first time when I was 19. That was my first girlfriend. I was engaged at 22 to another girl but that fell through. I was too young. I would say that I am about 60% straight and 40% gay. I didn't used to but now I do three-ways with a woman and another man. I used to do three-ways only with two women."

Of his work as the German Master, Dieter explains, "I began to work as a Master in Hamburg. There is a certain fashion show aspect to this S&M world. People like to come to bars and show off their outfits, men and women. In Hamburg I went to clubs and people would hire me. I had to force lesbians to suck a man's dick once. That kind of thing. What do I wear? I wear leather pants, boots, and a muscle shirt. I'm very average looking." One wonders.

As far as his pattern goes, he reports, "I work on weekends only and mostly with

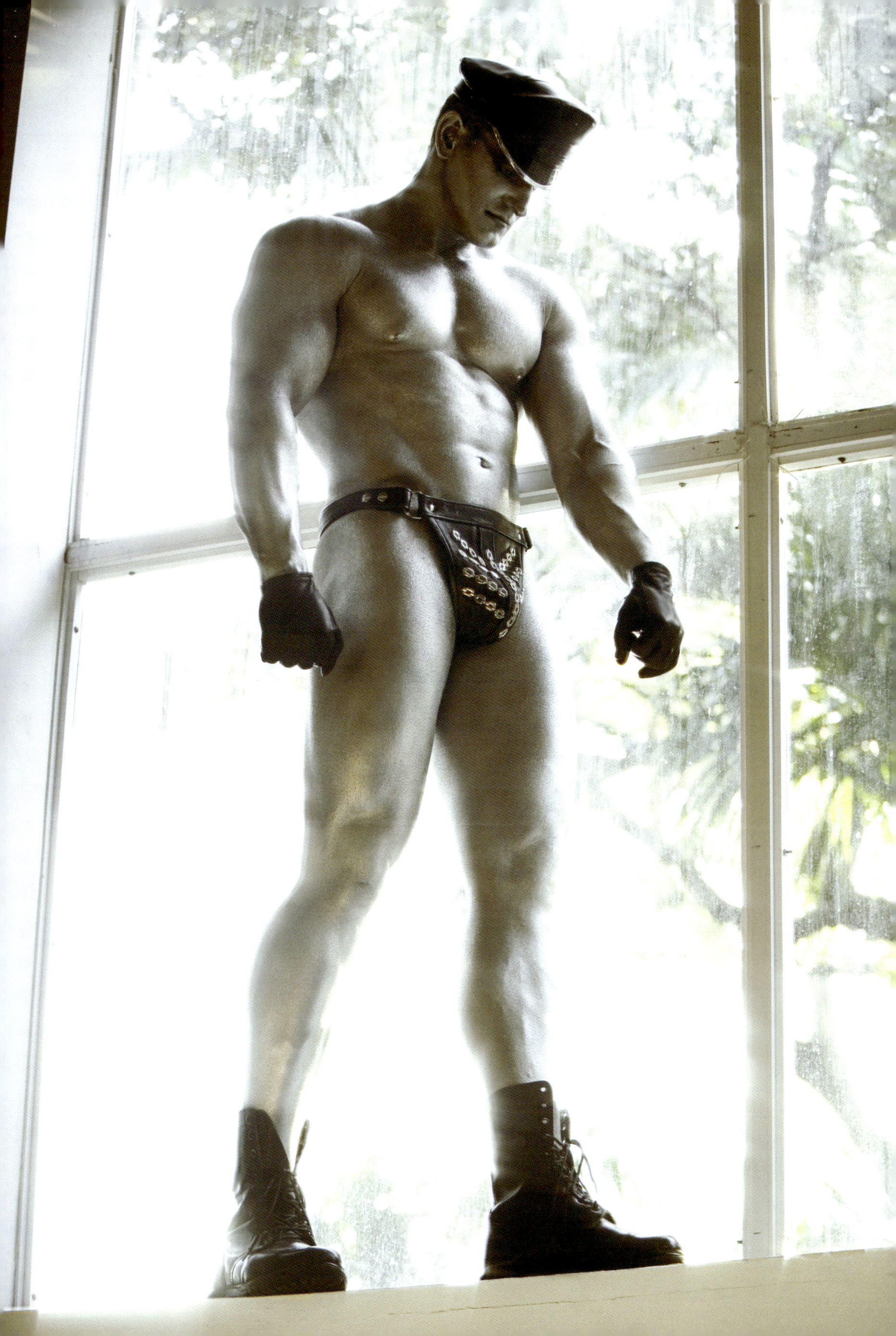

regulars. Mostly people call on weekends. They don't know really what they want. They want to be sucked or to suck cock. They want to be fucked. I only allow clients to give me a blowjob. Men clients. That's it. I meet women in bars or clubs. I go to fetish parties also. I would say that out of 100 women, two are into S&M. Many women are afraid of muscle guys although they may have a sexual fantasy about them. I don't go to gay bars. You can meet plenty of clients in straight bars and clubs.

"You know most of these male clients are school teachers, professors, doctors. They want to be discreet. I'd say about 80% are married and somewhere between 35 and 50. Breaking it down, about 70% of my clients are men and about 30% are women. And I get about 80% of my clients from ads. It's a service and you have to be sure they put the money on a table. They can't hand it to you. You have to be careful that you are not being set up by the police.

"For sex I prefer women. For domination I prefer men. There are some exceptions. I get young boys calling me and saying, 'I want to be a slave.' They don't know what that is. They just want to suck somebody's cock for free. And then you get clients who become friends and then they don't want to pay anymore. What people don't understand outside the S&M

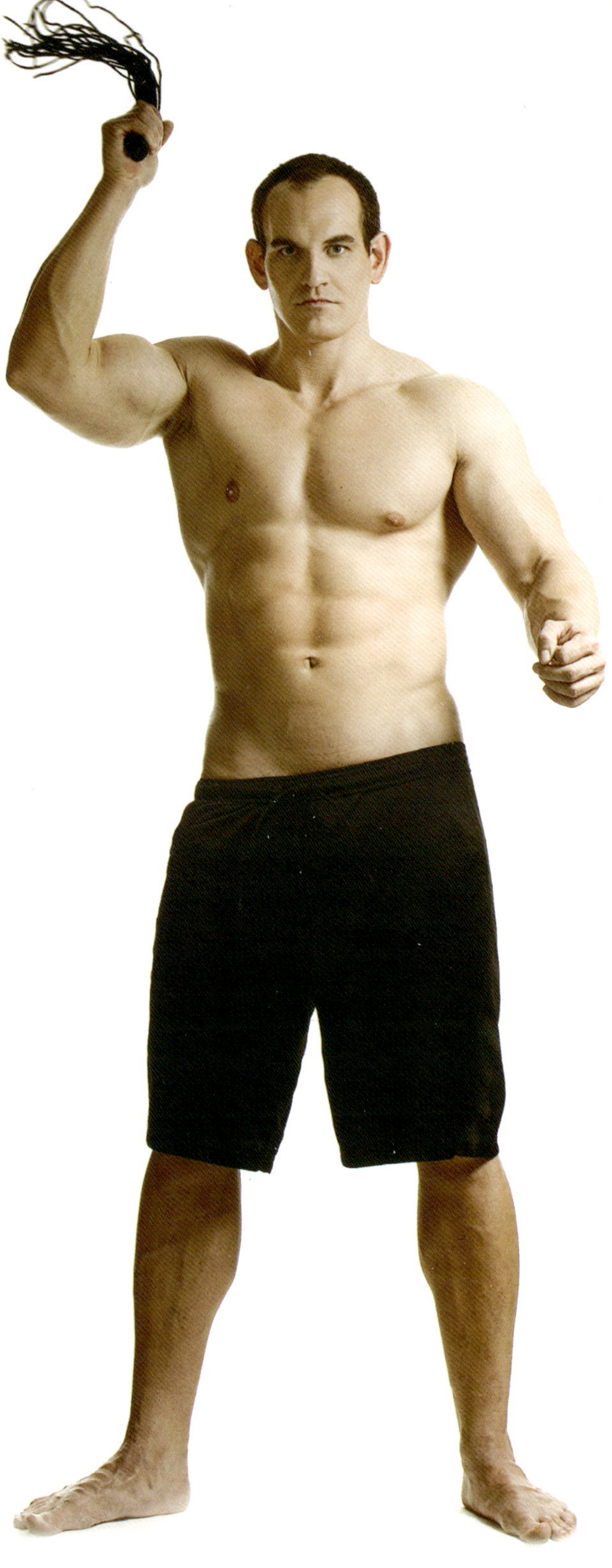

world is that the men are into pain because they then get an endorphin release. And that feels good.

"I could say about my work that I look over the edge. I want to know why people do it. I was told that 50% of men have a fantasy of having sex with another man. And that women often have a fantasy of seeing their husband or boyfriend sucking another man's dick. That's the world I see. I think a lot of this comes from Roman Catholic guilt repression. There's a certain comparison you could make with the Middle Ages when people were punishing themselves for their sins. More censorship and restrictions gives more thrill to the fantasy."

As far as S&M itself is concerned, the interviewers are told, "I learned about inflicting pain from a friend in Hamburg who did it to his girlfriend. He always said of himself that he was the German Master who taught women how to suck cock. "Most clients with some experience will know what they want. They have signs to indicate when they want more or less. Fisting isn't really S&M, although I know some women who like it. You know women have kinky fantasies and I'd say about 98% of the ones I've met are married.

"Most people who come to see me are experienced and tell me what they want, what they are into. And how much pain they can take. I don't train newbies. That could be dangerous for them. I can sense limits and clients give signs when they want me to stop. Bondage is just a fantasy. As far as I'm concerned, tying somebody up in a chair is like getting a package ready to take to the post office. It takes up too much time.

"My fee is $200 and the average client call is from one to one and a half hours. I will say this. I love doing it. I only do it on weekends and I get paid for it. I may have two or three clients in an evening and I work Friday, Saturday and Sunday evenings. It's a control thing for me. I wouldn't say that I was a sadist. It's more the pleasure of being in control of something. Sadists love their fantasies 24/7. I'm not that. I'm just a nice guy who enjoys playing a role… I'm just selling fantasies on the weekend. I'm a fantasy salesman."

About himself, aside from his weekend work, the German Master Dieter finishes by saying, "Friends and family don't know what I do. It's my own private business. I'm saving my money. I play soccer and I do power lifting to hang onto my body. My dream is to be an actor. I have a private life. I go to the Hard Rock café. I date girls. If I fell in love again I would give all of this up."

Thanks to Leatherwerks, Fort Lauderdale, for wardrobe.

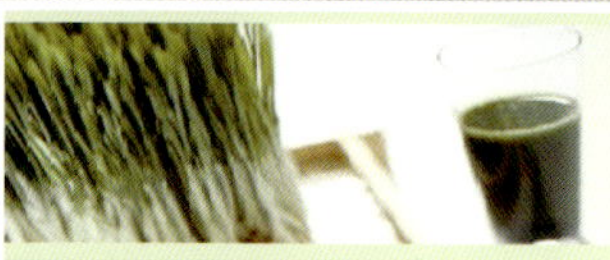

MASSAGE PARIS

Bodywork / Relaxation / Body Tensions Release / Muscles Stretching / Bodyrub / Détente / Bien-être

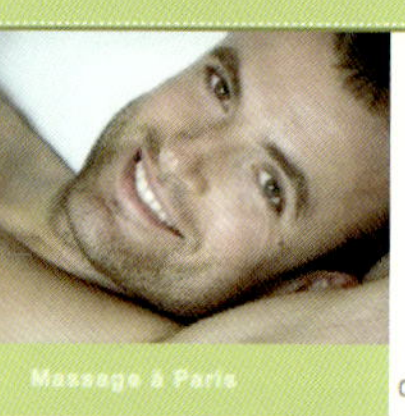

- Massage à Paris
- Les Massages
- Votre Masseur
- Votre Massage
- Votre Espace
- Bon à savoir / FAQ
- Tarifs
- Contact
- Liens

Évadez vous le temps d'un massage.

Relaxation musculaire, dénouement des tensions. Doux, apaisant et déstressant le massage vous apportera détente, bien être et douceur. Pour elle, pour lui, reçois, en plein cœur de Paris.

JOURNEE & SOIREE SEMAINE & WEEK END. SUR RENDEZ-VOUS A BASTILLE.

contact : **06 77 09 66 97**

paris.massage@free.fr

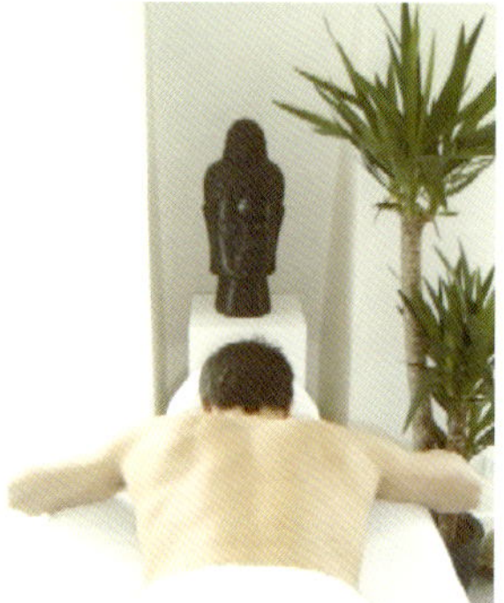

Let yourself escape the time of a massage.

It will help you to relax your muscles and undo the tensions. Gentle, and relaxing it will drive you to a higher level of well being. For Her, for Him, in the heart of Paris.

DAY & EVENING INCLUDING WEEK END. BY APPOINTMENT, BASTILLE AREA.

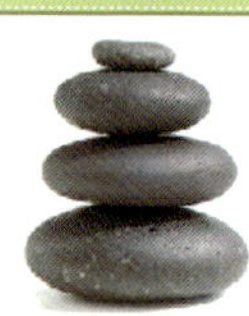

- Relax in Paris
- Massages
- Your Masseur
- Your Massage
- Where
- FAQ
- Rates
- Contact
- Links

DAVID HANDSOME

What to say of this good-looking man whose assumed name is very English but is in fact very French? His name is not his own, but his looks are. He IS very handsome.

His life now revolves around work in both Paris and Miami Beach. Among the escorts, he has a singular approach and perhaps would not truly classify himself as an escort but more as a masseur. Although it seems quite clear in his contact material that a "Happy Ending," as it is called, is quite within the possibilities of a booking with him.

David Handsome was born in Bordeaux and brought up north of Avignon in the French provinces. His was a life with nothing unconventional about it. He planned to earn his living with a career in business, continued his advanced studies in Paris and upon completion of his education served in the Army in what had been a former Moroccan regiment. He says, "It had a great uniform and we drilled all the time."

He had worked briefly at the front desk of a major hotel in New York before his military duty and returned there trying to find a job. His search was not rewarded and he took employment in a large department store in Edinburgh, Scotland. After a few years there he went to another branch of the same store in Madrid and then eventually to Paris. Paris was a brand-new experience for him, even though he was French. He explains, "I almost didn't go. I had never been there. But after two weeks I was in love with Paris."

As his thirties approached and seeking something a little more unusual, he moved to doing the same kind of job in London with a large store there. During this time he had two long-term relationships.

Continuing his itinerant work life, he then took a job traveling through Asia auditing branches of Gap stores, for whom he worked, and winding up at the headquarters in San Francisco. Returning to Paris he worked for a big electronics company and then returned to Madrid to work for a luxury goods company. His lover accompanied him and in Madrid their relationship came to an end. David Handsome decided he was tired and bored with the life he had been living and decided to try something different.

Despite his very good looks and lean, trim body, he did not at any time have a period of having many lovers or even briefer relationships pass in and out of his life.

Returning to Paris after living in Madrid, he discussed his life with a friend who had worked for many years as an escort in Paris. The friend said, "If you're bored and you don't like your life, why don't you work as an escort? If handled correctly the income is good, you can invest in real estate, and a solid retirement can be planned." It was an approach some might call very French. And advice that David Handsome took a few years ago. And it has worked to his satisfaction.

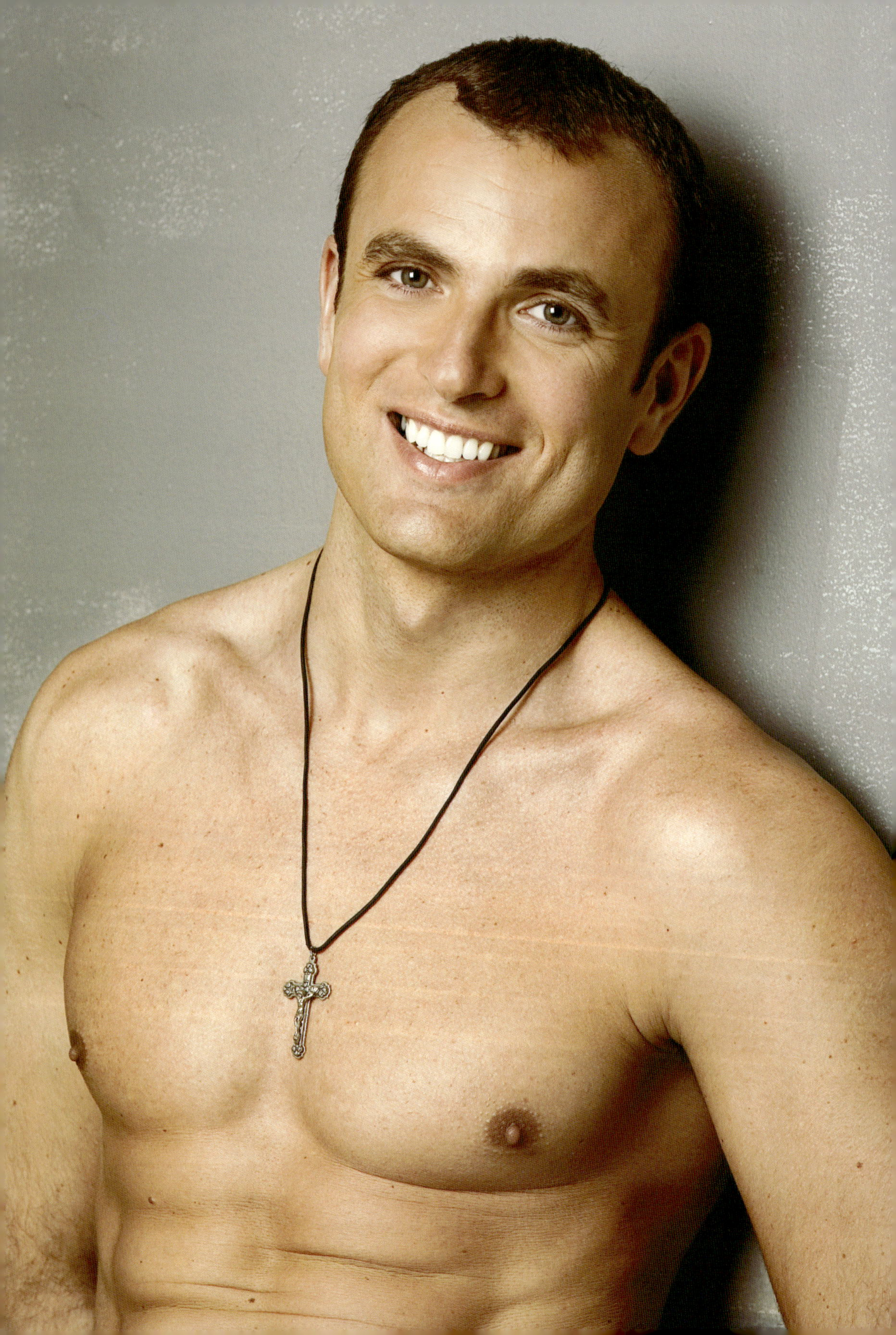

His technique is to advertise, work as a masseur, and try to have five appointments a day and charge a flat rate of $100 per hour. Some of his clients are only interested in a massage and that is their fee. If clients wish to have "release" that is possible for an extra $25. David Handsome works in the nude if a client wishes it but his fees never include intercourse or orgasm. That is not part of the service structure. As he says, "I could not possibly have five clients a day if I was having an orgasm every time."

He prefers his work time in Miami Beach to Paris as he says that Americans will always tip and often very well. The French he says, "...never tip."

He comes to Miami Beach at least twice a year and stays for some two months each time but is considering buying an apartment there as he finds he is not exhausting the market in a two-month stay.

Discussing his clientele, he remarks that, "...they are very often very attractive and have excellent bodies. There is no reason to try to find something attractive about them. They are attractive. And I like my work. I have a degree in massage therapy and I think I am very good at it."

To start his career in the U.S. he says, "I went on *rentboy.com* with vacation pictures. A man in Miami contacted from *bigcocksociety.com* and offered me photographs and a porn film. In my scene I was a French chef fucking in a kitchen. I started warming up by fucking my partner off-camera and when it was time to go on camera I was already pretty fucked out. I had to take Viagra."

David Handsome brings a kind of Gallic verve to his work. In his past he has had relationships with women and at one time visited New York regularly. Displaying himself and his body was no problem even then as he recalls, "...a girlfriend and I were having sex standing up and we noticed a man across the courtyard could see us and was standing in his window masturbating. We thought that was amusing so we continued to the finish and so did he."

He also laughs and remembers his first visit to New York. He thought everyone was very friendly and he was very popular. "I would go to bars and everyone immediately spoke to me and I made friends and went home with them. And then it finally dawned on me it wasn't so much friendliness but they wanted to get me into bed. And they did. It was perhaps then I realized that I could have a life as an escort."

He adds, "When I was young my mother used to tell my sisters, 'Don't tell him he's good-looking. It will go to his head.' So being told that I am good-looking and getting paid for it as an escort is something I enjoy."

In Paris his break down for clients is 80% Americans, 10% Saudi and Middle Easterners and10% Parisians. Among the French straight men he says, "When straight men come for a massage and I see they have an erection they will usually ask for a full release. Here in the U.S. guys are in their thirties, good looking with nice bodies. The rates are $90 an hour, $120 for ninety minutes. I get a $20 or $30 tip. I prefer working in the U.S. because in Paris they never tip."

"I have some kind of sex with almost all clients. I have six or seven clients a day. Of course I don't reach orgasm with them, that's their job. I like working with my hands. For years I worked with my brain. Here in Miami I strip and work with my clothes off. I would never do that in Paris." That may be because of cold Parisian apartments as well as for modesty reasons.

Negatives? David Handsome had one British client that text-messaged him after their appointment to say he considered him a rip-off. He thinks that was because the client wanted sex but never asked. He likes the U.S. and gives as an example, "Here the clients are always fifteen minutes early. In Paris they are always fifteen minutes late."

There is something brisk and no-nonsense about the handsome David Handsome's approach, as he is from a country that considers the *baise de santé* (the health fuck) as something every person may be in need of from time to time. For many clients it must be a relief to encounter this dashing masseur who is not from a puritanical culture and can consider his own beauty as something that is good for you. And of course you should pay for it.

David Handsome concludes, "I am different from the big muscle guys in this business. Clients often call me in Paris just to accompany them to dinner and I sometimes travel with them. They are usually foreigners. I am expanding my massage business and try to be consistent with five clients a day. I want to run a small-scale operation and although massage is something new in Paris, it's a good time to start."

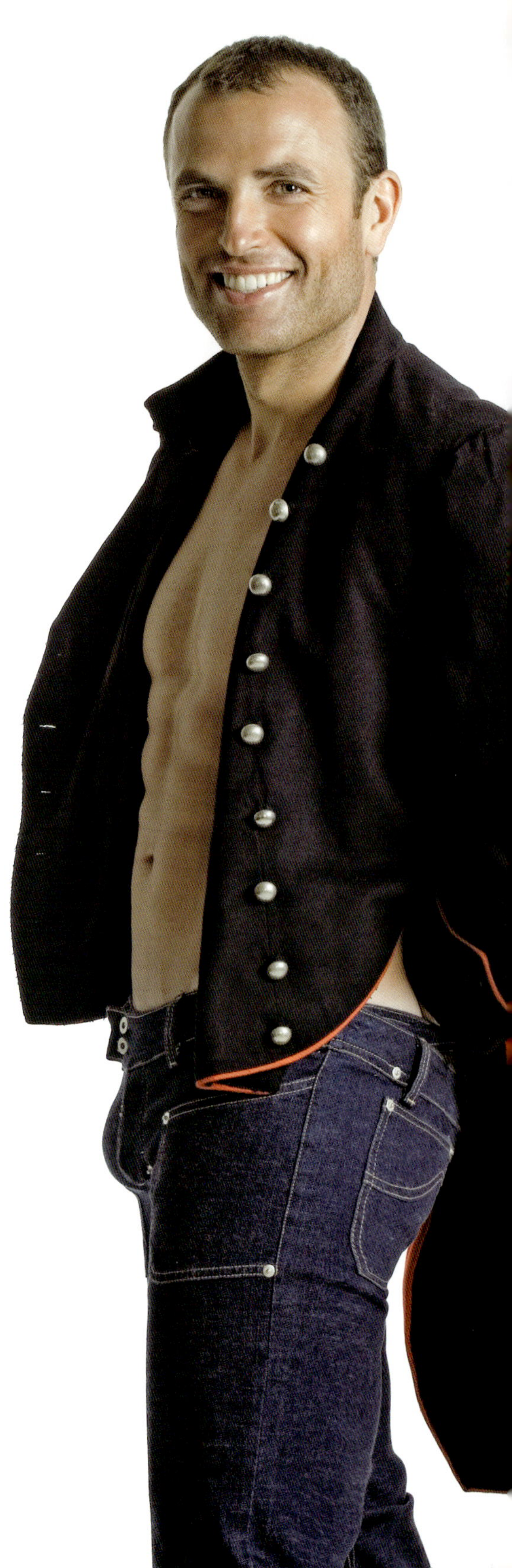

RICO SUAVE

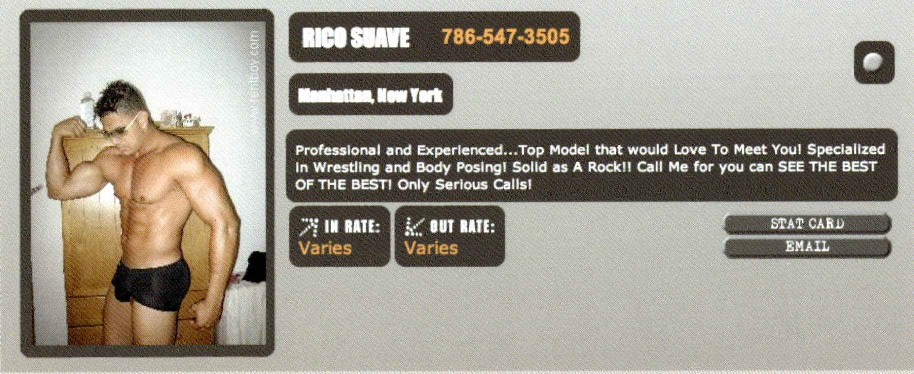

Rico Suave is a big guy. That's not his real name of course. He has rippling muscles from the top of his dark hair to the end of his toes, which are at least six feet away. He's something.

Rico is originally from Barranquilla in Colombia. His father was in the merchant marine, his mother a homemaker. He has two brothers and a sister. He came to Elizabeth, New Jersey when he was sixteen to finish high school. Eight years later he moved to Miami where he worked for two years as a personal trainer. He says, "I began to do body building because I felt skinny. I was passing a gym and I saw these guys who were built and I thought, 'I want to be like that.' So I got a membership to the gym and worked out seven days a week."

Taking supplements and working out Rico noticed one day he was just as big as the guys he'd seen hanging out outside the gym and started entering bodybuilding contests.

"I started dancing after that. I consider myself a very good dancer. I danced at Stella's in New York and the Paradise in Asbury Park in New Jersey." In Miami he has danced at the Boardwalk, Cactus and Twist.

He continues, "Once I started dancing I felt confident with my body. People like the combination of my body, my personality and my dancing."

Rico says that he poses for clients. "They touch me to feel the power," he tells the interviewer, "I like to help people with my energy. I give massages." His fees range from $200 to $300 an hour depending on the place He sees escorting as part time work. He adds that he sometimes gets calls from couples. And tells an interesting story: "In

New Jersey I had a woman call who was a virgin. I thought perhaps she was a transsexual. She was 28 years old. All she wanted to do was touch me. As far as I know she's still a virgin."

He adds another story. "I was dancing at Stella's and there was a young Chinese couple there. She was very beautiful." They introduced themselves to Rico and the man explained that his lady friend was a dancer, that she was 27 and that she wanted to give Rico a massage.

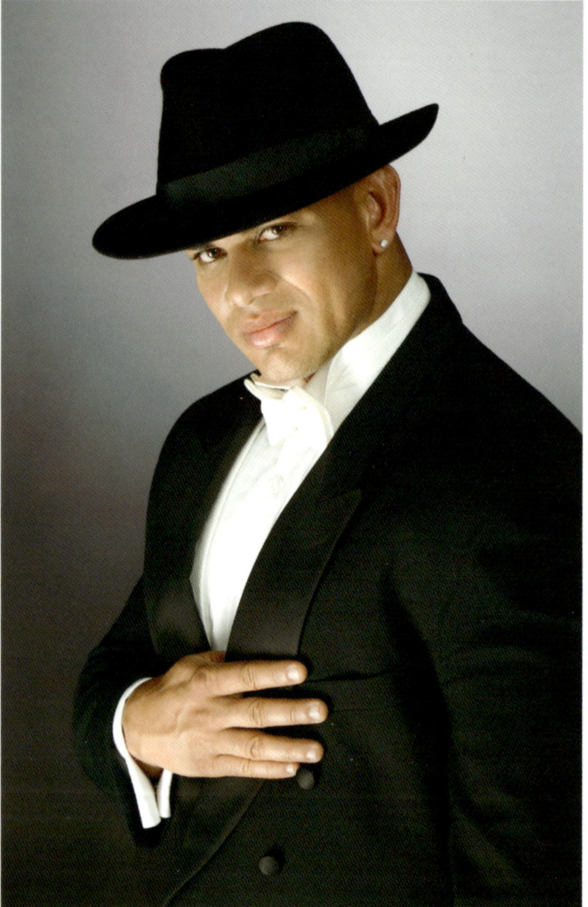

He continues, "At her apartment she had a massage table and massage oil and everything. I could see the guy behind a curtain. She began kissing me on the neck and I could see the man masturbating. Ten minutes later the guy came out and started kissing the girl. He said, 'Thank you, thank you. You made my fantasies come true. This is my wife'."

Another unusual client made a rendezvous with Rico at a hotel in Washington, D.C. Rico says. "The guy called on his way to the hotel. He was very serious and when he arrived he had a briefcase. He had to have been a lawyer or a diplomat. He wanted to be spanked. Very hard. With a belt until his buttocks were red like apples. I made four hundred dollars on that one. That was his fantasy."

Rico has been married for eight years and has two children, a seven year old boy and a two year old girl. He says, "My wife knows I do massage, and that's about it. I am studying singing and I write my own music. I want the world to know who I am and I want to express myself through song. I want everyone to know how beautiful the world is."

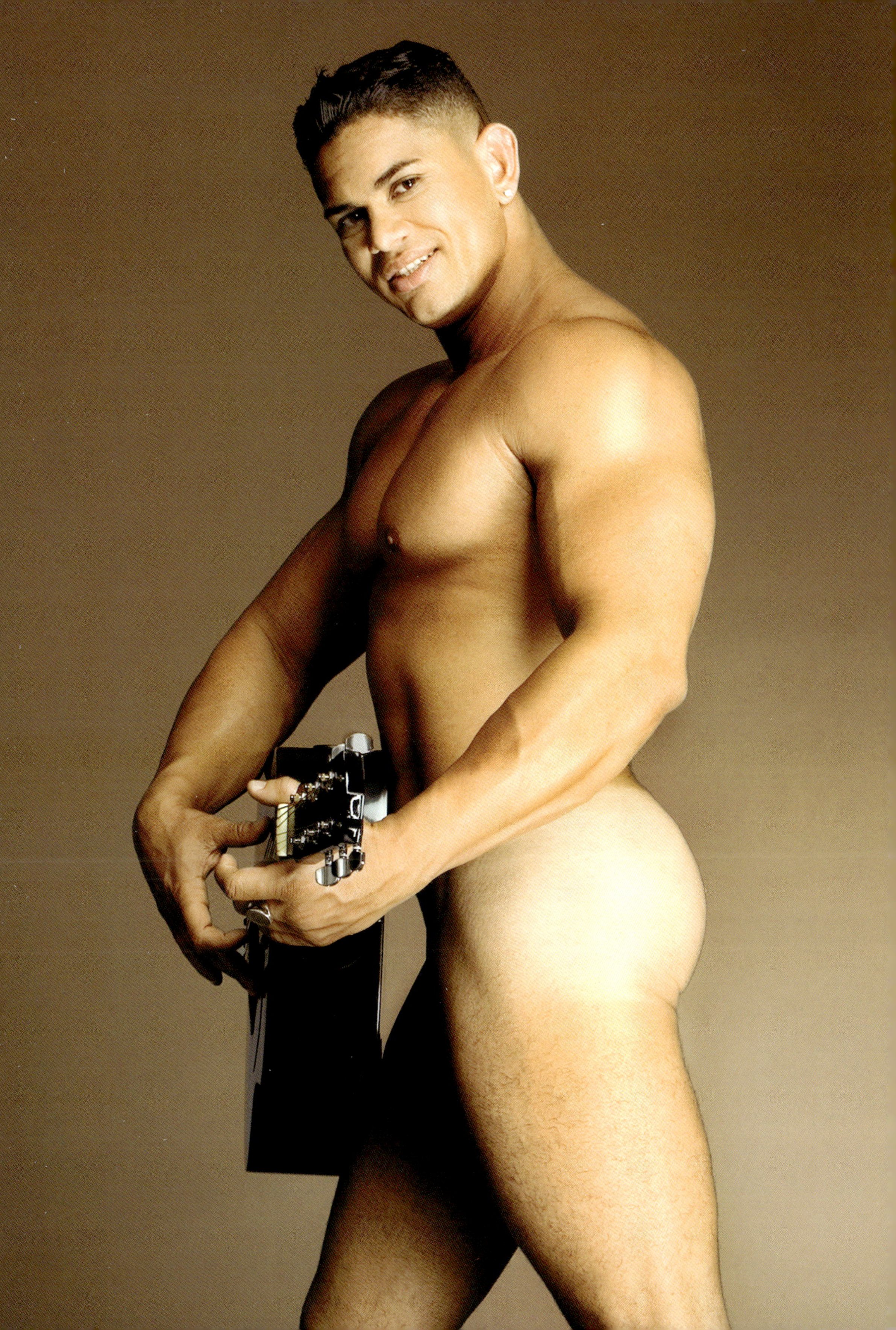

KACOROT

ENTIRE USA , Miami Beach

Send Email | Write a Review | Read Reviews | Tell a Friend | Add to Favorites

Join My Fan Club

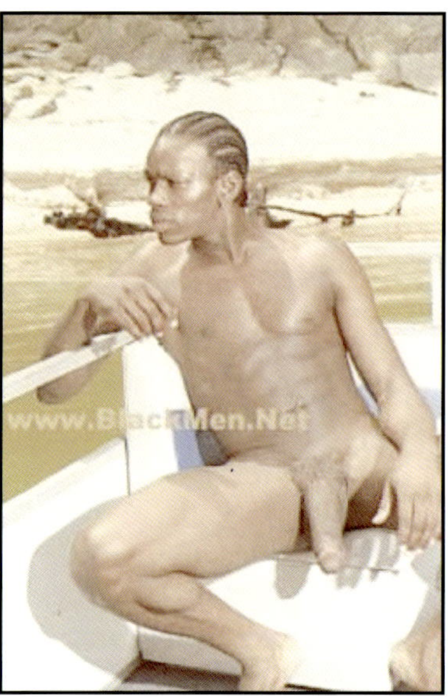

This Photo is 997 days old.
Photo Uploaded Here on 04/26/2004

Contact Information

Phone : 305-761-2962
Mobile : 305-761-2962
Pager :

Escort Description (Self-Described)

Age	**27**
Rates	**150.0**
Height	**6'2"**
Weight	**190**
Ethnicity	**Black**
Facial Hair	**no**
Body Hair	**little**
Hair Color	**Brown**
Eye Color	**Brown**
Dick Size	**11.5"**
Cut or Uncut	**cut**
Sexual Positions	**Versatile**
Incall/Outcall/Both	**Both**
Description	**Here you go! Come get into my life and let me help you have the best of the best I'm190 lbs of finely toned, dark chocolate with a smooth, hairless body and 11X8pleasure-filled reasons to contact me! All of it just waiting for you to call and discuss details (vidoes and parties are a specialty of mine!). I can travel to meet and greet whether you need a hot and sweaty workout partner, or an Armani-suited companion. Just call and we will talk schedules and other PERTINENT data my name is Kacorot, pronounced like "smack-alot" (WELL worth wrapping your lips around properly!)**

Last Logged by Escort:
Last Verified by Escort: 04/26/04
Ad Originally Listed: 04/26/04

Escort ID: 11314
Number of Reviews: 1
Number of Visitors: 14026

KACOROT

Kacorot seems like a very cool customer in his tight, white sleeveless t-shirt and straw cowboy hat, until you see his smile and realize what a kid he really is. His escorting name is taken from a Japanese animation cartoon.

He is from Philadelphia and in total with half-brothers and half-sisters from both parents there are nine boys and five girls in the family. Kacorot was brought up with his father's family. His father is an ex-marine and now is a construction worker.

Kacorot attended college in Milwaukee and prepared for a career as a chef. He has just gotten his culinary arts license and has been living in Miami for the past four years. The move came about when he was living with his lover in Atlanta and the boyfriend decided to move to Miami.

His career trajectory includes a move back to Philadelphia upon finishing his studies and working in a restaurant there. He then moved to New York and worked as an account analyst for a bank on Wall Street. "I was often approached on Wall Street," he says. "I saw things on Wall Street that amazed me. I saw sex, drugs, it was worse than the projects."

Unusually, he began doing porn films as a hobby before doing escort work. At the time he was working as a dancer in Fort Lauderdale and tells his interviewer, "People saw me in clubs and asked me, 'Are you a good dancer?' and actually I'm a very sexual dancer. I don't move much but I'm good so I got a lot of work."

Kacorot is still doing porn films in Fort Lauderdale. He says he started at $200 a scene but now gets $500 a scene. He has a half-brother, Tahreek, who is also an escort and makes porn movies also. Kacorot would like to start his own company and says he will not make more films without receiving royalties.

He came to Miami with a lover who answered his escort ad in Atlanta and flew him down for a rendezvous. Kacorot says, "He was all right with the money I earned as an escort but he was very controlling."

As an escort Kacorot reports that he works about ten times a week. He has an hourly rate of $200 and also, rather uniquely, has both an all-day or all-night rate of $700. He has a number of regular clients, among them one man in his 50s who hires him just to stay up and talk all night.

He travels occasionally for a day rate of $700, plus travel plus accommodations in a separate hotel. He doesn't like to stay with clients in their own home. He doesn't like going to rural locations, either. He says, "I can't. I'm a city boy." He has gone to the island of St. Thomas in the Caribbean but didn't like it. "There's no night life and all the

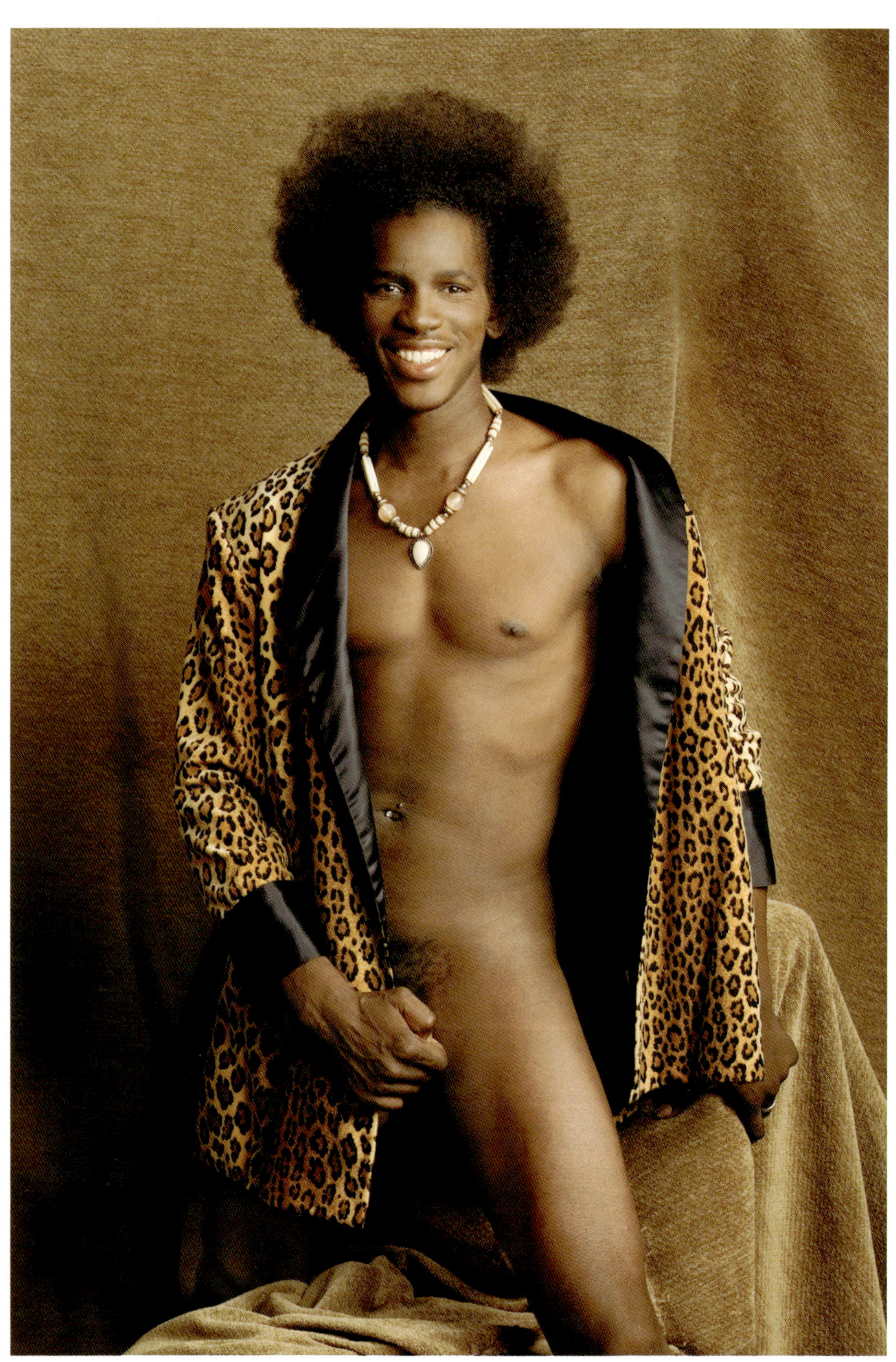

client wanted to do was bump and grind. I stayed one week and that was enough."

He identifies his clients as being primarily white, in their 40s and up and about 40% of them are married. Kacorot is African-American and does not particularly like African-American clients. He feels that they often try to drive too hard a bargain when it comes to paying fees and demanding sexual services.

His client who likes to chat all night would like to have a more personal relationship with Kacorot but the client was told, "If we have a relationship you have to support me. If you can't I can't stop working."

He has been in love with the boyfriend that he joined in Miami. He remembers, "He'd pick fights so I'd keep interested in him and he would try to have sex with me just so I'd be too tired to work. It just didn't work out." He adds, "I'm dodging and ducking love. When clients want the boyfriend experience and tell me they can deal with what I do, they never can. I fuck them, and then they fall in love. How do you fall in love for sex? They just do. On the other hand the words I hate most are, 'It's too big.' I have to wear extra-large Magnum condoms. Nothing else fits."

Of his good clients he tells about a man who wanted him to play the role of his mother's boyfriend. He supposedly has been caught with another man and gets spanked and has an orgasm in his underwear. Kacorot sees him as a not too-demanding client

Another client, a 50-year-old man in real estate, asks to be penetrated with a dildo and then whines and moans.

He has had a client who had oral sex with him for forty minutes and then suddenly ran out and into a nearby house. Of incidents like that Kacorot says, "I'm disappointed. I'm disappointed."

A recent bad client argued about the $200 fee and said, "If you were white and 21 it wouldn't be a problem." Just being seen as a piece of merchandise Kacorot finds particularly offensive. He says that when clients ask him if he can do something about the price, he replies, "I can go up." He adds about Latin American clients, "I get frustrated. How can you try to buy dick and can't speak English!"

He is very aware of the danger of AIDS and always uses condoms. Extra-large, he points out. He says, "Some clients want to bareback but I won't do it."

DYLAN

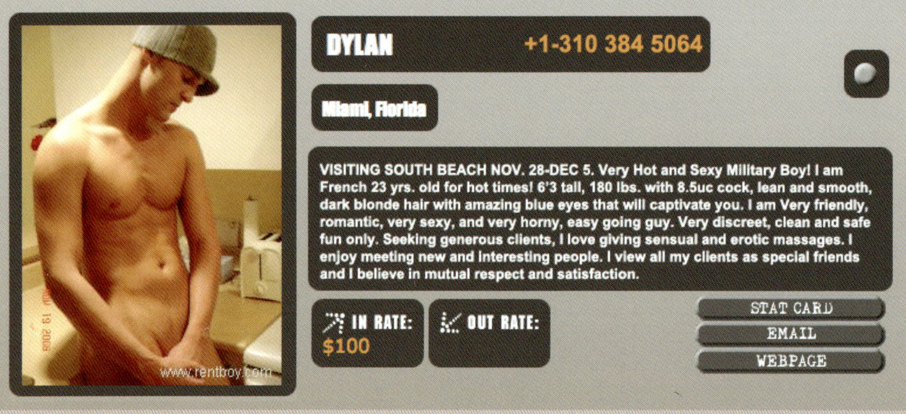

Dylan is tall, blond and beautiful. And French. French-Canadian to be exact. He is from Montreal. His escorting story is not long as he is only 23 years old.

He told his interviewers this much. He was brought up in a town near Montreal. His father works in a paper company. His mother is an *au pair* for a Montreal family. He has an older brother.

He started dancing in clubs last year in response to an ad he saw in a newspaper. That was in a gay club in the part of Montreal called Sherbrooke. The club is part of a complex that includes a female strip club.

A friend discussed escort work with him and he placed an ad on an American site. He reports that he works as an escort three or four times a week. His fee is $200 in and $250 out. He says that although his English is limited "…it's not necessary to talk much."

His clients are between 30 and 40 years old for the most part. He also does massage as part of his escort services and has regular clients. He was advertising in the Miami area when interviewed but actually was in Miami Beach for a vacation with his girlfriend. Dylan says he has no fantasies about his clients. "It's just business." Dylan says he is bisexual and that although he prefers women he is not insensitive to attractive men. His family does not know what he does. They believe he earns his living as a dancer. Of his clients, he says "…if they are not *hyper-joli* (super good-looking) but they are kind I can be with them without any problem." He feels that his clients like him because they are attracted to his photos and then when meeting him, particularly like his voice.

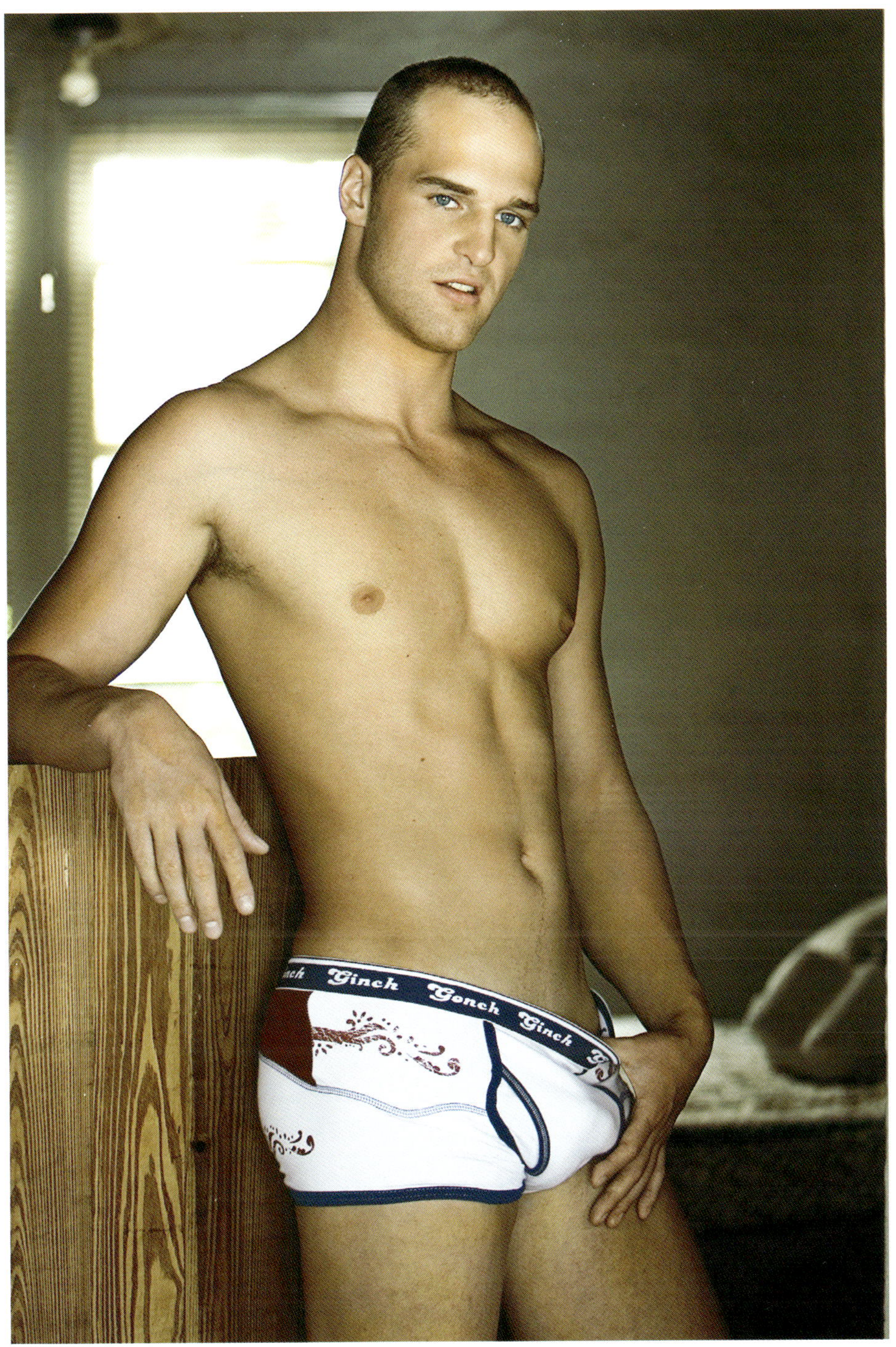
Ginch
Gonch
Ginch

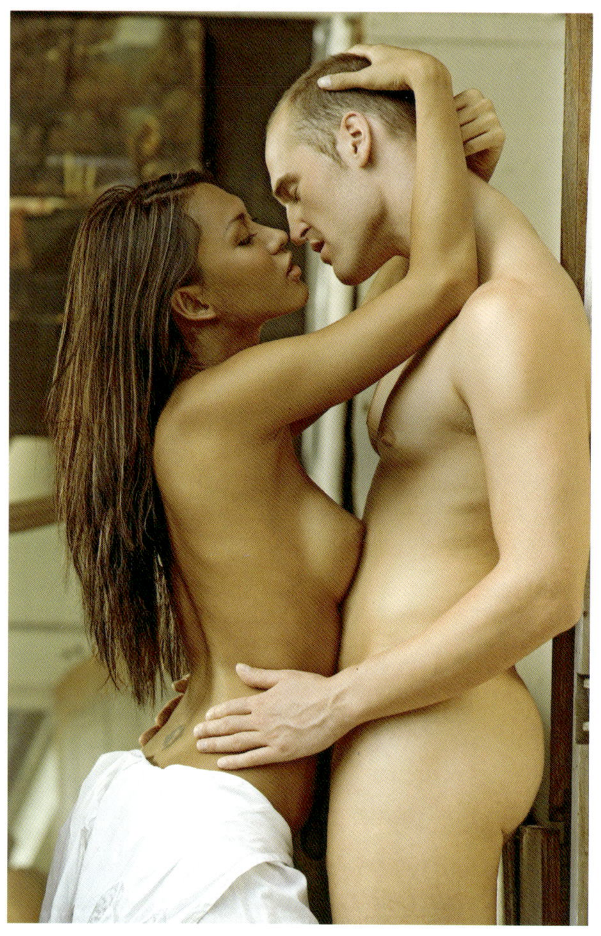

Dylan reports that he prefers clients in the United States to clients in Canada. "In Canada they always have to have sex. Here in the U.S. you can get away with just a massage and some fooling around. In Canada the people are more stressed and they are more demanding of the escort."

He adds that although prostitution is illegal in Canada, as it is in the United States, in the country north of our border the government provides free condoms and free testing for sexually transmitted diseases.

His girlfriend Joanne accompanied him to the interview and he said she serves as his agent and helps him write his ads. Joanne is of Filipino background and is from Toronto. Her first language is English. Originally Dylan and she met in a café in Montreal. She is a pretty, long haired brunette who wore a wraparound skirt and a brief beach bra-top to the interview. With her pretty body she was able to do this to great advantage. It was evident during the interview that Dylan and she are very romantically attached to one another. Joanne also works as an escort. Dylan's family likes his girlfriend, although he says that his father dislikes homosexuals.

During his photo shooting with David Vance, Joanne accompanied Dylan to the studio and it was revealed that she had begun life as a Filipino boy. She has made the transition to her new life successfully. Dylan and Joanne are a very Twenty-First Century couple.

Dylan and Joanne will return to Canada from their vacation in Miami Beach with more money than when they left. Dylan says, "...whenever I need more money we go on vacation."

DIEGO

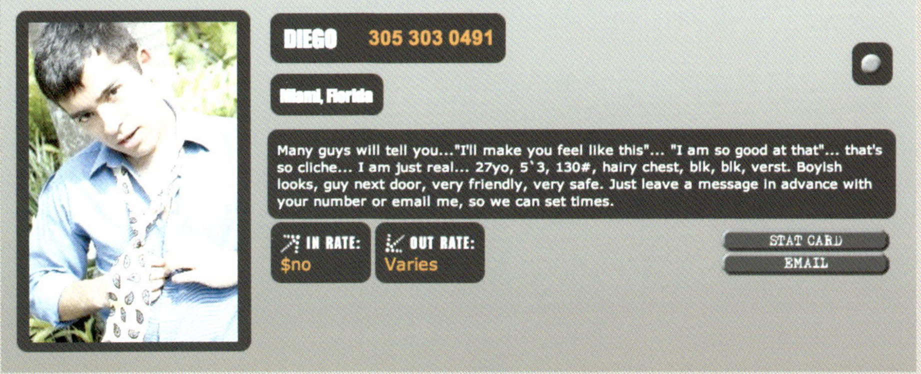

Boyish Diego looks much younger than he is. And he has a boyish personality to match his appearance. Originally from Lima, Peru he now lives in Miami, where his sister and mother also reside. He has two brothers who still live in Lima.

Diego first came to the United States in 1994 as a tourist. Still a student, he later began working as a steward on a cruise ship, a job that his mother discovered for him on a return flight between Miami and Lima. Seated next to her was a young man who worked as a cruise line steward and she made a contact for her son.

Diego says, "I thought it would be glamorous but it was anything but. Actually, it was like being in jail. You never got to leave the ship."

Diego then worked in the duty-free store at the Lima airport before moving to Miami. In Miami he first worked on the staff of a caterer but now is employed at a boutique hotel in the South Beach area of Miami Beach.

He remembers being interested in working as an escort when he was still in Lima. He answered an ad and went to a mysterious house where some disconsolate young boys were seated in a reception room. He was then shown into an office where an even more mysterious man in a hat and gloves seated behind a desk said, "I have to see your body. Drop your pants." He concluded with "You're fine," after taking a look. It wasn't fine with Diego, however. He departed not to return, deciding that he had stumbled upon something that was more of a bordello than an escort agency.

Once in Miami Beach, a friend told him about the Internet site *rentboy.com*. "I needed money," Diego says, "but I told my friend about my experience in Lima and my doubts about doing escorting." My friend said, 'Here it's quite different. Sometimes the

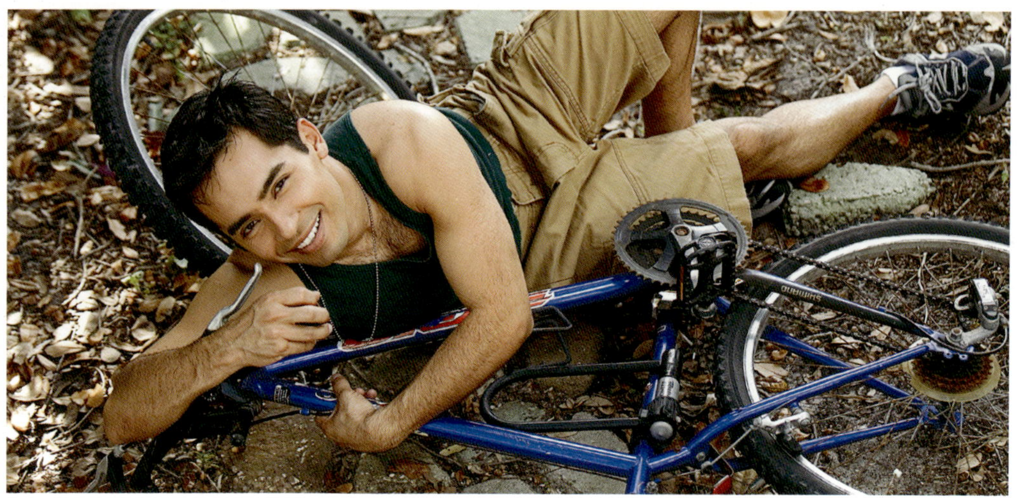

people who call are really quite cute." That was three years ago and Diego has been working since then.

He has a certain technique in finding clients. "I put an ad on a site or in a magazine for one month and then leave it out for three or four months. I will get enough clients from the one month insert to provide work for a longer period of time," he reports. His situation is unusual in that he at present lives with his mother and sister and only takes calls to go out. He works once or twice a week. He tells the interviewer, "I have regulars, as well, but from time to time they disappear. I don't have a real schedule. I plan to take an apartment on my own soon and then perhaps it will be different." He adds, "I would never call a client to ask if they want to see me."

Diego has a relatively modest fee of $130 an hour and no specific fee for overnight work or travel. He has a client in New York who flies him in on a Friday and back to Miami on Sunday and pays him $1,500 for what is in fact a short weekend visit. He also has a client in Orlando who pays $600 for an overnight visit, plus transportation.

Diego will tell you that most of his clients are "gringos," that is of non-Latin-American backgrounds and between 40 and 60 years of age. He says, "I have become friends with some people and they want to be nice to you. But it's difficult because they aren't people I would be friends with under normal circumstances."

He has never been in love and says, "I don't think I want to be in love right now. I can be attracted to someone but I don't really like the pressure. All those phone calls. When my ad is running I am concentrated on sex for business and I save my energy." However, he has had a relationship when he was still living in Peru and has had a long-term client who had a boyfriend with whom he no longer had sex. He liked the man and the man liked him because he reminded him of an earlier boyfriend. He remarks, "He was honest with me. He was HIV positive but even though he was very good to me it was stressful. I think I want to be with someone but not while I'm doing this.

"I feel the doors are not entirely open for me here in the United States. I think I need to learn more languages. Maybe I've lost my balls."

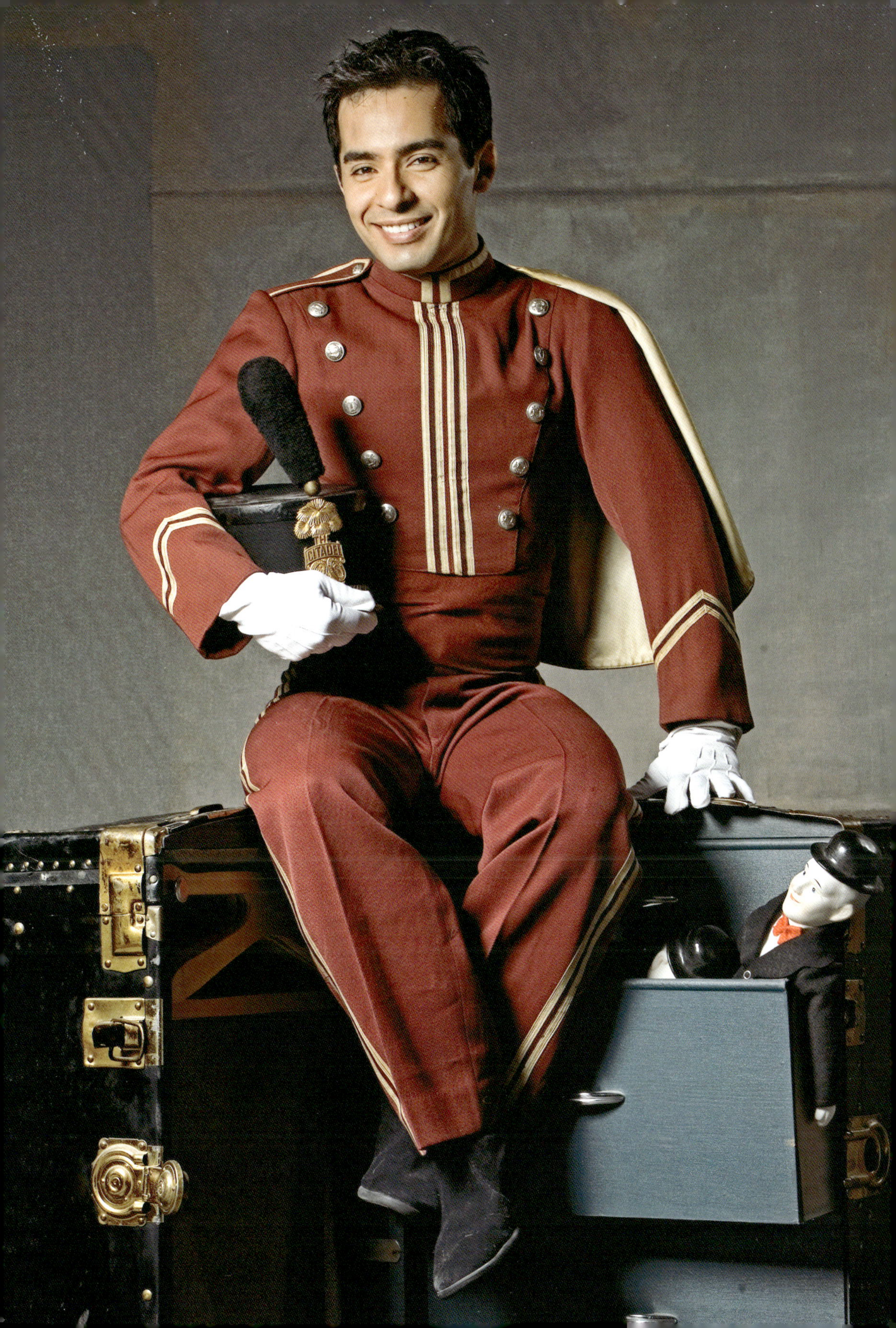
THE
CITADEL

MARCEL

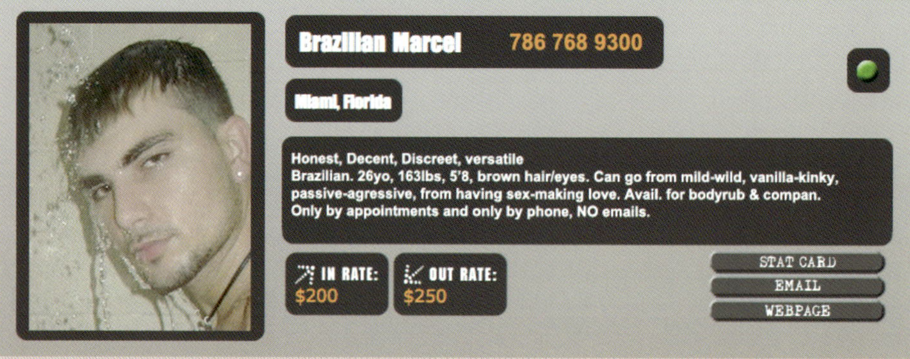

"My dream as a kid was to come to the United States and learn English. I had my visa request refused three times but I finally got here anyway." This is how the dark and dashing Marcel begins his interview. Very at ease and speaking very good English, Marcel seems to have made an excellent adjustment to his new life. He says, "My father repaired ships and traveled a lot. He spoke English very well. He spoke five languages altogether. I was about fourteen when he died. I have a sister and also two half-sisters by a previous marriage of my father's.

"I went to Sao Paulo for school. I had lived in other parts of Brazil before my school years. I planned to do something with computers but now I think I might be good with psychiatry. I know I'd be a good teacher. I give people advice on how to become an escort. I came to New York when I was 19 and stayed with one of my half-sisters who is a lesbian. She had gotten me a job cleaning at the Rockefeller Center with her. Then after awhile I moved out and worked in restaurants, a shoe store, a bar, in clubs, in a supermarket, as a superintendent in a building.

"I started escorting about four or five years ago. A friend of mine said, 'You're killing yourself for others and not making enough money.' I started thinking about my life. I thought about it a lot before I took the step, but now I look back it's not as big a step as I thought it would be then. I told my friend, who was working as an escort, 'The next time you have a client who wants a four-hand massage, call me.' I never had a problem.

"I placed an ad in a newspaper in Queens, where I was living. It was a gay newspaper, the New York Press. I was working in a bar in Queens as a waiter at the time.

Someone in the bar saw the ad with my picture. He wanted to have sex with me and we never did and that made him mad. He said to me, 'I saw your ad. That's not very nice.' I said, "I'm at a point in my life where I don't care what you think.' So then I heard they were going to fire me so I quit.

"After New York I moved to Washington, D.C. for about a year. Then I decided to go to Key West for Fantasy Fest and started dancing on a bar at Quest. I did some trips up to Miami and now I'm staying with some people here. I've only been here a month. Back in New York when I started escorting I had an apartment at Eighth Avenue and 51st Street. It wasn't very good and I didn't have a lot of clients. Then I got a better apartment, a studio, and presented myself as giving body-rubs. I would be nude, they could have a rub and then if they wanted more I would say, 'Do you need to stop by an ATM machine?'

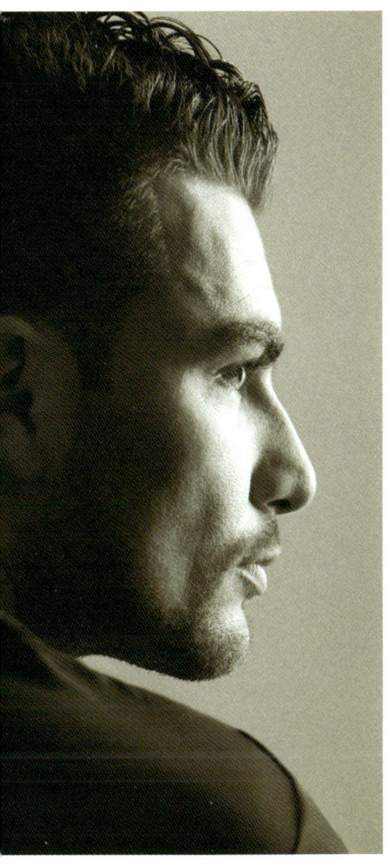

"In Washington it was easier to have clients and I had a lot more regulars there than in New York. In New York there are too many options. Clients want to have different experiences. Sometimes a client would sit down with a magazine and point out other escorts he'd hired and complain about them. "I had mostly local clients in Washington and I would say only about 15% were married men. Most clients were openly gay. I charged $120 for a body-rub in, $150 for a body-rub out. For full escorting, my fees were $200 in and $250 out. I could charge more in D.C. than I could in New York. When a client calls I can tell right away from the voice what that person is like. I would rather see two good clients a day than five of lower quality and I can tell a lot from their voices. I analyze them and don't talk about rates immediately. If you want me to be intimate with you I have to know something about you.

"My clients range in age from 25 to 60, I would say. I like younger clients myself although some escorts like older clients. But I've never had a client I turned down for physical reasons. Some clients are high on drugs and just want company. They just want someone around. I don't like that. They are filling up a hole in their lives; filling the gap of loneliness.

"Probably my best experience, financially speaking, was when I made $1,500 one night answering a call to Greenwich Village by a psychiatrist. I was his psychiatrist that night. I arrived at 9:00 in the evening and stayed until 10:00 the next morning. He just kept talking and handing out money all night long.

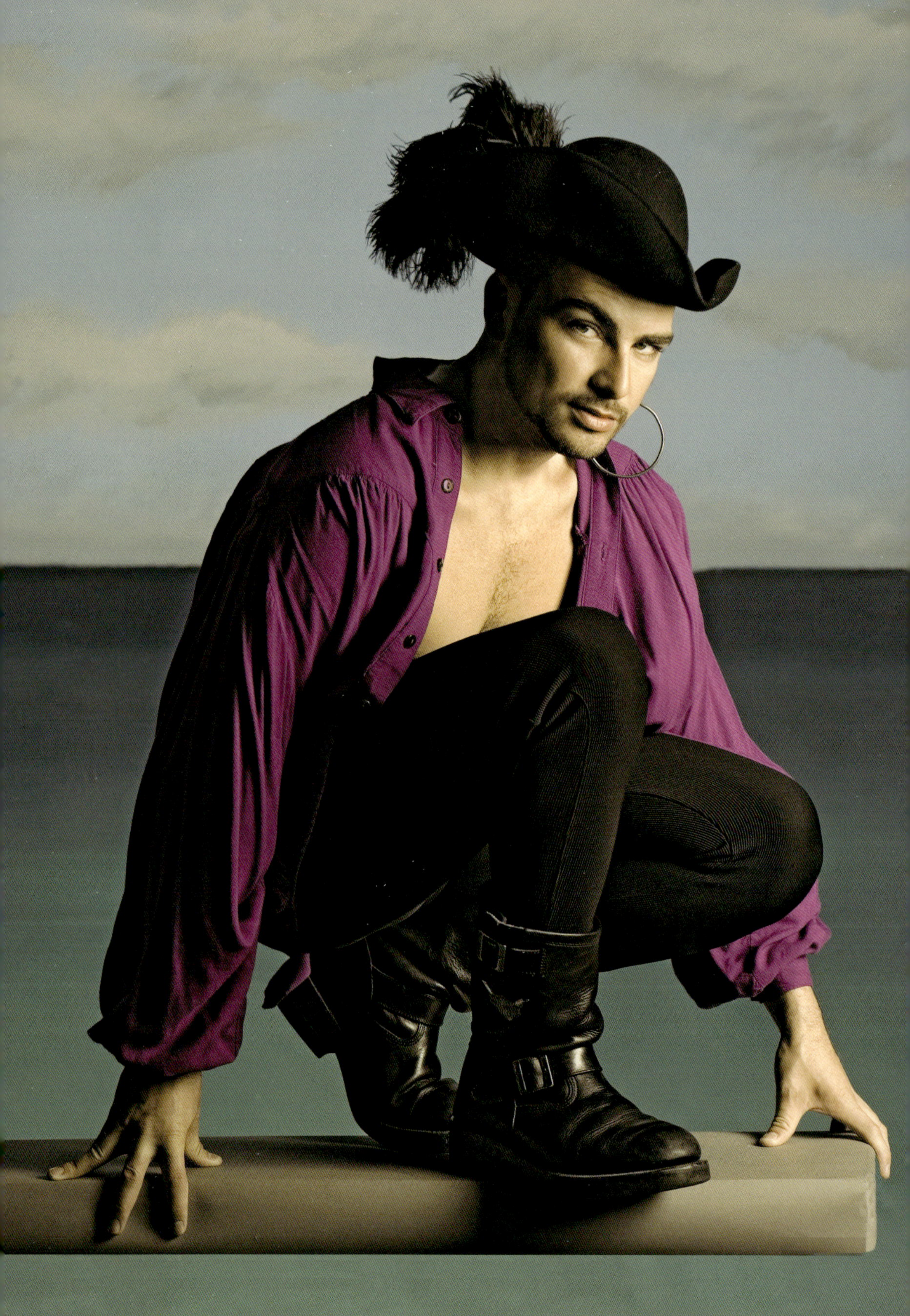

"My worst experience was in Washington. The client was into spanking and his ass was untouchable. I turned that one down. And I had a bad guy in New York who hired me for a massage but didn't want to take his shorts or pants off. He was high and began complaining that he wasn't getting what he wanted and asked to have his money back. I gave him half of it.

"When I first started advertising in New York it took a month before I got calls. The second issue of the magazine I began to get calls. Miami is nice because clients often will come pick you up and bring you back to where you're staying.

"I always wanted a perfect body but many clients don't want that. Sometimes they say, 'If you had that body I wouldn't have called you.' My plus is that I am Brazilian. I have clients who will call and book me two months in advance. I am one hundred percent versatile.

"One of my most interesting client contacts was with a guy who was very horny but didn't have any money. In lieu of payment, he told me he would give me some of his stuff. I got a great wardrobe of designer clothes including these Harley-Davidson boots that I am wearing right now.

"I had one funny experience because I am 100% versatile. I really am. When I was in New York I used to travel down to Washington from time to time. I had three different ads where I was a top, a bottom, and a third where I was versatile. Advertising as a versatile I had a call from a Washington man and I went there. He wanted a real bottom and he got one. About a week later I got a call. It was the same man, I could tell the voice. He wanted a top, a real top. When I showed up he took one look, recognized me and said, 'There is no way you could be a top the way you bottomed.' I said, 'I take that as a compliment.'

"I also have a private life. I date guys. My wish would be to have a lover who was also an escort-masseur. There should be a matching-up service for escorts so we could find the kind of partner we want. I'm often recognized as an escort. Many men I meet don't say anything. They just want to have the chance to be with an escort for free.

"As for my sexual history, I knew as a child that I was gay. At about the age of eight I played around with cousins. I slept with a lot of boys when I was a teenager, too. I was very sexual. When I told my mother I was gay she freaked out. It was very hard for her to accept it. She talked to my lesbian half-sister in New York a lot about it. My mother confronted me about it as I was getting all these phone calls from boys. Never any girls. I always felt intimidated by girls.

"Strangely enough, although my mother doesn't know I escort, I suspect there is a history of escorting in her life, also. She may have been a stripper.

"I try to save but it's difficult in this line of work. At first you are unsure if you will stay doing it. Sometimes I get depressed about this.

"It's curious, when you're in this business you're already in before you decide whether you'll stay or not. And then you can't really stop because you need the money.

TONY SERRANO

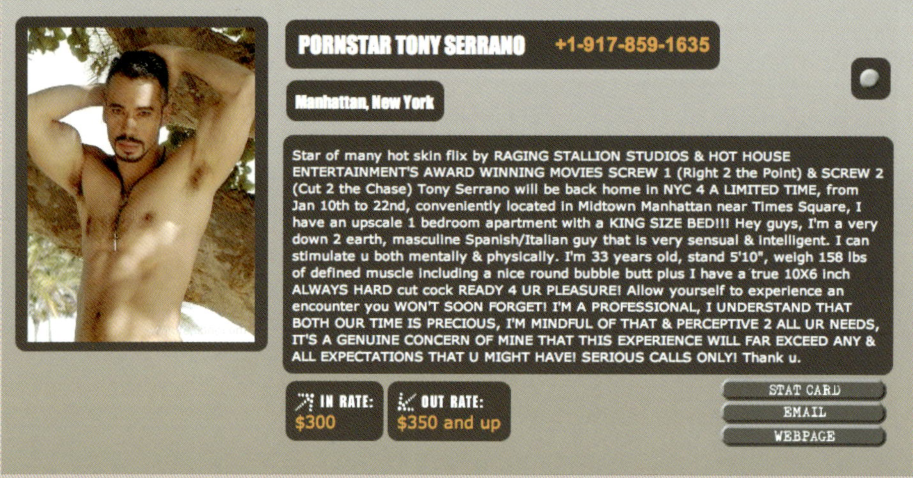

There is something dreamlike about Tony Serrano. And very well it may be, as his life has been in many ways like fiction. Dark and handsome, he tells the story of his childhood. "I was adopted with my twin brother in Barcelona, Spain. My adoptive parents were American, my father being in the military and stationed in Europe at the time.

"I was eighteen before I found out some of the facts about my birth. My biological mother and father were lovers, young lovers. When my mother discovered she was pregnant my father abandoned her. When my brother and I were born, my mother put us up for adoption as it was impossible for her to care for us. Her only request was that we be kept together. We are fraternal twins.

"My adoptive parents were originally from Harrison, Oklahoma and had been high school sweethearts before they married. When my mother thought she was having her first pregnancy it turned out to be a tumor. So serious that once it was removed she was only given six months to live, but she beat it. And a result of the tumor she could never hope to have children."

Tony's given name was already Timotheo Antonio Serrano and his brother had been named Ricardo Raul Serrano, Serrano being his birth mother's name. He was brought up using his adoptive parents' name of Wells, but has now returned to his original given name. As an Army "brat" he was brought up on Army bases around Europe and as a teenager went to live in Peachtree City, near Atlanta.

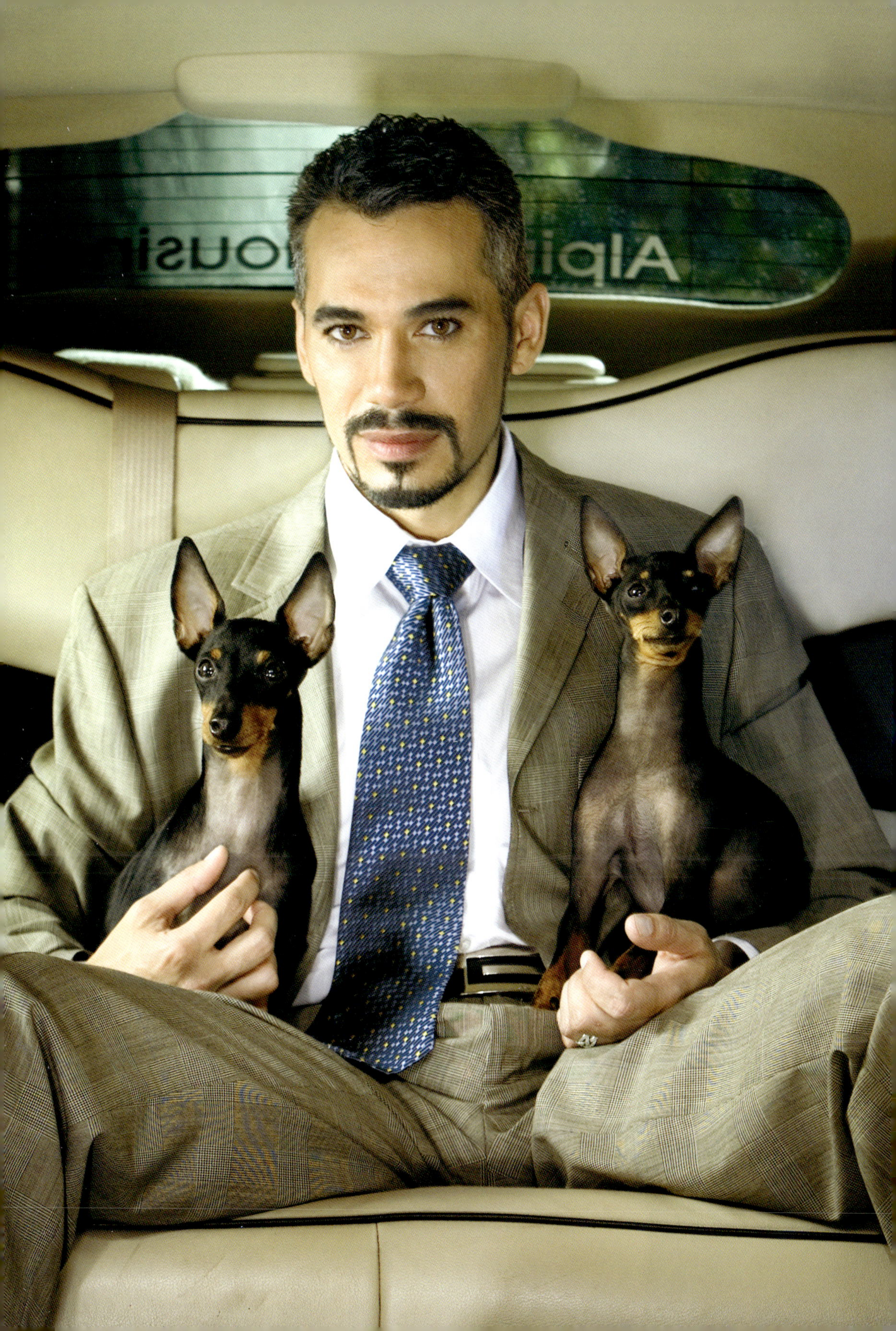

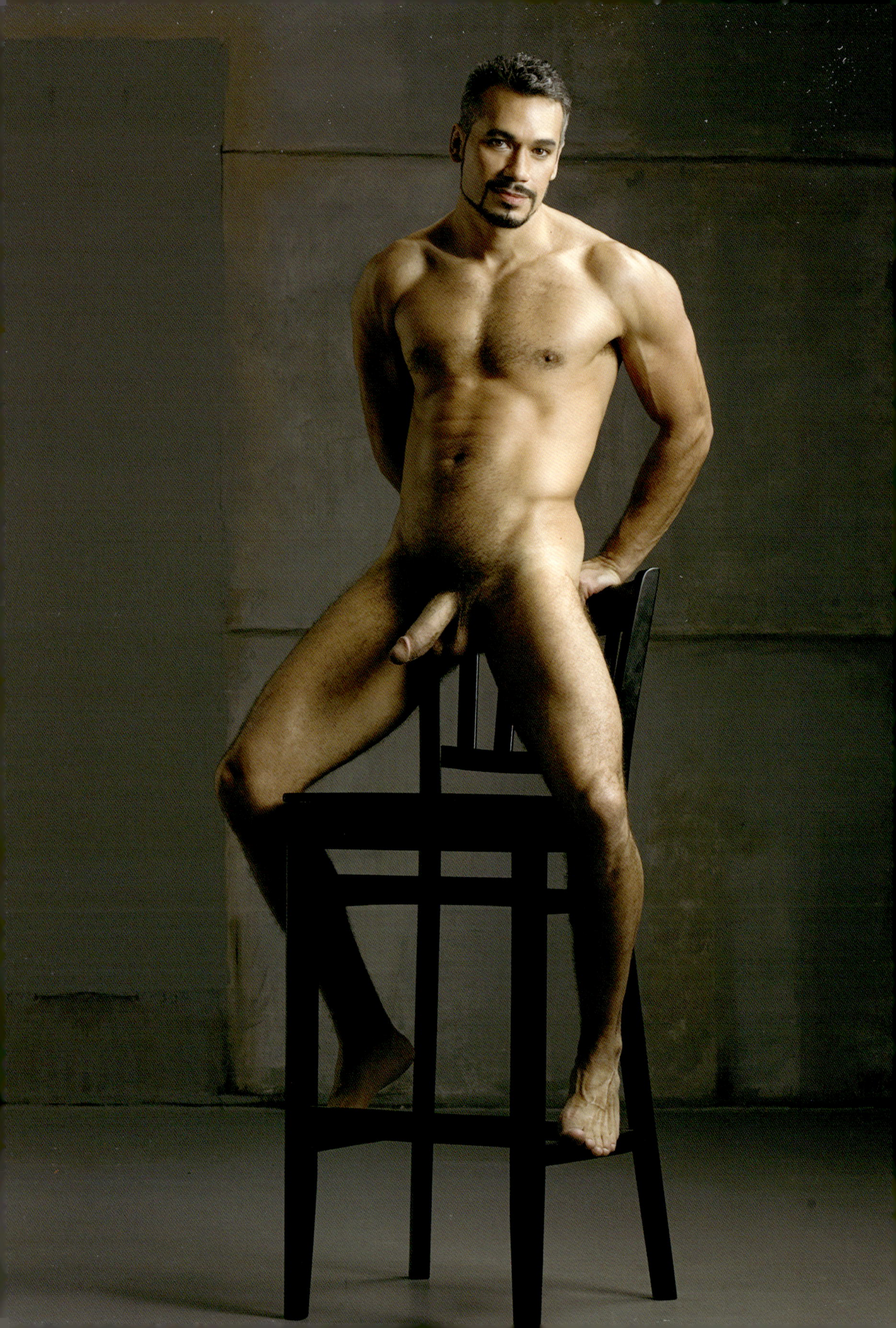

He says, "I was rebellious and I joined the Navy at 18. I joined to get an education. Growing up my brother and I weren't exactly alike. He was more adventurous physically but I was more at ease and more adventurous socially. In the Navy I served in San Diego under my adoptive name of William Allen Wells. My brother joined the Army a little later and is still in that service. I actually have other siblings because after our adoption my new mother was thought to be very ill again, but when she was hospitalized it was found that she was in fact pregnant. And she had a daughter and subsequently another son.

"In the Navy I graduated from the Naval School of Health and served the Medical Corps. In the service I was able to feel comfortable with being gay. When I was at home I felt bad and wrong because of what the church and society were telling me. But in the military I met a lot of other people like myself.

"I stayed in San Diego after I left the Navy. I had a very close friend, a lover, in Los Angeles who was a newspaper editor and he encouraged me to come there and begin to study psychology. The plan was to attend UCLA. But that got very de-railed in July of 1995."

Tony hadn't moved to Los Angeles to attend college yet when he got involved in an incident that altered his life a great deal. After a party there he had stopped to get something to eat at a diner. There had been drive-by shooting and incidents in the neighborhood where hitchhikers had been picked up and then robbed drivers. The pick-ups might have been of a sexual nature, also. On his way from his car to the diner a man had stopped and asked him if he wanted a ride and had been told "No." Shortly thereafter that man had been robbed and shot and managed to drive into a gas station where ambulances and police soon clustered. Walking into this situation on his way back to his car, Tony was identified by a street person as having fled the scene of the crime and was arrested. He was kept in jail as a suspect until October. His parents rallied to him, found him a homicide lawyer and finally the case was dismissed because the homeless man who had identified him could not be found.

Out of jail he found that his newspaper editor lover, who had been supportive and helpful while he was being unfairly held, had found a new lover. Tony was on his own and looking for direction. At this time another friend introduced him to a rendezvous restaurant called Numbers and there he began a career in escorting. He had been working out in jail and had a good body and needed the money. In 1998 he moved to New York.

Still somewhat traumatized by his arrest, he was further disturbed when an L.A. woman police detective showed up at his apartment in New York. She had been the detective on the case and had come to apologize for all the trouble they had caused in his life. She told him they had captured a man who had confessed to the crime.

Before leaving Los Angeles Tony worked as a travel agent as well as doing escort work. He was approached to do porn videos but his first film was done for Michael Lucas and he traveled to New York to shoot it. Subsequently he worked as a flight attendant for

US Airways, but was let go when they merged with another airline. For the last two years he has only worked in the porn industry and as an escort. He estimates that he has done about two-dozen films for Raging Stallion, Falcon, Hothouse, Catalina and Titan, as well as others. Originally he had been approached in Los Angeles to do sports and recreation videos for Falcon with the director Chichi LaRue. However his first films were with Michael Lucas in New York. He says, "For the performer the amount of time against the dollar is good, but you have to remember that the producers make millions. It is certainly the best marketing tool for escorting."

Looking back on his life as a gay man, Tony remembers, "I knew I was gay even as a young boy. I identified with the same things my sister enjoyed. My first gay encounter was with a neighbor boy who was eager to explore sexually. It didn't matter with which sex at that age.

"We were living in a brownstone in New York then and we had a recreation room in the basement where all the neighborhood kids came for sleepovers. I had a pal and we played with each other sexually while the others slept. I actually was in love with his older brother.

"My first real lover was an officer in the Navy. This was in an early stage of my attraction to men. Carl had light hair and blue-green eyes. My other major lover was a banker in San Diego. We were together for two years. He was one of what I consider the two great loves of my life. The other was a Cuban from Havana whom I met at my Aunt's home in New York. We met about five years ago and were together for two years.

"Now as an escort I have a regular clientele all over the world. I have a personal website but *rentboy.com* is also good for New York, London and Paris. I also can be found on *Men4Rent* now and *Gaydar*, *Escupido* and *Gay Romeo* are good international sites. My hourly rate is $300, overnight is $1,700, weekend rate is $2,500 and a week rate is $4,500. Plus travel expenses, of course.

"I like to think that I provide an uplifting experience for my clients. We all need tender, loving moments with another human being and if I can provide that I am happy to do so. I should add that I do everything but I am primarily a top because of my size."

Tony reports that although bad experiences are rare, he recently had one with a very well known person who was very negative and unhappy. "He wanted everyone to be unhappy around him and I picked up on that right away. I told him so and couldn't work with him. But I also dated another very well known person with much pleasure. He wouldn't appear in gay venues and although he is not a celebrity he is very well known in the entertainment industry.

"I would say that perhaps 40% of my clients are married and I do have appointments with married couples. I can have a fulfilling sex experience with a woman but I have a more complete relationship with a man. It's a more passionate, total experience. In the future I would like to attend NYU and get a degree in psychology or a Masters in Social Work. I'd like very much to be a therapist and write a book."

ANTTON HARRI

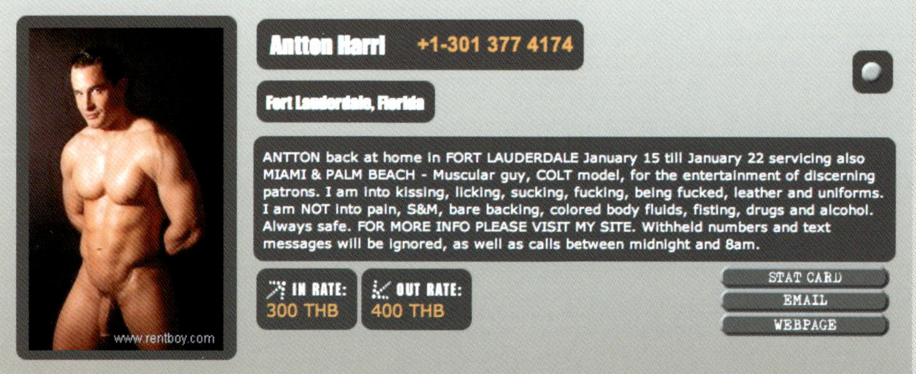

Antton has a beautiful peaches and cream complexion and is extremely muscular. He has the appearance of the wholesome, sporty jock next door, far from what one might think a porn star/escort would be like. Both in appearance and in personality. His warm manner and readiness to laugh made him an easy interview. As well, he is very ready to talk on many subjects like history, politics and travel. Throughout the lunch and later during a stroll down Lincoln Road, the see-and-be-seen pedestrian main street of Miami Beach, Antton got a lot of looks.

Antton is originally from a city called Donostia near San Sebastian in the Basque country (the border of Spain and France). He came to the United States for the first time when he was seventeen as a high school exchange student in Sacramento California. He found the educational system here much different from the European, with many more social activities and more parties. He says, "I had a great experience. More than anything, my host mother made me like this country and the experience was great. Since then I had the desire to return to this big country, the land of plenty."

Antton is a university graduate with a BA in Business Administration. He studied in San Sebastian and then transferred to a college in Madrid. He wanted to have more freedom than his parents allowed with their strict curfew. His parents would stay up and wait for their fully-grown children (3 brothers and 3 sisters) to return home after their late outings on Saturday nights.

He did porn back in Europe before doing porn in the US. His first film ever was shot in Barcelona and his second one was shot in Catania, Sicily. He is currently working exclusively with COLT studios.

In April 2006, He did a film for Black Scorpion Videos with Rafael Alencar who also appears in this book. The film was titled "Dreams of Rafael" and his scene was a sex scene set in a limousine. He explains, "Rafael was the wealthy landowner and I was the chauffeur. I wore sunglasses with a hot chauffeur uniform. I loved it! I had never worn that kind of an outfit before. Due to Rafael's large endowment my acting was very realistic. The camerawoman, Mr. Pam, said that my acting was great! My moaning and groaning was all real."

He was already escorting by the time he got involved in porn. He started escorting in Madrid during his final year of university as a way to pay for Russian language courses that his parents refused to pay. He joined a male bordello in Topete Street and used to spend his Friday and Saturday evenings there. He worked a lot which allowed him to pay for his language courses and still save some money to move to London.

Antton says that his work pattern is very irregular. Much depends on whether he is at home in Fort Lauderdale or whether he is traveling. He usually gets busier when traveling, especially in bigger cities like New York, San Francisco, London and Paris. Fort Lauderdale is rather quiet. In Fort Lauderdale he has mostly a clientele of regulars. During a New York visit he never does more than two or three jobs a day. He does not want to be exhausted to a point were he is not feeling at his best when working. So he prefers not take a fourth.

His rates for in-calls are $300 per hour, outcalls $400 per hour and overnights $1,500. Any other length needs to be discussed. He says, "I am not a clock-watcher. Usually my appointments last more than the agreed time. I usually take appointments every 3 hours to take a little rest and be ready for the next. I always shower before and after.

"There is no specific profile for my patrons; they are very diverse, young, old, married, single, partnered, divorced. I do take calls from couples but I've never had a single woman call me. I never ask anything. I just let the clients tell me what they want themselves. I respect their privacy. If they want to be anonymous that is fine. Regulars are willing to get more personal and exchange real names. It is up to the patron."

Antton has had many good experiences in escorting, most of them being related to unforgettable trips. A client took him to Scottsdale and Sedona, Arizona. He loved the Far West. Once Antton spent an entire week in Singapore with a client who sent for him. He was fascinated by the Asian culture. For him, his most amazing trip was a voyage to Dubai in the Near East. He found himself very impressed by all the construction, the buildings, the modern architecture and the openness and diversity of the people.

His worst experience was with a patron in Los Angeles who tried to get him drunk, exceeded the agreed time and at the conclusion of their time together didn't have the cash to pay. He paid with a check that he cancelled two days after Antton made the deposit in the bank. " Nasty conman!" was Antton's comment on that client.

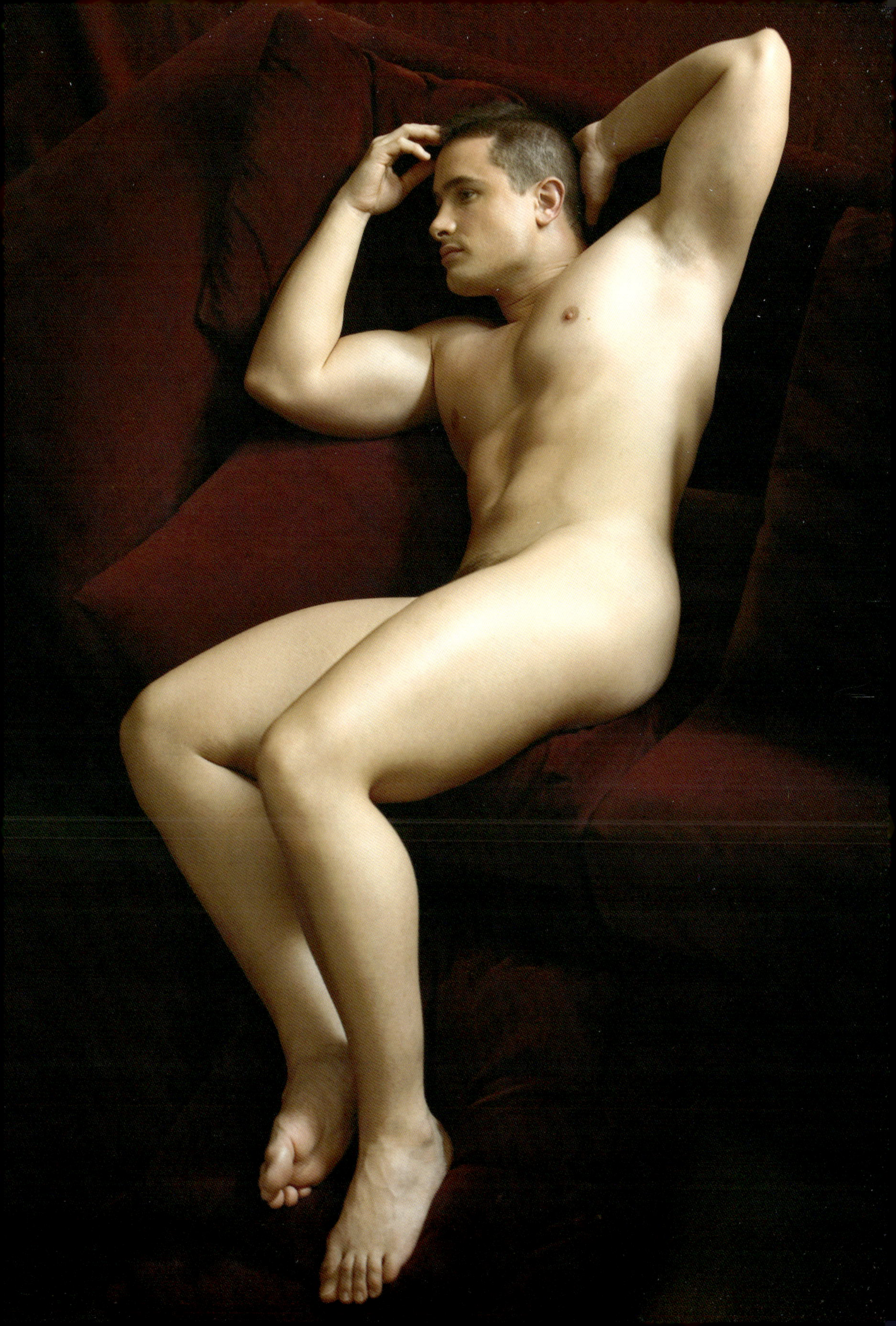

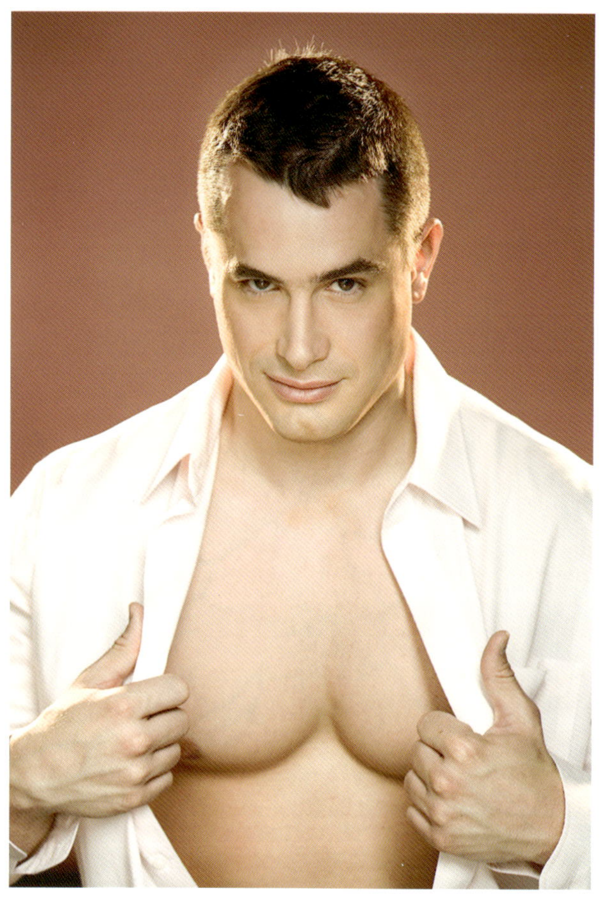

Another bizarre request came from Amsterdam. In his site Antton is very specific that he doesn't do anything kinky, so most clients don't ask. However, there was a call from Holland from a man who "... wanted to lick my ass after having a poo. I agreed to do it as long as he would not kiss me after licking my ass. At the end he ended up canceling the appointment.

"Another time, I was the birthday present to a woman in London. Her husband was more excited than she was. She was a bit stiff and uneasy. She refused to kiss, kept her mouth pursed tightly, even though I kissed her on her lips, I licked her nipples and belly, she did not feel anything until I got down to her pussy and then she started enjoying herself and reacting like a human being. I had never been with a woman before so I had higher expectations of pleasure than I got. I did get aroused but she laid there like a chunk of wood so there was no interaction. She probably did not enjoy the fact that her husband was next to us. But he enjoyed it thoroughly. It seemed more of a gift for him than for her. I never interacted with him. We double-fucked her with her sitting on top of me and the husband up her ass."

Regarding ever being in love, Antton admits he has been in love and has had relationships, but previously to escorting. He believes it would be difficult to escort and to be in a relationship at the same time. The only relationship that he could be in that might work would be with another escort he thinks.

Antton's clients find him a very patient and attentive person. In his own words "Whenever I am with a patron I make sure that he is the only person I care about during the time he is spending with me. I never rush. There is always a little talk at the beginning. I always welcome my patrons with a kiss. Then after a little talk I approach the patron and then I start some foreplay with him." Clients say he is very gentle and patient. Many times the client is an older person and he does not rush them in any way as he wants all enjoyment to be mutual. He always stresses that they are there to enjoy their time with him. He adds, "Sex is not a competition. Therefore there is no need to be in a hurry, there is no pressure to perform and the whole point is to enjoy it, regardless of what we do. I'm very versatile."

Antton was first aware of his gay feelings when he was fifteen years old. His parents were very strict and sex was a taboo. "We had the kind of family life where sex was out of the question. I only socialized with my siblings and cousins. Whatever I learned I had to discover myself. When I started masturbating I discovered that I could not ejaculate when thinking about a woman. I had to fantasize about men. I also got visual pleasure from looking at men. I was always aware of getting visual pleasure from men but I did not realize I was gay until I started masturbating. I often looked at pictures of men in sports magazines and I liked looking at bodybuilders. Then at 15 I realized I liked men more in a sexual way versus an intellectual way.

When asked about what he wanted to be when he grew up he says that he thought about many things, including becoming a lawyer or a diplomat. Even a teacher. And he thinks that he still might. He also writes. "I write poems about everything, including some homoerotic ones as of late."

All his close friends and some members of his family know what he does for a living. But only one of his brothers knows. By chance, his brother saw him on the internet and sent Antton a very understanding message. Antton thought he would be upset. His brother's message said that he was very puzzled by what Antton did but that he wanted to let him know that he was not one to judge him. He also added that he would not let anyone else know what Antton does. "My brother also urged me to be careful because there are many nasty men out there and that he is there for me should I ever need him. I sent him a link to my website *antonharri.info* to make sure he was looking at the right site. So he could learn with more details about what I do. I suspect he had a look." Antton adds he hopes to find the right moment to tell his sister without alarming her. He wants very much to explain to her that what is important is an honest relationship. Most of his friends and family think he is doing some boring administration job in an obscure consulting company.

When asked about his future plans and if he's saving his money, he says he is trying to and that he is tired of renting. In the future, he would like to own his apartment. So far, he is enjoying being an escort and maybe will continue for two or three more years. Perhaps someday he will direct his own movies, either in the United States here or Buenos Aires where there are so many handsome men.

"I think I would say to a prospective escort that you should be yourself and not have multiple personalities. It can get confusing and is unhealthy mentally. Play safe and always use a condom. Never do barebacking" And he would advise any prospective escort to maintain a muscular physique by observing a strict diet and regular exercise, as he does.

CHAD BROCK

Chad Brock

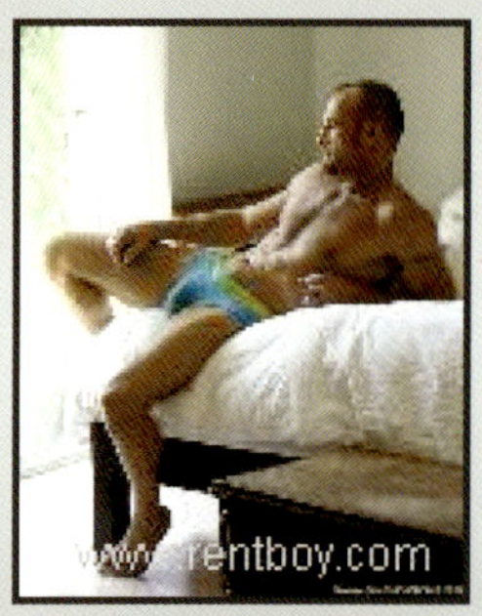

Click here for more pics

Very attractive straight acting and looking versatile all American guy. Laid back and passionate. Mild to Wild !! Swimmers build 5' 10' 165 lbs 8 inch cut. Available for your pleasure !!

Currently Serving	
Ft Lauderdale	
My Phone Number	
+1 954-240-8859	
Email	
In Rate	**Out Rate**
$150.00	**$200.00**

Chad Brock is fit, good-looking in a very American way, well-spoken and confident. He is not slow to admit that he is 45 years old, although his physique and overall appearance suggests a much younger person. He is presently employed as the manager of a major chain book store in Fort Lauderdale, Florida but has found that his salary is in need of financial augmentation if he is going to have the lifestyle that his previous career afforded him. A longtime airline employee, Chad Brock has worked as an attendant for a number of the major companies, enjoyed it very much and now is moving on to another chapter of his life.

Talking about relationships, Chad says, “You have to be very open with each other and discuss your fantasies and what you want to explore sexually. If not, your partner will let it out somewhere else. And as cheating goes, how much do we want to have sex with someone if it makes our partner, the person we love, feel insecure?”

Chad Brock is originally from Los Angeles and was a business student in college there before working for the Aerospace Corporation. He realized in his early teens he was attracted to men and moved to Denver in his early twenties with his lover. The work situation was not good there so they moved on to Orlando, Florida because of his partner’s job. He says, “It had been my dream since childhood to work as an airline attendant and in Orlando I applied to Eastern Airlines and was accepted. I worked for them for two years until they went under.

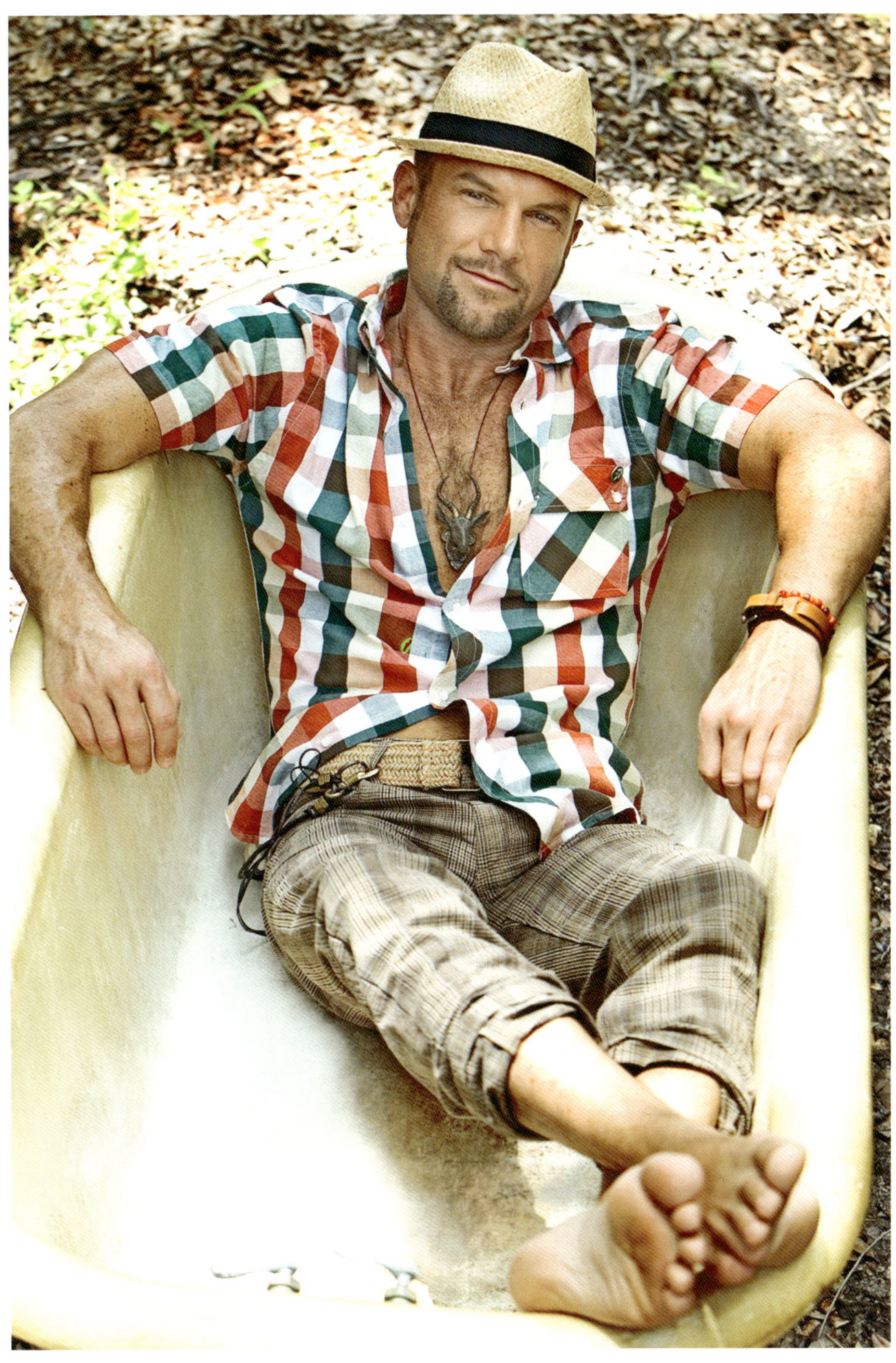

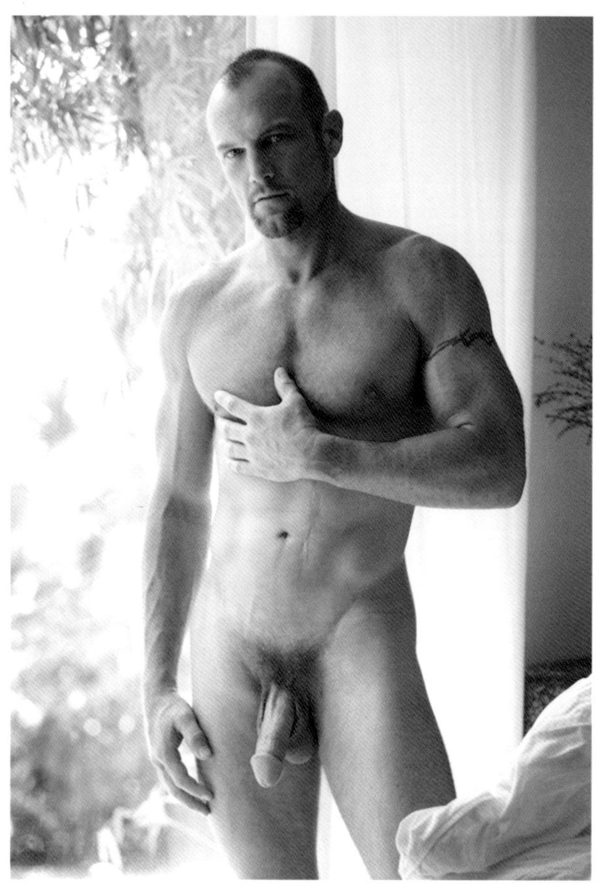

"I then decided to work for Delta and was transferred to Salt Lake City. My relationship with my partner hadn't worked out and I was single. In Salt Lake City I met a great guy and we became very attached to each other. But he was a very devout Mormon and was not out to his family or friends or at work. I finally told him we could not continue seeing each other if it all had to be hidden and lied about. So he came out to his parents and they were amazing. They accepted me like a son and respected us as a couple. We had dinner together every Sunday, I was with that partner for six years. But my career wasn't going where it should with my being located in Salt Lake City. I needed to move to Boston and my lover wasn't prepared for that. Unfortunately I had met another man, a flight attendant who worked for Delta also, and I left.

"I'm a very 'relationship' kind of guy and with my new lover I was with him almost all the time. We worked the same flights and spent all our time together and it got to be too much for him. And you have to face that after 9/11 the world and life of airline attendants changed drastically. The airlines began to struggle, working hours and schedules became much tougher. Much that was attractive about working as a flight attendant just wasn't there anymore."

After 19 years as a flight attendant Chad Brock moved to Fort Lauderdale and began working as a designer of showrooms for a home furnishings company. He found he had a knack for this that the company liked very much but with the recession and economic downturn the company went out of business.

Living in Fort Lauderdale Chad made new friends, among them a handsome man who was working successfully as a performer in porn movies. He suggested that Chad add this to his work schedule in addition to his new job as a manager for the book chain. He has done a number of these films and his agent for the films suggested he might try working as an escort also. He put ads on *rentboy.com* and *men4rentnow.com* and has been working in the escort industry since.

Discussing this work he says, "There will be weeks when you have a client every day. And then there are weeks with no clients at all. It's very inconsistent and hard to analyze. Some of my escort friends will be working a lot when I 'm not. And vice versa." His rates are $200 out and $150 in and most of his clients prefer to come to his apartment. He says that 90 per cent of his clients are unmarried, 90 per cent are white. Perhaps 25 per cent are sixty years old and up. A few are quite young and the majority are between the ages of 40 and 60. "I have had one very beautiful Asian client," he adds.

He reminisces and says he had a call from a quite young man who had been hanging out with his friends looking at the escort websites. His friends dared him to call Chad and he did. Chad told him "It's $150." The young man replied, "I only have $50." Chad says, "He sounded like a nice kid so I said, 'Okay, that's fine.'. So he came over and he was really a beautiful guy. It was a very unusual experience."

At the other end of the spectrum he had an elderly client who lived in complete disorder in a large and not clean apartment. After a few sporadic attempts at sex Chad decided he was well out of there and would have left without payment except the man insisted he take a check. Then not many hours later the man called and said, "I'm putting a stop on the check. You were a complete failure as an escort." And proceeded to rant on in the same vein and finished by threatening him with the police. Chad had already deposited the check and says of the episode, "I didn't care that he put a stop on it. I was just happy to get out of there."

On the other hand he has a client in Miami whom he sees at two week intervals, spends perhaps four hours with him and is paid $1,000 for the visit. "He's a very nice guy, good-looking; that's a really great client."

He, too, has experienced the client who wants the relationship to become more personal and permanent. What escorts call "the boyfriend thing." He has some clients who will spend their hour with him just talking.

His family understands that he works in the escort industry and makes porn films as he has shown pictures to them of his well-known porn industry friend. They recognized his friend and they only find his porn work interesting.

He is in a relationship at the present time with a partner who is twenty years his junior. They met on the set of a porn film and he says, "We just hit it off immediately. I think we can make this thing work as long as we are open and honest with each other. There is a difference in sex where there is love and commitment and sex that is just for variety and enjoyment." Chad adds, "He tells me he's really looking forward to when I am 50 and a really hot Daddy."

As for the future, Chad Brook has high hopes that with the economy rallying he can return to the field of designing showrooms. He says, "I have a real talent for it and I love it. I can see myself doing that in my fifties."

Thanks to Base, Miami Beach, for wardrobe.

JOE KENT

KEY WEST
JOE KENT
(Falcon/Catalina Video Model)
Personal Escort
Bodywork
Out Only
Very Friendly
24 Hours
305.587.3667 cell
800.632.3469 pager
joekent.com

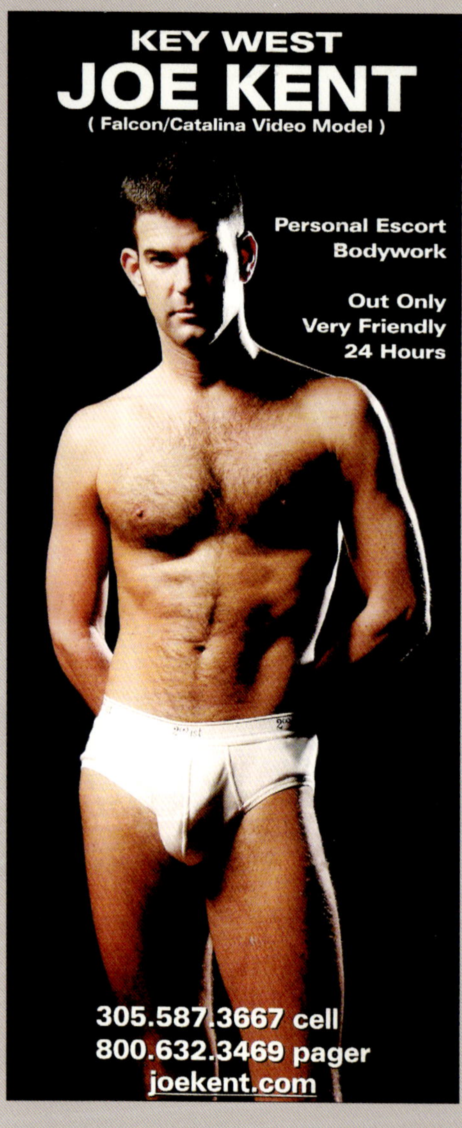

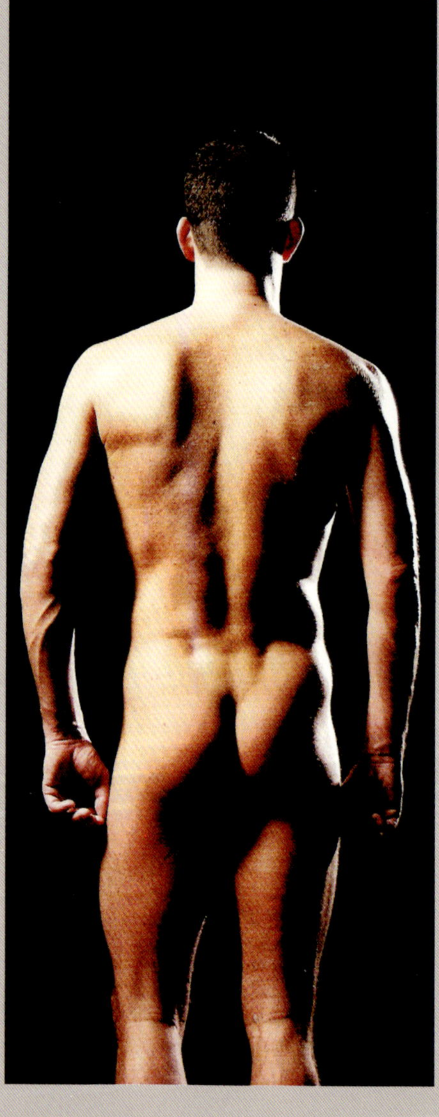

Joe Kent is dark and slim with piercing eyes. He is very verbal and speaks very cogently about his life as an escort. He was born and raised in New York and attended the University of New York in Purchase, N.Y. He went there to get a degree in psychology.

He originally wanted to be a flight attendant and while in school found jobs working as a security guard and in a tanning salon. In a magazine he read an article by an escort called "All in a Night's Work" and decided to try it. He says he had always been fascinated with the idea of working in the sex industry. He was 22 at the time.

He started by going to the bar/restaurant Rounds on 51st Street in New York and found that some escorts were in and out of the bar several times a night while he was only finding clients three or four times a week. He says, "I was jealous. I thought, 'What am I doing wrong?' No one would tell me." He adds that the going rate at that time was $150 an hour and that Monday and Tuesday nights were the best nights for him although the weekends could also be busy.

"One night I wrecked my car. I needed money so I put an ad in a magazine. I was still in college so I was bringing guys to my dorm room for massages. They were men from Westchester County. I never thought of it as a job. It's more like an additional way to make money," he says. "But you wind up always waiting for the phone to ring and you don't get a real job." Joe moved to Key West after visiting several times and found escorting was easier there. He says, "I was just in my own little world there. Now I'm in my thirties. I want to do something else, but what?

"Sometimes you have clients that are a nice surprise. You don't really want to leave. Some of them want you to be their boyfriend. The ones from Wisconsin. I had a boyfriend... a client... who was from Wisconsin. He ran a dairy farm. He would fly me up there. He would send me money and he bought me a ring. I would stay for long periods of time with him but he was always up at seven every day and I was left alone in the house. We were completely different. Then his dairy business went bust and he was broke. He moved in with his mother. But when I was up there I would go to Minneapolis to work. That was very good. There's a lot of money there."

About his private life Joe tells the interviewer. "I have one adopted sister. My father is still alive. He re-married 20 years ago. I love my stepmother. When I was staying with my parents once I heard my stepmother telling him very loudly, 'Your son is peddling his goods for older men. He's doing favors for older men.' My father denied it but he suspected it. He just didn't want to raise questions. He just didn't want to bother.

"Now I'm living with a friend in Fort Lauderdale and I am working to pay off some credit card debts. I'm getting clients who are younger than I am now, too. I had a 21-year-old Arab prince who flew in from Los Angeles. We didn't even really do anything. My clientele is late thirties, professional, and gay for the most part. They come from the internet. The older clients who want to meet in hotels are usually married and kind of inept at the gay scene. They say things like, 'Do you do oral?' as though they're in some kind of supermarket.

"When I was in high school I had a teacher take me out and then to his home and he showed me a porn film and wanted to have anal sex. I don't like that much. I will top if they want me to but I prefer oral sex. I might bottom if I'm charmed. I don't like clients who take drugs. It makes them very unstable. There are so many people these days into crystal meth. It's the devil's elixir. These days everybody wants to bottom. Right away they're legs up in the air and they want everything in the house put up there.

"Bad clients? I had one who didn't have money on him and had to go downstairs to get money. Once we were in the street he jumped in a cab and split. I really felt raped and victimized.

"On another occasion I had been seeing a client in the Trump Tower in New York and after sex he said that we would have to go down to the street to an ATM so he could pay me. The guard on duty didn't notice me when I had come in the first time and anyway the guards had changed while I was there. Once on the street the guy darted back into the building and the guard wouldn't let me enter. You get all kinds of weird stuff when some guy is trying to avoid paying.

"My good clients include couples, which I had quite a few in Key West, five to be exact. The husband would call me for a massage. The wife would watch and then I would have sex with the wife. I love it. I've been with a number of straight couples. Sometimes when I fool around with the husband the wife gets jealous. It's never the reverse. I've done it enough that I think I'm more or less bi. My very best experience was when I was lying on the beach in Key West and my phone rang. It was a cruise ship captain from a hotel right next door. He was Scandinavian, very manly; my face was all roughed up from his kisses. He had quite a beard. The sex was great. And then he paid me and left."

When asked about his first awareness of his homosexuality Joe Kent remembers, "I was three when I knew I liked guys. I had a little friend and I chased him about. When I was ten I took his hat home and smelled it. I was a schoolyard bully. I had sex with a friend when I was ten. I had a babysitter who used to rub up against me. Then her brother babysat me and I took him to the bathroom. He showed me his penis, coming out of that hair. It was the most exciting thing that ever happened to me. He fucked me. Ever since, I have had an obsession with penises. Also when I was 15 I got drunk and called a gay bar and they sent over a very drunk gay guy who was hot to trot. It was very exciting.

"I suppose my eyes and my ass are my best features. I really want to get out of escorting but I feel trapped now. You become very dependent upon escorting and waiting for the phone to ring becomes an addiction. You don't have a job. Escorting generates cash but I don't consider it a job and it discourages you from pursuing other things. I need the money and I really can't do anything else. I feel as though I am in a trap. All the things I was supposed to do at a certain time, like jobs and education and things like that, I did not do. And now I suspect it's too late."

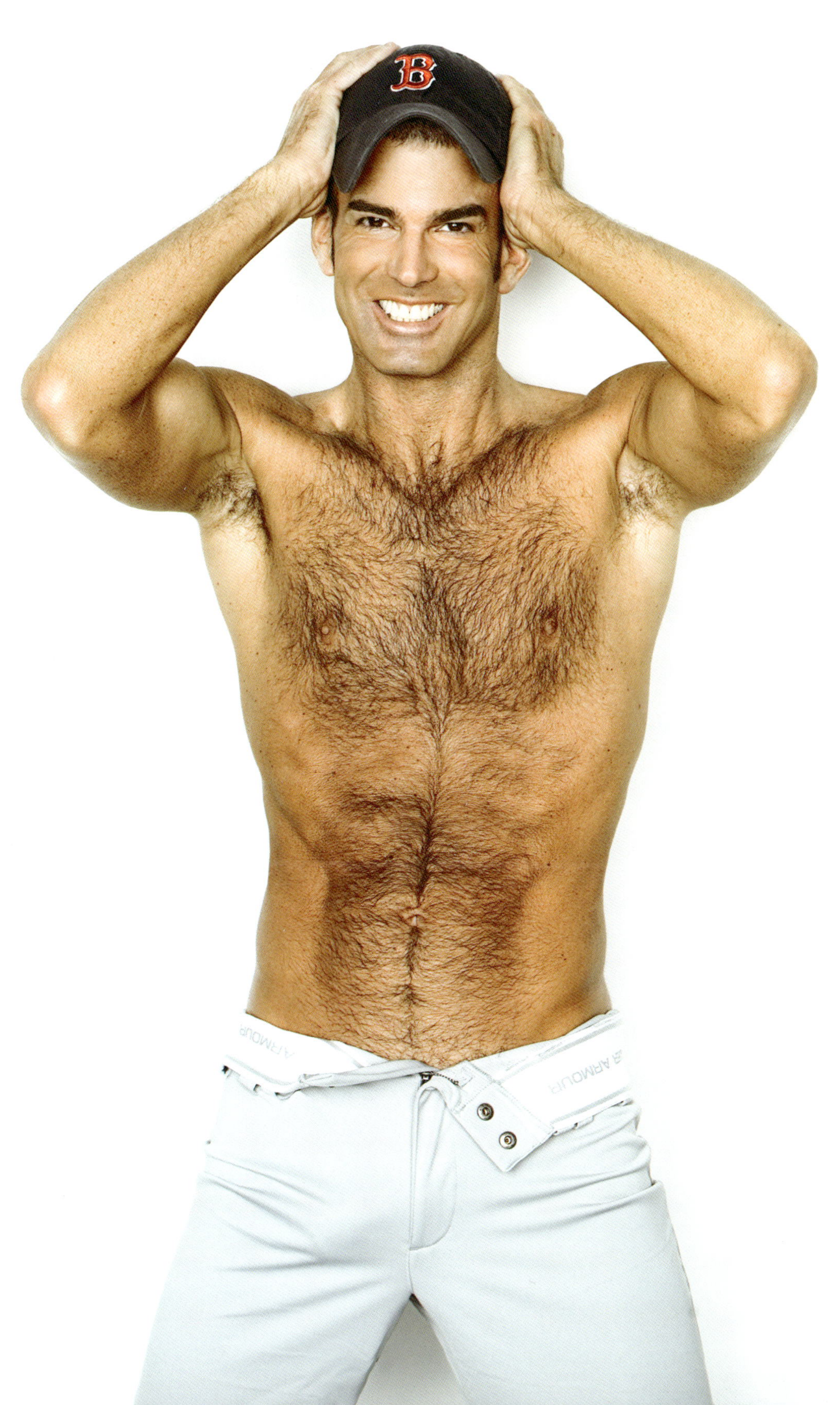
B
ARMOUR
ARMOUR

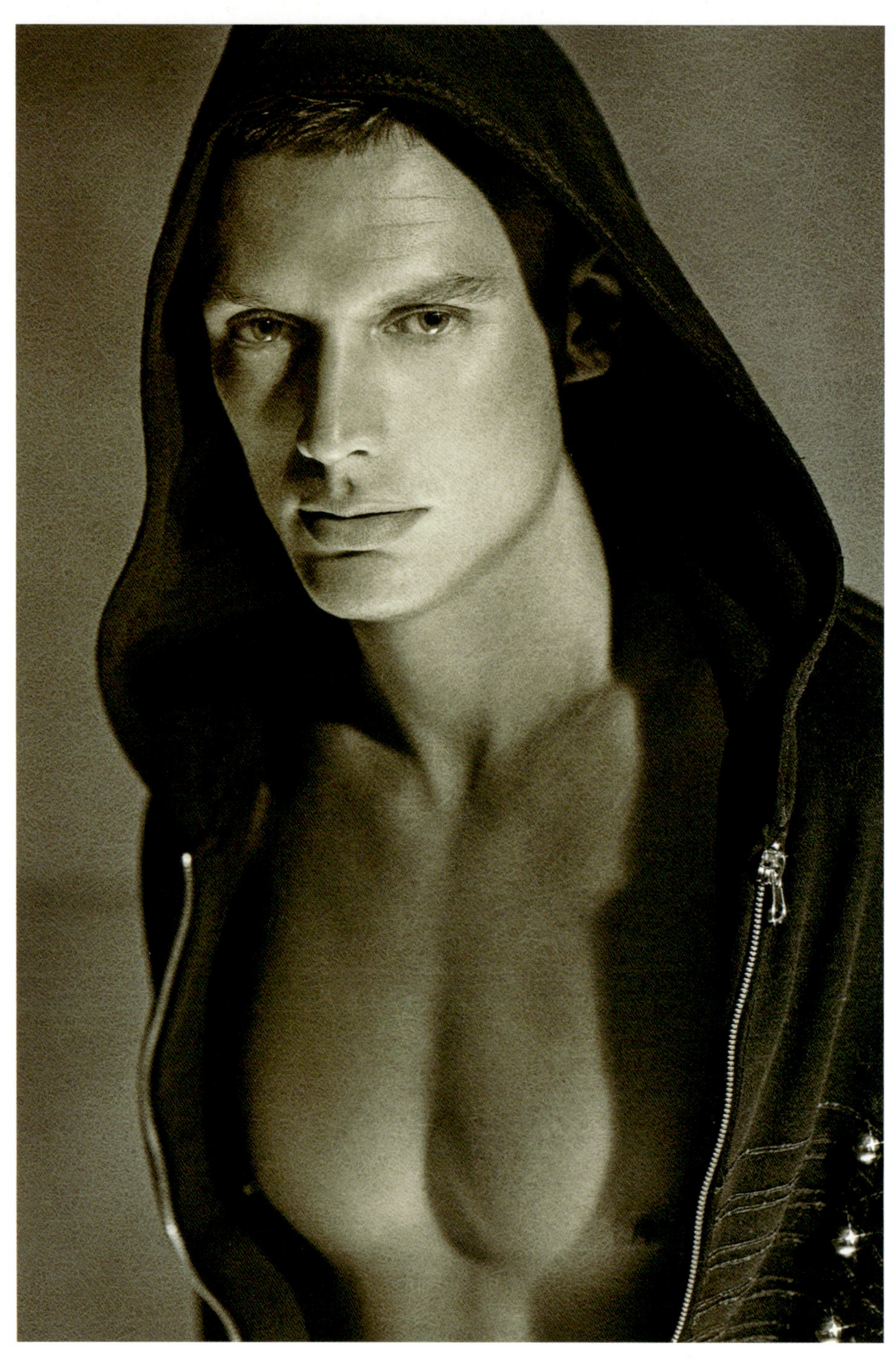

ABOVE: BOBBY BROCK
OPPOSITE: GERONIMO

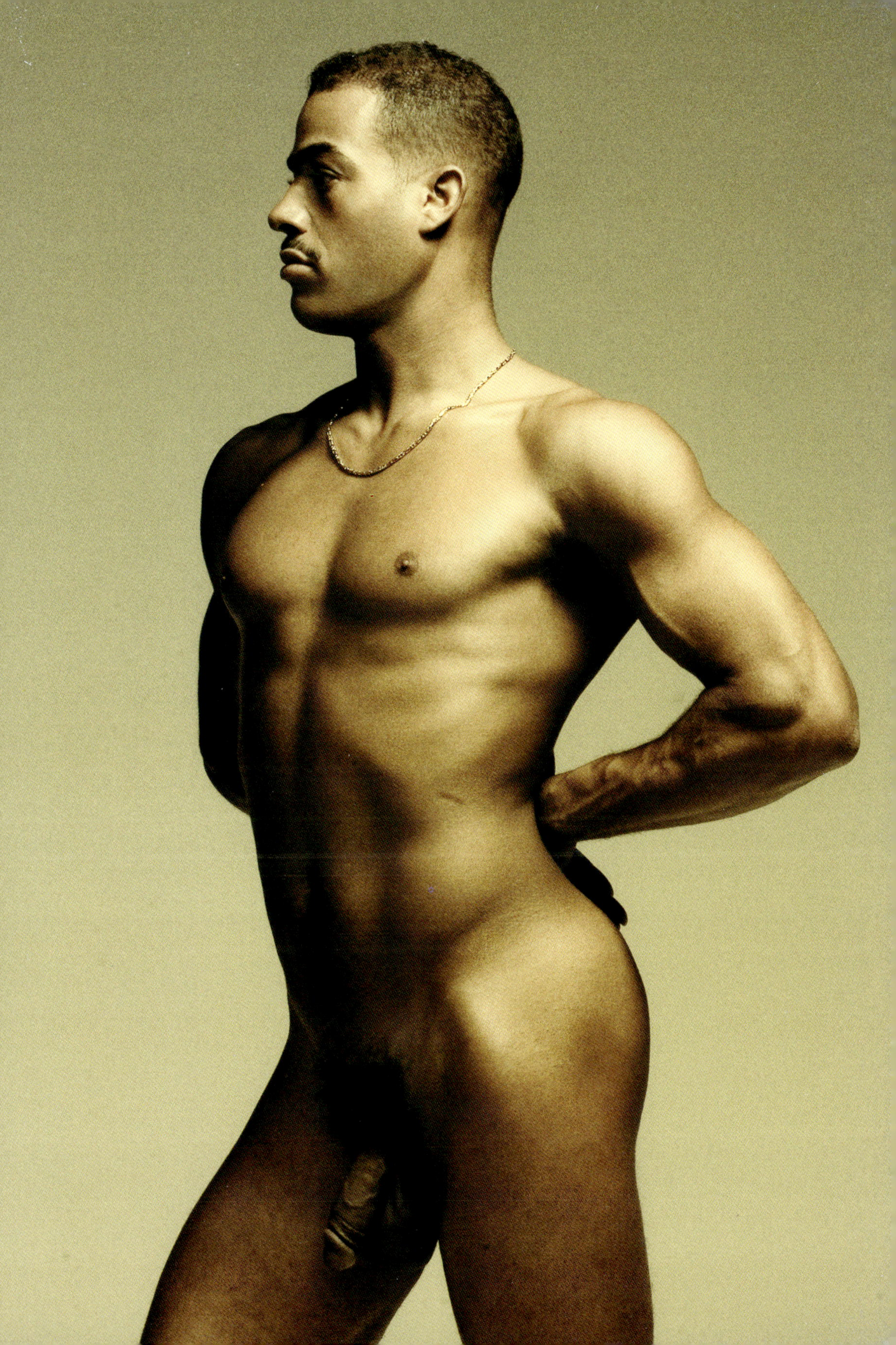

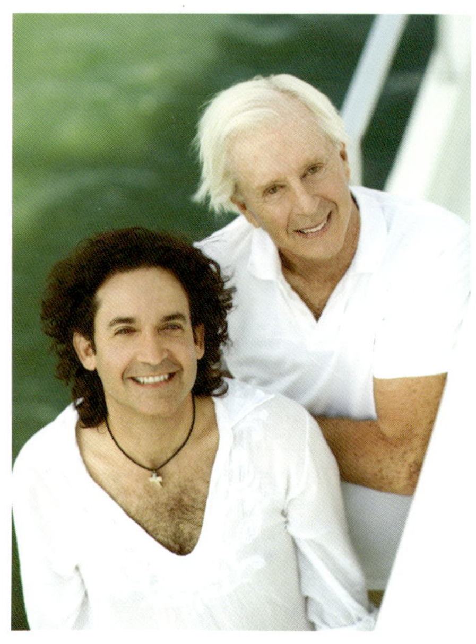

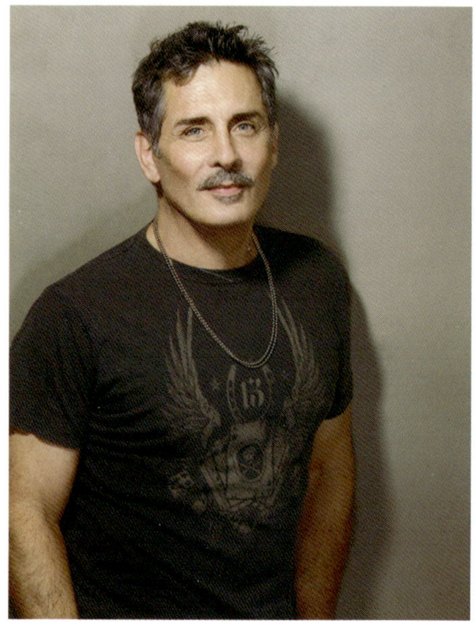

David Leddick (right) is the author of five novels, six books on the male nude, a biography of art figures in the 1930s and 1940s and the non-fiction book "The Secret Lives of Married Men." His most recent book is "In the Spirit of Miami Beach." He lives in Miami Beach, Paris and Montevideo, Uruguay.

David Leddick is also a stage performer, currently performing in a musical version of this book called "Escort."

For **Heriberto Sanchez** this has been his first photo-journalism book project. He has previously collaborated with Mr. Leddick on other stage and film projects. Mr. Sanchez has appeared on Spanish TV programs, soaps and commercials. He is originally from San Juan, Puerto Rico, and attended the Sorbonne in Paris. He resides between Miami Beach and Paris.

Of Italian descent, **David Vance** has been surrounded by the atmosphere of his heritage since childhood. The art, the sculpture, the music, the literature and the cuisine of his world exposed him at an early age to the classic in observing life. He sees beauty through the eyes of his ancestors and creates beauty in their same vision.

Vance lives in Miami and works around the globe. His advertising and editorial assignments include Cosmopolitan, Men's Health, Rolling Stone and many others. Among his clients are Revlon, Rolex and Coca-Cola. Celebrity portraits include Luciano Pavarotti, Sophia Loren and Andy Garcia.

To purchase a photograph from the great David Vance collection please contact him at www.DavidVancePrints.com